INSPIRE / PLAN / DISCOVER / EXPERIENCE

PARIS

PARIS

CONTENTS

DISCOVER 6

EXPERIENCE 64

NEED TO KNOW 306

Left: Classic Parisian rooftops
Previous page: The city of Paris in springtime
Front cover: Arc de Triomphe, a symbol of French
patriotism, in the heart of Paris

DISCOVER

WELCOME TO
PARIS

Sweeping, tree-lined boulevards and beautifully manicured parks. World-class museums and cutting-edge haute cuisine. The inspiration of countless artists, writers and philosophers, Paris is a city that speaks to the soul. Whatever your dream trip to Paris includes, this DK Eyewitness Travel Guide is the perfect travel companion.

1 Admiring art in the Musée du Louvre

2 Irresistible *macarons*, a patisserie favourite

3 The cobbled streets of Montmartre

4 Taking a break in the Jardin des Tuileries

The birthplace of the French Revolution, Paris is steeped in history. From the Gothic magnificence of Notre-Dame, through the Second Empire opulence of the Opéra Garnier to the elegance of the Eiffel Tower, the city's landmarks are a testament to its enduring status as a political and cultural powerhouse. Art is everywhere: lose yourself in the galleries of the Louvre and marvel at the Impressionist masterpieces in the Musée d'Orsay, or visit Belleville to view the ever-changing street art on Rue Dénoyez. Paris's renowned food scene is equally rich, with an enticing array of boulangeries and bistros that reflect each neighbourhood's local flavour. Stalls overflow with fresh produce at the Marché d'Aligre, while La Cuisine offers the opportunity to learn to cook your own French classics.

The city's charms extend beyond its centre and it's well worth heading to Versailles to experience the royal splendour of the palace and gardens. Alternatively, escape the crowds and play *flâneur* for the day at the Bois de Vincennes or Bois de Boulogne, exploring their winding trails, stately châteaus and serene boating ponds.

Compact enough to travel around easily, Paris can still overwhelm with the volume of unmissable sites on offer. We've broken the city down into easily navigable chapters, with detailed itineraries, expert local knowledge and comprehensive maps. Whether you're staying for a weekend, a week or longer, this DK Eyewitness guide will ensure that you make the most of all that the city has to offer. Enjoy the book, and enjoy Paris.

REASONS TO LOVE
PARIS

It's soaked in history. It's steeped in culture. It's a gourmet's delight. Ask any Parisian and you'll hear a different reason why they love their city. Here, we pick some of our favourites.

1 EIFFEL TOWER

The most iconic symbol of Paris. Some people scale its full height while others view it from a distance, but no one forgets the first time they see the Iron Lady (p200).

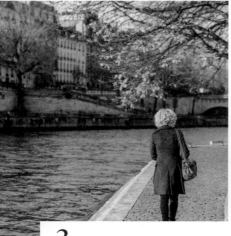

COFFEE AND CAFÉS 2

Centuries-old cafés are the place to sit and sip a dark espresso while watching the city saunter, sashay or scurry by – an endlessly fascinating spectacle.

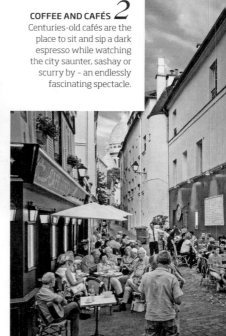

3 PLAYING FLÂNEUR

Parisians invented the concept of the *flâneur*, an aimless wanderer. Whether it's the Seine's footpaths (p210) or the boutique-filled Marais (p84), there's always a reason to put one foot in front of the other.

MUSÉE DU LOUVRE *4*

Home to the *Mona Lisa*, the Louvre *(p184)* houses over 30,000 works from across the ages. It's easy – and recommended – to get lost in its seemingly endless galleries.

NOTRE-DAME *5*

The huge outpouring of grief that followed the 2019 fire at this massive cathedral *(p70)* is a testament to how dear it is to the city's heart. Damaged, but defiantly still standing, this national treasure is an enduring icon.

CLASSIC FRENCH CUISINE *6*

French food is unrivalled, and eating at a restaurant is a total experience, where service is an art and every server can recommend a stellar wine.

VERSAILLES 7

Built to wow the world, Louis XIV's epic château and gardens are true marvels. Find yourself awed at every turn by the opulent display of wealth and grandeur *(p296)*.

RIVER SEINE 8

Paris's identity flows from its beloved river. Car-free paths on both banks offer romantic strolls or cycle rides past eye-catching street art and historic landmarks *(p210)*.

9 PATISSERIES AND BOULANGERIES

Baguettes and pastries fuel Parisians, and a daily trip to the bakery is routine for most. A buttery croissant anywhere else will never compare.

10 MARKETS

Rain or shine, Paris's street sellers spring to life each day. Bustling food markets colour nearly every neighbourhood, while the flea markets brim with hidden treasure.

OPERA AND BALLET 11

France raised the bar on ballet and opera under the Sun King, Louis XIV. Savour the fruits of that legacy in the ornate Opéra Garnier *(p172)* and the modern Opéra Bastille *(p106)*.

HAUTE COUTURE 12

Paris is a fashion capital and its designer stores are veritable temples to couture. Marvel at the dazzling displays that elevate clothing into fine art.

EXPLORE
PARIS

This guide divides Paris into 15 colour-coded sightseeing areas, as shown on the map below. Find out more about each area on the following pages. For areas beyond the centre see p290.

Cimetière de Montmartre

MONTMARTRE AND PIGALLE
p152

Place de Clichy

Parc Monceau

OPÉRA AND GRANDS BOULEVARDS
p168

Opéra National de Paris Garnier

Place de l'Opéra

Arc de Triomphe

CHAMPS-ÉLYSÉES AND CHAILLOT
p212

Place de la Concorde

Jardin des Tuileries

LOUVRE AND LES HALLES
p180

Musée du Louvre

Palais de Chaillot

La Seine

Jardins du Trocadéro

Musée du Quai Branly-Jacques Chirac

Eiffel Tower

EIFFEL TOWER AND INVALIDES
p196

Parc du Champ-de-Mars

Musée d'Orsay

Place Joffre

Dôme des Invalides

ST-GERMAIN-DES-PRÉS
p234

Place de Breteuil

Jardin du Luxembourg

MONTPARNASSE AND JARDIN DU LUXEMBOURG
p278

Cimetière du Montparnasse

Place Denfert-Rochereau

WESTERN EUROPE

UNITED KINGDOM

NETHERLANDS

BELGIUM

GERMANY

Lille

PARIS

Strasbourg

Rennes

SWITZERLAND

FRANCE

Atlantic Ocean

Bordeaux

Lyon

ITALY

Toulouse

Marseille

SPAIN

Mediterranean Sea

Cité des Sciences
et de l'Industrie

Parc de
la Villette

Sacré-
Coeur

LA VILLETTE
p138

Place de
Stalingrad

Parc des
Buttes-Chaumont

Canal St-Martin

**RÉPUBLIQUE AND
CANAL ST-MARTIN**
p114

Parc de
Belleville

Place
de la
République

**BELLEVILLE AND
MÉNILMONTANT**
p126

Pompidou
Centre

Musée
Picasso Paris

Cimetière du
Père Lachaise

Place
de l'Hotel
de Ville

THE MARAIS
p84

Place
Voltaire

**ÎLE DE LA CITÉ
AND ÎLE ST-LOUIS**
p66

**BASTILLE AND
OBERKAMPF**
p100

Place
de la
Bastille

Musée de
Cluny

**LATIN
QUARTER**
p248

La Seine

Panthéon

Jardin des
Plantes

Muséum National
d'Histoire Naturelle

Parc de
Bercy

**JARDIN DES PLANTES
AND PLACE D'ITALIE**
p262

Place
d'Italie

0 metres 800
0 yards 800

N

GETTING TO KNOW
PARIS

Paris is a patchwork of neighbourhoods, each with a history and essence of its own. The Seine runs through the heart of the city, creating its Right and Left banks, while the main sightseeing areas are enclosed by the Périphérique, a ring road that separates the city centre from the suburbs.

PAGE 66

ÎLE DE LA CITÉ AND ÎLE ST-LOUIS

Located in the heart of Paris, these two islands are cornucopias of must-see sights. Île de la Cité houses both Notre-Dame and Sainte-Chapelle, masterpieces of Gothic architecture, while Île St-Louis is full of boutiques and cafés. Former royal palaces – such as the Conciergerie, where Marie-Antoinette was held prisoner – double as administrative buildings, giving even the day-to-day a frisson of enthralling history. Both islands are an essential, and inevitable, part of a Parisian excursion.

Best for
Sightseeing and strolling along the river

Home to
Notre-Dame, Sainte-Chapelle

Experience
The awe-inspiring Gothic architecture of Notre-Dame and Sainte-Chapelle

THE MARAIS

PAGE 84

Full of fashionable boutiques and restaurants, the Marais is the neighbourhood visitors return to over and over again. Its noble origins are apparent in the Renaissance mansions repurposed for the likes of Chanel and the Musée Carnavalet. Along Rue des Rosiers, the scent of freshly fried falafel wafts through the air as the city's best Jewish bakeries prepare poppy-seed pastries. Parisians spend afternoons mingling at the Place des Vosges, with its lime trees set against the rosy bricks of a former royal residence.

Best for
Shopping, dining, history, architecture, LGBTQ+ life

Home to
Musée Picasso Paris, Pompidou Centre

Experience
The trendy boutiques and the scenic Place des Vosges

PAGE 100

BASTILLE AND OBERKAMPF

Gritty and lively, these areas east of the Marais make up for a lack of major tourist attractions with stellar dining options. Trendy coffee shops, independent boutiques and innovative bars draw a younger, multicultural crowd from across the city. *Flâneurs* can enjoy the elevated Coulée Verte René-Dumont for a bucolic stroll above the streets, or wander the markets at Aligre and along Boulevard Richard Lenoir – both sell fresh flowers and mounds of seasonal produce. Those looking for a taste of local life will find it here.

Best for
Nightlife and restaurants

Home to
Place de la Bastille

Experience
The magnificent Colonne de Juillet and a stroll along the elevated Coulée Verte René-Dumont

→

RÉPUBLIQUE AND CANAL ST-MARTIN

These areas have recently transformed into exciting, somewhat quirky destinations. Characterized by the *bobos* (bohemian-bourgeois Parisians) who helped gentrify it, the canal is a hotspot for daytime coffee dates and evening picnics, fuelled by an extensive selection of cafés. Shoppers should head to the pockets of boutiques specializing in homewares, clothing and jewellery. This is the side of Paris that few visitors see but are exceedingly happy to find.

Best for
Coffee lovers and getting off the beaten track in style

Home to
Canal St-Martin

Experience
The Musée des Moulages medical museum and a pizza picnic beside the canal

BELLEVILLE AND MÉNILMONTANT

Far from the beaten path, Belleville and Ménilmontant are local enclaves that are little visited by tourists. Artists toil away in their galleries and in the streets, turning thoroughfares such as Rue Dénoyez into open-air artworks, while Asian restaurants and shops attract locals who want a break from duck *confit*. Hipsters and international residents have made their home in these characterful areas, which offer a rewarding glimpse into everyday Parisian life.

Best for
Global cuisine and experiencing local life

Home to
Cimetière du Père Lachaise

Experience
A hunt for the tombs of famous figures such as Edith Piaf and Oscar Wilde at the Cimetière du Père Lachaise

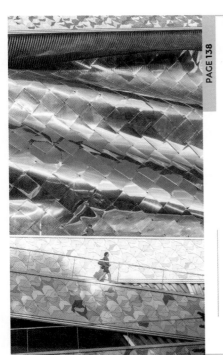

PAGE 138

LA VILLETTE

On the city's northeast edge, the canal cuts a broad path through this green park that's as family friendly as it is cultural. The stunning Jean Nouvel-designed Philharmonie towers like a spaceship while the science centre and playground across the water provide endless entertainment for kids. Joggers and cyclists appreciate the traffic-free pathways, and in spring and summer concerts and outdoor movies sound-track the evenings. Parisians of all ages head here to while away the time with a glass of rosé as the clinking of their *pétanque* balls echoes over the water.

Best for
Music lovers and getting some fresh air

Home to
Parc de la Villette, Cité des Sciences et de l'Industrie

Experience
Playing pétanque *along the canal or taking in a show at the Philharmonie de Paris*

PAGE 152

MONTMARTRE AND PIGALLE

Although the area around the Moulin Rouge is still dotted with sordid "love" shops and seedy bars, Montmartre and Pigalle have become fashionable destinations for diners and shoppers. Pigalle's red lights have given way to some of the city's best pastry shops, boutique hotels and designer stores. Visitors still love browsing the art at Place du Tertre and soaking up the view of Paris from atop hilly Montmartre, where the cobbled streets and quaint houses retain a 19th-century village feel that few other districts reproduce.

Best for
A night out and great views

Home to
Sacré-Coeur

Experience
The sound of buskers on the steps in front of the Sacré-Coeur while watching the sun set over the city

$\rightarrow$

PAGE 168

OPÉRA AND GRANDS BOULEVARDS

Studded with theatres and crowned by the Opéra Garnier, this district epitomizes Baron Haussmann's plans for Paris, with monuments at every intersection. Its broad avenues, lined with exquisite churches and wallet-emptying department stores, attract Parisians and camera-toting tourists alike. This is the place to stroll, shop and repeat, whether it's for rose-flavoured *macarons* from Ladurée's original shop or a luxury bag from Printemps.

Best for
Shoppers and theatre-goers

Home to
Opéra National de Paris Garnier

Experience
Shopping for perfume under the Art Nouveau cupola of Galeries Lafayette, before heading next-door to Printemps' rooftop café

PAGE 180

LOUVRE AND LES HALLES

Paris's former royal palace and central market are as lively as ever. The Musée du Louvre, with its infamous glass pyramid and the *Mona Lisa*, needs no introduction. The stately manicured gardens of the adjacent Tuileries house cafés and other art galleries. Les Halles was historically the hub of food distribution in the city, and the smells of ripened cheeses and fresh baguettes still tempt shoppers along Rue Montorgueil. It's all about cuisine here, from fine dining to street food, and wine bars and cocktail clubs shake up the nights.

Best for
Shopping, dining and history

Home to
Musée du Louvre

Experience
Coming face to face with the Mona Lisa *before sampling pastries along Rue Montorgueil*

PAGE 196

EIFFEL TOWER
AND INVALIDES

This corner of town is grandiose and ornate, with the gold-topped Dôme des Invalides soaring against the skyline. Full of history and artifacts, it plays second fiddle to the neighbourhood's real star: the Iron Lady herself, the Eiffel Tower, rising at the edge of the river. Away from the chaos of tours and elevator lines, this district also offers quaint streets such as Rue Cler, where colourful, buttery pastries await. Some of the city's top restaurants aren't far away. If Michelin stars seem overly excessive then a picnic on the Champ-de-Mars underneath the tower will do, with the appropriate bottle of oaky red wine, of course.

Best for
Sightseeing and fine dining

Home to
Eiffel Tower, Dôme des Invalides, Musée du Quai Branly–Jacques Chirac

Experience
Stunning views from atop the Eiffel Tower before paying homage to Napoleon at his tomb at the Invalides

$\rightarrow$

PAGE 212

CHAMPS-ÉLYSÉES AND CHAILLOT

The world's most famous avenue still has a shine to it. Although its shops are mainly frequented by tourists, it's worth a visit for the iconic stores and the monumental Arc de Triomphe. Well-heeled Parisians do live nearby, but are more likely to be found at one of the museums at the Palais de Chaillot. Luxury shoppers will revel along the Avenue Montaigne, and the area's palace hotels are the perfect place for a ritzy afternoon tea or evening cocktail.

Best for
Window shopping and Michelin-starred dining

Home to
Arc de Triomphe, Palais de Chaillot

Experience
A dip into the Petit Palais exhibition hall before splashing out on a terrace coffee on the Avenue des Champs-Élysées

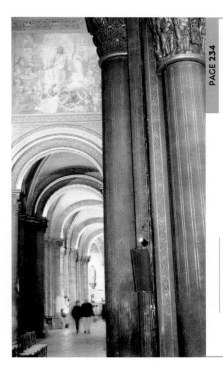

ST-GERMAIN-DES-PRÉS

Cafés line the streets and squares of this iconic district – the chocolates and pastries are some of the city's best. Shoppers delight in the boutiques and art galleries found here – Le Bon Marché in particular captivates shoppers who walk through its perfume-laden halls. A smattering of museums and centuries-old churches attracts tourists, but locals continue to lay claim to this bohemian enclave. There's no better place to rub elbows with true-blooded Parisians than in one of the neighbourhood's plentiful cafés and bars.

Best for
Strolling and people watching

Home to
Musée d'Orsay

Experience
Local life at one of the legendary cafés while nibbling macarons

LATIN QUARTER

From Roman ruins to Hollywood backdrops, the Latin Quarter is beloved by Parisians and travellers alike. Café crowds are decidedly younger than most, filled with university students from the Collège de France and La Sorbonne. Every block seems to have a bookstore, from obscure academic shops to the bursting shelves of the famed Shakespeare and Company. Peppered along the tiny twisting streets are crêpe stands and dive bars, all offset by the grandeur of stunning sights such as the Panthéon, Musée de Cluny and Church of St-Étienne-du-Mont.

Best for
Budget travel and history lovers

Home to
The Panthéon

Experience
Shopping for a picnic at the Marché Maubert and discussing philosophy with students around the Sorbonne

→

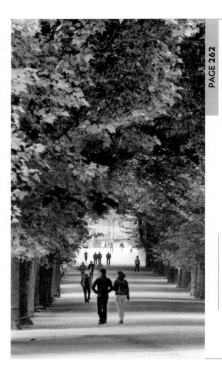

PAGE 262

JARDIN DES PLANTES AND PLACE D'ITALIE

Many people stop at the Latin Quarter, leaving this corner of the Left Bank less busy than the rest. The flowering Jardin des Plantes is home to natural history galleries and a zoo, and is a popular spot with Parisian families at weekends. A stroll along Rue Mouffetard delights with cheese and pastry shops, while architectural surprises such as the mosque or the national library make an exciting break from the traditional Parisian cityscape.

Best for
Family days out in any weather

Home to
Muséum National d'Histoire Naturelle

Experience
Sipping mint tea at the Grande Mosquée de Paris after visiting Europe's second-oldest zoo

PAGE 278

MONTPARNASSE AND JARDIN DU LUXEMBOURG

Old and new Paris come together in this patch of the Left Bank, where traditional cafés nestle alongside modern tower blocks. Parisians gather al fresco in the gorgeous Jardin du Luxembourg, while in-the-know visitors head to the Tour Montparnasse and the Catacombs. Locals still congregate at the *belle époque* brasseries, where the appetizing smell of lentils and sausages is accompanied by the sound of clinking beers.

Best for
A day at the playground and belle époque dining

Home to
Cimetière du Montparnasse

Experience
The cavernous underground Catacombs before ascending the Tour Montparnasse for a unique perspective of the city

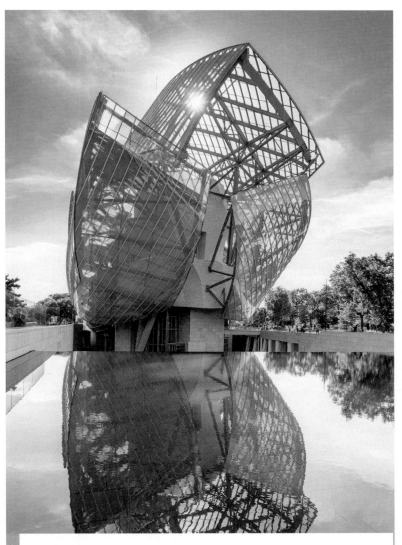

BEYOND THE CENTRE

Beyond the Périphérique (Paris's ring road), two natural parks act as the city's green lungs. The Bois de Vincennes and Bois de Boulogne offer lakes for boating, paths for strolling and châteaus for exploring, as well as attractions such as the contemporary Fondation Louis Vuitton art gallery and an innovative zoo. Disneyland® Paris grants families another day-long escape, while history buffs will enjoy an outing to the palace and gardens at Versailles, a 17th-century Disneyland® in its own right.

Best for
Days out and escaping the crowds

Home to
Bois de Boulogne, Bois de Vincennes, the Palace and Gardens of Versailles, Disneyland® Paris

Experience
The sumptuous estate of Versailles or taking some air in one of Paris's green lungs

←

1 The interior of Notre-Dame, before the 2019 fire

2 The Pont des Arts

3 Shakespeare and Company bookshop in the Latin Quarter

4 Jardin des Tuileries

Paris is a treasure trove of things to see and do, and its relatively compact size means that much exploring can be done on foot. These itineraries will inspire you to make the most of your visit.

5 HOURS

If you only have a few hours in Paris, a stroll along the River Seine is an ideal way to take in a plethora of sights. Begin in the Marais at the Hôtel de Ville (p95), the ornate city hall. Cross the river onto Île de la Cité, one of the oldest areas in Paris and home to major attractions such as Notre-Dame (p70). Pause outside the splendid cathedral to see the latest developments before continuing your walk past the similarly impressive Sainte-Chapelle (p74). At the island's western tip, a statue of King Henri IV stands on the Pont Neuf (p78), the city's oldest bridge. Cross the bridge and head west towards the Louvre (p184), rising majestically just a few blocks away. Walk through its courtyard and admire the elegant wings and iconic pyramid, after stopping for coffee and a snack at Le Fumoir, located on Rue de l'Amiral de Coligny, behind the massive museum. There's no time to go inside to admire the art, but the beautifully manicured Jardin des Tuileries (p191) offers an inviting stroll through flower beds and leafy walkways lined with statues. Enter the gardens through the Arc de Triomphe du Carrousel (p192), one of two monumental arches built by Napoleon.

At the gardens' far end, looking onto the Place de la Concorde (p222) and its Egyptian obelisk, splendid sweeping views take in the Grand Palais (p223), the Arc de Triomphe (p216) and the Eiffel Tower (p200). Walk down to the square and cross the river towards the National Assembly (p210), home to the lower house of the French Parliament. Follow the reclaimed riverbanks of the Berges de Seine (p210) east towards the Musée d'Orsay (p238), identifiable by its twin clock towers. Continue on charming Quai Voltaire towards the Pont des Arts (p245), which affords great photo opportunities.

Proceed back along the Left Bank, browsing the stalls of the *bouquinistes* (used-book vendors), arriving at Place St-Michel (p256). Visit one of the many nearby bookshops, such as Shakespeare and Company (p258), before heading past Notre-Dame to intimate Île St-Louis. This little island sports no grand tourist attractions, but is the place to grab a cone of Berthillon ice cream (p77). End your stroll with a glass of wine and dinner at the Brasserie de l'Isle Saint-Louis on Quai de Bourbon, enjoying views of the Seine.

←

1 Pretty Canal St-Martin

2 The Colonne de Juillet and Bassin de l'Arsenal marina

3 Les Philosophes café

4 An exhibit in the Muséum National d'Histoire Naturelle

24 HOURS

Morning

Start with coffee and a pastry along the Canal St-Martin (p118). Hipster coffee joints are in abundance here, and a take-away cappuccino pairs perfectly with a chocolate croissant from Du Pain et des Idées, the district's best bakery, on Rue Yves Toudic. Sit with your breakfast beside the canal, its green bridges arching gracefully over the water. Stroll the area and its shops on your way to the Upper Marais, just across nearby Place de la République, then live out noble fantasies while exploring the 17th-century mansion that houses the Musée Picasso (p88). Browse the art and relax with a drink on the rooftop terrace before continuing.

Afternoon

Enter the heart of the Marais by foot, stopping for lunch in a café such as Les Philosophes on Rue Vieille du Temple, or queueing for the entirely worthwhile falafel at L'As du Fallafel (p92) on Rue des Rosiers. Indulge in some retail therapy before ducking down onto the Seine, along the Berges Rive Droite. This riverside pathway allows traffic-free strolling and features boats doubling as cafés. Cross a bridge onto Île St-Louis and make your way over to the Left Bank. Just to the east is the pristine Jardin des Plantes (p268), an enclave for botany enthusiasts and a haven for anyone who appreciates natural beauty. It's also home to the Muséum National d'Histoire Naturelle (p266), which is worth a quick look. At the far end of the garden, pause for some mint tea at the Grande Mosquée de Paris (p268), just beyond the garden's gates.

Evening

Head back to the river and cross, walking along the stretch of canal that leads towards Place de la Bastille (p104). Its Colonne de Juillet is visible from a distance. Plan on eating somewhere in the neighbourhood, such as Bistrot Paul Bert on Rue Paul Bert or Septime (p107) on Rue de Charonne, for a true Parisian dinner. Then hang around for drinks and cocktails in the vicinity of Rue de la Roquette (p107), where the nightlife is sure to catch you up in its excitement.

1 The opulent Hall of Mirrors in the palace of Versailles

2 Cruising the Seine at sunset

3 A classic French breakfast

4 Art for sale in Place du Tertre in Montmartre

3 DAYS

Day 1

Morning Start the day in St-Germain-des-Prés with coffee and a croissant at any café, then take a leafy stroll through the nearby Jardin du Luxembourg (p286). Dip into St-Sulpice church (p243) to inspect the Delacroix paintings before going shopping along Boulevard St-Germain.

Afternoon Follow Rue de Seine towards the river, stopping for lunch at La Palette, a traditional café serving delicious *croque monsieur*. Stroll the Île de la Cité, home to Notre-Dame (p70), before renting a Vélib' bicycle and heading west to explore the Eiffel Tower (p200). Dare to walk the stairs if the queue for the elevator is too long.

Evening Have dinner nearby at Le P'tit Trouquet (p209), which serves classic French dishes. Follow this with a boat ride down the Seine as the sun sets.

Day 2

Morning Begin in hilly Montmartre, with a quick visit to the Sacré-Coeur basilica (p156). Browse the artists selling their wares in the open-air gallery of Place du Tertre (p158), then visit the Musée de Montmartre (p160) for a quick lesson on the 19th-century artists that made the district famous.

Afternoon Have lunch at Le Sancerre on Rue des Abbesses before heading down the hill towards Rue des Martyrs (p165), laden with pastry shops and boutiques. Consider a late afternoon jaunt through the Louvre (p184) to see the highlights, including *Mona Lisa* and the *Venus de Milo*. Soak up the views of the exterior with a coffee stop at the Café Marly, under the arcades of the Richelieu wing.

Evening Head to Les Halles for dinner at Champeaux (p189). Sip wine and people-watch for the rest of the evening along charming Rue Montorgueil, or take in the dreamy, late-night cityscape from the banks of the Seine, watching out for the Eiffel Tower's on-the-hour light show.

Day 3

Morning Travel less than an hour out of the city by train to Versailles (p296). Wander the world-famous gardens and 17th-century château, renowned for its opulent Hall of Mirrors.

Afternoon Splurge on lunch at Ore (p299), an ornate little restaurant situated inside the château. Be sure to visit the outer estates, including the queen's fairy-tale hamlet with a working farm.

Evening Head back to Paris and share a bottle at an intimate venue like Willi's Wine Bar on Rue des Petits Champs, near the Louvre. If you've still got room after your lunch, have dinner in style at one of the city's iconic belle époque brasseries such as Bofinger (p107) or La Rotonde (p147).

PARIS FOR
ART LOVERS

Numerous figures have shaken up the art scene from the French capital, from Monet and the Impressionists to Dalí and the Surrealists. Countless masterpieces adorn Paris's greatest museums, while private galleries and even the streets offer a more personal look at contemporary art in the city.

World-Class Museums

Whatever your interest in art, one of Paris's museums has a collection of it. Highlights include the soaring gallery of the Musée d'Orsay *(p238)*, a former train station famed for its Impressionist works, and the fascinating modern galleries of the Fondation Louis Vuitton *(p292)*. Try to escape Mona Lisa's gaze while exploring the superlative collection at the Louvre *(p184)*, before snaking up the panoramic escalator of the Pompidou Centre *(p90)* to marvel at Mondrian's deceptively simple squares. Smaller museums dedicated to Monet *(p304)* and Picasso *(p88)* will leave you swooning for these artistic icons.

↑ The courtyard of the Louvre, home to many world-famous works

Create Your Own Collection

Paris is a nirvana for art collectors with any budget. High-end art galleries along the Left Bank sell some of the city's most sought-after works, while at Place du Tertre in Montmartre *(p158)* you can mingle with local artists selling their canvases for a bargain. Visit the studios of little-known artists in Belleville *(p137)* – they might end up selling you something you didn't even know was for sale.

←

Place du Tertre in Montmartre, a hotspot for local artists exhibiting and selling their work *(below)*

TOP 5 ART MUSEUMS

Musée du Louvre
The world's most visited museum and home of the *Mona Lisa (p184)*.

Musée d'Orsay
Dedicated to Western art between 1848 and 1914, its main draw is Impressionism *(p238)*.

Musée Picasso Paris
The greatest collection of the legendary artist's iconic works *(p88)*.

Pompidou Centre
An eye-catching modern building that houses an equally memorable art collection *(p90)*.

Palais de Toyko
A daring, and often overlooked, contemporary collection *(p229)*.

Striking Street Art

From the wily Space Invaders that dot the city to the work of the iconic Miss.Tic, Paris is a haven for street art. Some of it appears clandestinely overnight while other murals, especially around the Canal St-Martin or even along Rue Dénoyez in Belleville *(p133)*, are city initiatives to encourage street artists. Explore these ever-changing works by taking a wander around eastern Paris, or booking a tour with Street Art Tour Paris.

↑ Some colourful street art in front of Le Barbouquin on Rue Dénoyez

The Sprint for the Yellow Jersey

The world's biggest annual sporting event, the Tour de France sees around 200 cyclists covering an astounding 2,000 miles in 23 days. The race culminates in late July at the Champs-Élysées *(p212)*, where cyclists race through several laps before the final sprint for the coveted *maillot jaune* (yellow jersey). It's a thrilling end to the long race – best of all, it's free to watch; just arrive early to grab a coveted spot at the front, mere inches from the cyclists as they race past.

→

Cyclist Chris Froome leads the peloton riding past the Arc de Triomphe

PARIS FOR
SPORTS LOVERS

Hosting a busy schedule of events throughout the year – including, in 2024, the Summer Olympic Games – the city is often abuzz with sporting fever. Whether you are passionate about cycling, racket sports or *le foot* (football), it's hard to beat congregating in a stadium or a packed-out bar.

Battle of the Nations

Rugby fans flock to Paris every February and March to watch the French rugby union team compete in the Six Nations Championship. French home matches are played at the Stade de France in St-Denis in northern Paris – expect a rowdy, good-natured atmosphere. On non-game days, a tour of this magnificent stadium can be booked online (www.stade france.com/tour-pass). Sports bars also stream the action live, particularly those around Montparnasse *(p279)*.

France competing against Ireland in the Six Nations rugby championship

TOP 4 SPORTS VENUES

Accor Arena
The Paris Masters tennis tournament is played here.

Parc des Princes
Home to Paris Saint-Germain football team.

Stade de France
The stadium will house most major Olympic events in 2024.

Stade Roland-Garros
This is the home of the French Open tennis tournament.

Clay-court Grand Slam

The origins of tennis are thought to lie in 12th-century France, so it's apt that one of the Grand Slam tournaments takes place in the capital. The French Open is held in late May at Roland-Garros stadium *(p152)*. Tickets are in high demand, so matches are also streamed at the Hôtel de Ville, where the atmosphere is no less lively *(p95)*.

US tennis player Coco Gauff serves during the French Open in Paris

The Beautiful Game

With the Eiffel Tower on their crest, it's no surprise that football club Paris Saint-Germain are also known as *Les Parisiens*. Though they are France's most popular club, evidence of the country's love for football is found everywhere in Paris. The city has many great public pitches, including the Émile Antoine stadium near the Eiffel Tower *(p197)*.

Fans watch Paris Saint-Germain in training at Parc des Princes

Explore Paris's Green Spaces

The city is replete with numerous wonderful green spaces to be enjoyed, for free, by the whole family. The Parc des Buttes-Chaumont *(p42)* is one of the highlights, and is perfect for kids to explore. There are sailing boats for hire at the Jardin du Luxembourg *(p286)*, and the fantastic playgrounds at Westfield Forum des Halles *(p190)* are always a winner.

$\longrightarrow$

Soaking up the sun in Parc des Buttes-Chaumont, one of Paris's loveliest parks

PARIS FOR
FAMILIES

Paris is a playground for kids, with engaging parks and gardens. Children – and adults – will delight in riding the carousel in the Jardin des Plantes, floating a colourful wooden sailboat in the Grand Bassin at the Jardin du Luxembourg or enjoying the beaches of the Paris Plages.

Take a Boat Trip

Boat cruises along the Seine or on the Canal St-Martin are a family favourite. Parents have the chance to relax while kids watch the city pass them by. Options along the Seine include Bateaux Mouches, Vedettes du Pont Neuf and Bateaux Parisiens, while the main company for the canal is Canauxrama. The 19th-century locks of the canal are especially curious, as is the cavernous tunnel that the tour takes you through.

Boat tour cruising along the Seine, past the Eiffel Tower $\uparrow$

Be a Chef for the Day

The kitchen is the heart of any family, so learn to cook together with a class at La Cuisine Paris (p96). This well-appointed cooking school in the Marais offers English-language lessons in making a variety of traditional French dishes. Here you will discover how to make buttery croissants or roll out your own baguettes before tasting the fruits, or rather pastries, of your labour. It's a sure-fire way to keep the whole family busy and smiling for a few hours, even if you all end up covered in flour.

Learning
the basics of
French baking
at a cooking school

TOP 4 RAINY DAY MUSEUMS

Muséum National d'Histoire Naturelle
Home to thousands of impressive animal specimens (p266).

Musée de la Chasse et de la Nature
A collection of hunting trophies (p96).

Aquarium de Paris
An underwater wonderland situated across from the Eiffel Tower (p221).

Cité des Sciences et de l'Industrie
A huge science museum, packed with interactive exhibits (p144).

INSIDER TIP
Eating Out

Parisians don't typically take their children to higher-end restaurants, so choose somewhere more family oriented, such as the chain Hippopotamus or the budget-friendly Chez Gladines (p255), where the food is still good but the atmosphere more relaxed.

Search for Hidden Treasure

Paris's museums are huge, but a treasure hunt provides an exciting new way of exploring them. A little rivalry, a bit of learning and a whole lot of fun await anyone who embarks on a hunt with THATMuse at the Louvre (p184) or Musée d'Orsay (p238).

→

Children enjoying a
treasure hunt at the
Musée d'Orsay

Daily Bread

Although French bread needs no introduction, there is, nevertheless, an art to choosing it. In Paris, all baguettes are not created equal. Ask for a *baguette de tradition* to get the Parisian favourite, a regulated loaf that has nothing beyond the essentials inside. Crusty and handmade, these baguettes are tastier and delectably chewier than some regular crumbly baguettes. Try a *baguette bien cuite* if you like your bread well-baked and extra crispy.

→

Fresh, crunchy baguettes, available for sale at any neighbourhood boulangerie

PARIS FOR
FOODIES

Paris is legendary for its cuisine, so make sure you pack your appetite. Whether it's haute cuisine, rich, buttery pastries or rustic regional dishes, the city's delectable array of fresh, quality produce will delight your taste buds – though perhaps not your waistline.

Flavourful fromage

Cheese is a way of life in France and punctuates any worthwhile meal. Cheesemongers dot Paris's streets and markets with hundreds of different pungent, subtle and salty varieties, their shops lined with huge, aged wheels and fresh, delicate discs. Try a bit of everything, following the vendor's suggestions, and don't be shy to ask for tips on assembling the perfect mix of creamy, sharp and stinky goat, cow and sheep's milk cheeses.

←

An array of delicious cheeses on display at a market stall

TOP 4 GLOBAL CUISINES IN PARIS

With its multicultural population, the city also offers diners an amazing selection of world flavours – particularly those of France's former colonies.

North African
Couscous and tagine are popular dishes.

Vietnamese
Waves of immigration mean stellar *bo bun* and *banh mi.*

Middle Eastern
Falafel in the Marais is unparalleled.

Japanese
Ramen around Rue Ste-Anne is worth the wait.

→

Mouthwatering pastries for sale in one of the city's many patisseries, where delicate *macarons (above)* are a regular feature

MARKET STREETS

Shop like a Parisian on market streets, where stores focus on specific goods and outdoor stalls often pop up at weekends. Trendy Rue Montorgueil is a good stop for bread and cheese, while pastries are the draw on Rue Cler *(p209)*. Sample caramels and candies on Rue des Martyrs *(p165)* or shop for fresh produce along Rue Mouffetard *(p269)*.

Heavenly Patisserie

From the mighty *macaron* and spongy madeleines to creamy éclairs and tangy lemon tarts, Paris's patisseries are where taste buds go to be reawakened. Every corner bakery produces its own sweet, buttery or otherwise decadent versions of the classics. If there's a queue at your chosen boutique, chances are you've made the right choice.

Opera and Ballet

The palatial Opéra Garnier *(p172)*, home to the ballet, is a fairy-tale experience. Showing both opera and dance productions, it's a classic dose of Paris's musical heritage. The more modern Opéra Bastille *(p106)*, a stunning glass venue, lacks the romance but delivers on acoustics. There's not a bad seat in the house from which to take in a production.

←

A ballet performance at the Opéra Garnier, the historic home of the ballet

PARIS FOR
LIVE MUSIC

From elegant symphonies to buskers in the Metro, Paris is a constant concert. World-class singers belt out centuries-old operas on stages that also welcome contemporary musical comedies or the latest pop artist. In the streets, the hum of accordions and bluesy jazz renditions infuse the air.

Paris Philharmonic

The glittering Philharmonie de Paris *(p147)* immerses spectators in the musical experience. You're never more than 32 m (105 ft) from the conductor, and cutting-edge acoustics mean you won't miss even the softest flute. Home to Paris's symphony, it's a daring space that will envelop you in sound.

↑ Chinese pianist Lang Lang performing at the Philharmonie de Paris

Contemporary Music

Contemporary music flourishes in Paris, and local venues such as La Maroquinerie *(p134)* host up-and-coming artists. Familiar faces grace the stages of L'Olympia, where Edith Piaf famously sang, while smaller venues like La Cigale offer a more intimate concert experience. Major pop and rock acts pass through the arena by Bercy *(p111)*, or even the Stade de France, for massive, bass-blowing concerts.

←
Rock band Uria Heep performing at La Cigale

 INSIDER TIP
Music Festival

Celebrate the summer solstice with street buskers and concerts during June's all-night Fête de la Musique *(p58)*.

Musical Theatre

Paris has no Broadway or West End, but its growing musical theatre scene has French audiences applauding at the stage call. Experience classics such as *My Fair Lady* and *Singin' in the Rain* in English amid the splendour of the revamped 19th-century Théâtre du Châtelet. For French versions of modern musicals, from *Grease* to *Mamma Mia!*, head to the Théâtre Mogador *(p175)* in the Opéra district.

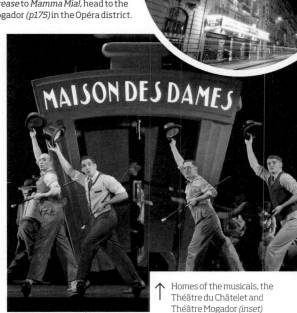

TOP 5 JAZZ VENUES

Sunset Sunside
An intimate venue in Châtelet.

La Petite Halle
A newcomer on the scene in La Villette.

Duc des Lombards
In the Latin Quarter and practically a pilgrimage for musical artists.

New Morning
An obligatory stop for real jazz enthusiasts.

Chez Papa
An elegant jazz venue with restaurant.

↑ Homes of the musicals, the Théâtre du Châtelet and Théâtre Mogador *(inset)*

Idyllic Gardens

Flowers seem to bloom year-round in Paris's gardens. The hidden Jardin du Palais-Royal *(p188)* features fragrant roses, while the Jardin des Plantes *(p268)* grows exotic specimens from around the globe. The Luxembourg *(p286)* and Tuileries *(p191)* gardens are exquisite examples of royal property turned public.

An avenue of trees within the arcade-lined enclosure of the Jardin du Palais-Royal

PARIS FOR
GREEN SPACES

Perfectly manicured flower beds, sheared and shaped shrubbery, and spouting fountains decorate every corner of Paris. Former royal hunting grounds and private gardens are today lush green spaces where locals congregate to stroll or play a friendly game of *pétanque*.

TOP 4 LOCAL FAVOURITES

These lesser-known green spaces are popular spots where locals relax.

Parc des Buttes-Chaumont
Hilly, picnic-friendly and popular on weekends *(p146)*.

Parc Monceau
Well-heeled Parisians picnic here *(p226)*.

Parc de la Villette
The place for football matches and jogging *(p142)*.

Place des Vosges
A tiny green space in a royal setting *(p92)*.

Innovative Reclaimed Space

Some of Paris's most successful modern green spaces have flourished out of former industrial expanses. Visit the Coulée Verte René-Dumont *(p106)*, an elevated train track that traded trains for tulips – the entire walkway is akin to a hanging garden sitting above the city. The Berges de Seine *(p210)*, a pedestrianized roadway along the river, features barges doubling as floating gardens.

→

The Coulée Verte René-Dumont, on a former railway track

INSIDER TIP
Flower Market

The Marché aux Fleurs Reine Elizabeth II *(p77)* is a gardener's playground. Flowers spill onto the street, while bulbs, seeds and tools fill the market stalls.

Relaxing Parks

In the 19th century, city planners built two green lungs – the Bois de Boulogne *(p292)* and Bois de Vincennes *(p294)* – on either side of Paris. Natural woodland, peaceful ponds and seemingly endless trails form this pair of bucolic havens. Each houses botanical gardens and various architectural features, as well as surprises such as an open-air theatre. Beyond the gardens of Versailles *(p296)*, the vast Parc de Versailles allows visitors to wander through pristine parkland.

↑ The verdant parkland of the Bois de Vincennes and Bois de Boulogne *(inset)*

On Stage and Screen

As the location of Molière's final performance (at the Palais-Royal) and home of the world's oldest continuing theatre – the Comédie-Française, founded in 1680 – Paris has a rich pedigree when it comes to the stage. On the silver screen, the city has notably provided the backdrop to New Wave classics such as *Breathless* and *Jules et Jim*, and more recently to *Amélie*'s heartfelt quest for love in Montmartre – the Café des 2 Moulins, where she worked, can be visited on Rue Lepic.

← Audrey Tautou as the title character in 2001's charming *Amélie*

  INSIDER TIP
Famous Tombs

Visit icons such as Oscar Wilde and Edith Piaf at their final resting place in the Cimetière du Père Lachaise *(p130)*.

PARIS FOR
INSPIRATION

Paris has inspired countless thinkers and artists over the years. The centre of the Enlightenment, a fashion hub and a popular location for films since the Lumière brothers invented the cinema, the city is rich in cultural capital. Trace the steps of its icons to stimulate your own imagination.

Iconic Residents

From Chanel and Marie-Antoinette to Voltaire and Pasteur, Paris has hosted a long list of world-famous icons who have contributed to philosophy, art, science and culture. See Marie-Antoinette's bedchamber at Versailles *(p296)*, sip coffee in Les Deux Magots as Hemingway did *(p244)* and pay homage to Chanel at her first boutique on Rue Cambon.

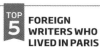

↑ The iconic Les Deux Magots on Boulevard St-Germain

← Inside the opulent bedchamber of Marie-Antoinette at the Palace of Versailles

Literary Paris

The iconic Shakespeare and Company bookshop *(p258)*, a Left Bank institution, is a testament to the staying power of the written word. Paris has been the backdrop for countless epic novels, including *Notre Dame de Paris* and *Les Misérables*. Search for the phantom at the Opéra Garnier *(p172)*, stroll Rue Montorgueil like Florent in *The Belly of Paris* and keep an eye out for *Les Misérables*' Gavroche around the Bastille *(p104)* – or maybe in Victor Hugo's house *(p93)*, where he penned his most famous work.

←

The Opéra Garnier, the setting for *The Phantom of the Opera*

TOP 5 FOREIGN WRITERS WHO LIVED IN PARIS

Ernest Hemingway
The US author wrote *A Moveable Feast* about his time living in Paris from 1921 to 1926.

F Scott Fitzgerald
US writer Fitzgerald lived in Montparnasse in the 1920s.

George Orwell
The English novelist tells of his experiences living in poverty in *Down and Out in Paris and London* (1933).

James Joyce
Irish writer Joyce lived in Paris from 1920 to 1940. *Ulysses* was published here in 1922.

Anaïs Nin
Novelist Nin met her lover, fellow American Henry Miller, in Paris.

Visitors walking through the beautifully landscaped Jardin des Tuileries ↑

PARIS ON A
SHOESTRING

Paris attracts droves of budget travellers with good reason. Free museums and green spaces keep visitors active during the day, while low-cost street food and happy hours make evenings a pleasure. And what beats a picnic along the Seine with a bargain bottle of wine, a baguette and some cheese?

Churches

Most churches in Paris are public property, open to visits for no fee. Avoid the tourist crowds at Sainte-Chapelle and the Sacré-Coeur, head instead for the beautiful St-Sulpice *(p243)*, Paris's second largest church, which houses paintings by Delacroix. St-Étienne-du-Mont *(p257)*, next to the domed Panthéon, is often deserted, despite containing the tomb of St Geneviève – the patron saint of Paris. With stunning stained glass and countless artworks, these monuments are as awe-inspiring as they are budget-friendly.

→

The magnificent St-Étienne-du-Mont church

Parks and Gardens

From the top of Parc des Buttes-Chaumont (p146) to the furthest reaches of the Bois de Boulogne (p292) and the Bois de Vincennes (p294), greenery in Paris is, generally, free. Discover the ornate Médici Fountain in the Jardin du Luxembourg (p286) and view the obelisk at Place de la Concorde from the Jardin des Tuileries (p191). Have a pond-side picnic in Parc Monceau (p226) or join a game of pétanque in the Jardin du Palais-Royal (p188). It's astonishing that these pristine parks and gardens require no fee, but such is the magic of Paris.

← Locals playing a game of *pétanque* in the Jardin du Palais-Royal courtyard

Did You Know?

Many ticketed museums are free on the first Sunday of the month – check websites for details.

One of the lavishly decorated rooms in the Musée Carnavalet ↑

Municipal Museums

A number of city-run institutions such as the Maison de Victor Hugo (p93) and the Musée Carnavalet (p97), dedicated to Parisian history, are free. While special exhibitions are ticketed, the main collections are open to the public. Even contemporary art at the Musée d'Art Moderne de la Ville de Paris (p228) is accessible for visitors to view. The quaint Musée Cognacq-Jay (p92) fills a historical mansion, while the soaring Petit Palais (p223) is housed in an exhibition hall built for the 1900 Exposition Universelle.

High-End Shopping

The home of Chanel, Dior and Gaultier, Paris excels at high-end boutiques. Avenue Montaigne *(p226)* is a sight in and of itself, with all of the designer names that most will recognize and few can afford. These aren't places to wander in casually in your trainers and shorts, they are the real deal – just ask the security guards who double as bouncers. Equally prestigious shops exist around Rue St-Honoré and in the St-Germain neighbourhood *(p241)*, while the Marais has recently become a centre for men's haute couture.

→

Legendary Chanel boutique on Avenue Montaigne and *(inset)*, L'Avenue bistro on the same street

PARIS FOR
SHOPPERS

Paris is synonymous with fashion, and for many people Parisian style is the ultimate in chic. In addition to clothing, the city is also a treasure trove of boutiques selling one-of-a-kind items that you can't find elsewhere. Whether it's a flea market find or a scarf from Hermès, the fun is in the hunt.

Department Stores

Paris brought department store shopping to life with Le Bon Marché *(p243)*. Today there are several emporiums to choose from, but the formula is the same. Browse the designer outlets on the ground floors, amid masses of visitors queueing for the latest bag, before ascending the escalators through floor after floor of multi-brand bliss. When it all gets too much, take a breather on the rooftop in the scenic café at Printemps *(p177)* or the deck at Galeries Lafayette *(p175)*.

 ←

The stunning Art Nouveau interior of Galeries Lafayette

COCO CHANEL

Born into poverty and raised in an orphanage, the iconic Coco Chanel (1883–1971) opened her first shop in Paris in 1913. It sold hats and sportswear made from simple fabrics such as jersey, which proved popular with women seeking relief from restrictive corsets. The designer revolutionized fashion in the 1920s with the introduction of the little black dress and the launch of Chanel No.5, the first perfume to bear the name of a designer.

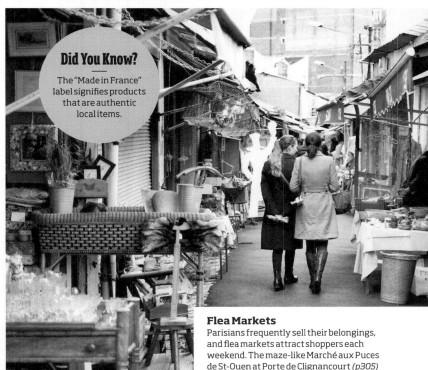

Did You Know?

The "Made in France" label signifies products that are authentic local items.

Flea Markets

Parisians frequently sell their belongings, and flea markets attract shoppers each weekend. The maze-like Marché aux Puces de St-Ouen at Porte de Clignancourt *(p305)* is the place to spend money on antique lamps, chairs and other homewares to create your own personal Versailles. Browse, feign interest and bargain when necessary – perhaps not on the €5 trinket box, but the €5,000 Louis XV chair may be negotiable.

Shoppers browsing the ↑ wares at the Marché aux Puces de St-Ouen

World War II Scars

Hitler gave orders for Paris to be levelled at the end of the Nazi Occupation, but they were disobeyed by the general in charge of the city, who instead surrendered. Relatively few physical scars remain from the Occupation of 1940–44, but marks on the front of the police office on Île de la Cité *(p77)* recall skirmishes between Resistance fighters and German forces.

←

The police office on Île de la Cité, the scene of fighting during World War II

PARIS FOR
HISTORY BUFFS

There are more than two millennia of history to discover in Paris. From Viking invasions and plagues to Revolution and Nazi Occupation, the city's tumultuous past comes alive in its museums, streets and cafés.

TOP 4 HISTORY MUSEUMS

Musée de l'Armée
Military history from medieval knights to Charles de Gaulle *(p204)*.

Musée Carnavalet
An in depth exploration of the history of Paris, located in two former mansions *(p97)*.

Pavillon de l'Arsenal
Houses an exhibition charting the evolution of architecture in Paris *(p93)*.

Musée de Cluny
Specializes in medieval history, and also houses Gallo-Roman ruins *(p254)*.

→
The Arc de Triomphe du Carrousel at the entrance to the Jardin des Tuileries

Napoleonic Memorials

The mark of the 19th-century emperors Napoleon I and his nephew, Napoleon III, is visible throughout the city. If you see an "N" on a bridge or monument, as on the façade of the Louvre *(p184)*, it's easy to date that particular work to one of those men. Napoleon I also commissioned several monuments in his own honour, including the Arc de Triomphe *(p216)*, the smaller Arc de Triomphe du Carrousel *(p192)* and the bronze column in Place Vendôme *(p193)*.

Roman Remains

Few are aware that Paris was once a bustling Roman town. Boulevard St-Michel is a former Roman road, and ruins of the baths there are still on display next to the Musée de Cluny (p254). The enormous Arènes de Lutèce (p268), which today hosts football matches and playdates, once was a staging ground for Roman theatre and combats.

→

The ruins of the Arènes de Lutèce, once a vast Roman arena

💬 INSIDER TIP
Historic Tales

Test your French by reading the 700 or so Histoire de Paris signs all over the city, which recount historic events at the location where they happened. The oar-shaped plaques were designed by Philippe Starck.

The Flame of Liberty

More recent history is commemorated by inventive memorials such as the Flame of Liberty. A copy of the torch held by the statue of the Lady Liberty in New York, it originally symbolized French-US relations. Today it informally honours Princess Diana, who tragically met her fate in 1997 in a car accident in the road tunnels below.

The golden Flame of Liberty, a tribute to Princess Diana ↓

↑ Napoleon's commemorative column in Place Vendôme

PARIS
RAISE A GLASS

Parisians have always enjoyed their tipples. Wine, imported from all over France, remains a staple, while a new wave of cocktail bars have reinvented how the city enjoys spirits. Beer, once brewed in belle époque brasseries, now gets the craft treatment in hip, upstart breweries.

Craft Beer

French beer has historically never been something to write home about. Today, however, bolshy breweries like Goutte d'Or and Paname Brewing Company (p151) are changing all that. The brasseries of the 19th century have ceded their hops and barley to younger brewers bringing craft beer to Paris. Sample their wares at establishments like La Fine Mousse (p108), which specializes in French and international craft beers.

$\rightarrow$

The impressive beer selection at La Fine Mousse

Innovative Wine

Parisian wine tastes have moved far beyond the clichés of red with meat and white with fish. While there's no reason to stray from French wine in the city, prepare to experiment with pairings that you might not have considered. When in doubt, always trust your server, who can advise you which bottle will suit your needs. And if you're still unsure, sample the house wine – often a sure-fire monthly offering.

←

Red wine flowing at a dinner among friends, and for sale at one of the city's many wine shops *(below)*

Creative Cocktails

Bars like Candelaria and Prescription Cocktail Club have fully opened Parisian eyes to cocktails, a revolution that began over a century ago with the legendary Harry's Bar *(p175)*. A new wave of bartenders play with a variety of ingredients and flavours, creating a host of inventive concoctions. Sit back and enjoy the show, and have your patience rewarded with an Instagram-worthy cocktail that also tickles the tastebuds.

↑ Popular cocktail bar Candelaria, a true hidden gem on Rue de Saintonge

Above the Skyline

Paris rose to new heights in the modern era. At first declared an eyesore, the 19th-century Eiffel Tower *(p200)* became a symbol of the city with its brown iron lattices. Enjoy a bird's-eye perspective of Paris from its viewing gallery. Alternatively, ascend the 20th-century Tour Montparnasse *(p284)* for panoramic views from a different angle. While not as elegant as the Iron Lady, its green makeover for the 2024 Olympic Games promises a change, joining shimmering contemporary structures like the Fondation Louis Vuitton *(p292)* and the Philharmonie de Paris *(p147)*.

→

The view from the Tour Montparnasse, looking towards the Eiffel Tower

PARIS FOR
ARCHITECTURE

Planned and perfected, Paris showcases centuries of architectural styles. Jagged Gothic façades, soaring Neo-Classical domes and dazzling modern buildings dot the city. Admire Paris from a fresh perspective by tracing the city's architecture from its subterranean depths to the tip of the Eiffel Tower.

KEY ARCHITECTURAL STYLES

Gothic: this imposing style flourished in France, most famously at Notre-Dame *(p70)*.

Baroque: the lavish decoration of Versailles *(p296)* is typical of this style.

Neo-Classical: inspired by ancient Greece and Rome, this style is epitomized by the Panthéon *(p252)*.

Art Nouveau: incorporating curves and natural motifs, Art Nouveau details are still visible in the Metro station entrances.

Overhead

Most of Paris's architecture dates from the 19th century, when the city planner Baron Haussmann redesigned most of the city. His fashionable architectural innovations spread across France, and even to other countries. Amble along Haussmann's sweeping tree-lined boulevards and gaze up at the uniform façades that are a signature of his style. He was also known for the monumental intersections he created around lofty buildings, such as the cupcake-like Opéra Garnier *(p172)*.

Avenue de la Grande Armée, designed by Baron Haussmann ↑

Street Level

Medieval half-timbered houses and Renaissance palaces still dot the Marais, where history survived the ravages of conflict and city planning. See examples on Rue François Miron, or head over to the palatial Place des Vosges (p92), lined with pretty pink brick façades, for a taste of French Renaissance architecture under Henri IV. The courtyards of these mansions once welcomed the regal carriages of Parisian nobility.

← Hôtel de Soubise, one of the numerous historic mansions in the Marais

BARON HAUSSMANN

Lawyer by training and civil servant by profession, Georges-Eugène Haussmann worked under Emperor Napoleon III to redesign Paris. Working with the best architects and engineers of the day, he tore down old buildings and cut new boulevards across the city. His controversial plans angered many, but the result was, arguably, quite striking. During his time, modern sewers, green leafy parks and strict building regulations gave us the Paris that we adore today.

Below Ground

Underground, Paris is a world unto itself. Discover the 18th-century Catacombes (p285), a dark and twisted tangle of limestone quarries that house the bones of millions of Parisians, transferred from overflowing cemeteries. The 19th-century sewers (p209) are also open for visits, showcasing the potent and often rat-infested network to daring tourists.

↑ The macabre Catacombes de Paris, decorated with millions of bones

Walk the Canal Towards La Villette

Head to the Canal St-Martin *(p118)* to experience a local vibe. Few tour groups make it to the green bridges arching over the water, flanked by cute boutiques and coffee shops. Walk north along the canal to La Villette, a district worth the trek. The modern park *(p142)*, with its concert hall and science museum, draws Parisian families.

Canal St-Martin, a popular spot with locals for strolling and picnicking

PARIS
OFF THE BEATEN TRACK

It's easy to escape the crowds without going too far. Hidden courtyards and museums in the centre lure those who want something different, while the outer districts hold charming cafés, monumental churches and oddball galleries. Discover where the Parisians live and see the local side of the city.

Explore Multicultural Belleville

A bustling Vietnamese and Chinese district, Belleville is an enclave for Parisian artists and a new generation of hipsters. Take a rewarding excursion through the hilly Parc de Belleville *(p132)* for sweeping panoramas of the city, then be enticed by the smell of *pho* (Vietnamese soup) wafting along Rue de Belleville *(p132)*. Street art and quaint cafés decorate the district, which is especially lively during the market on Tuesday and Friday.

↑ Shoppers browsing a neighbourhood flea market in Belleville

Shop with Parisians at the Marché d'Aligre

Live like a Parisian for a day at the Marché d'Aligre (p106), one of Paris's most vibrant food markets. Barter for strawberries and have some mid-morning wine and oysters while filling your canvas bags with treats. The covered market, the Beauvau-St-Antoine, is the best place to head for succulent sausages or tangy goat's cheese, while outside are fresh flowers, mountains of lettuce and stalls full of seasonal produce that will provide endless meal inspiration. The outdoor market also features stalls selling bric-a-brac and second-hand books.

←

Food stalls at the Marché d'Aligre, packed with an array of quality fresh produce

---

💬 INSIDER TIP
Quiet Spots in the Louvre

Even the Louvre, the world's most-visited museum, has plenty of spots for quiet contemplation. Head where tourist groups rarely go, upstairs to the Northern European painters or to the wings housing Islamic art and Near Eastern antiquities.

Make an Excursion to Paris's Green Lungs

Rowing lazily across one of the lakes in the Bois de Vincennes (p294) or the Bois de Boulogne (p292), you'll wonder why all the tourists are still queuing for a boat ride along the Seine. These two large parks – lush green spaces situated on the outskirts of Paris – are often overlooked by visitors to the city. Stunning châteaus, exotic botanical gardens, a zoo, a mini amusement park and even the Fondation Louis Vuitton contemporary art gallery (p292) await those who make the trip across the Périphérique into these natural havens.

→

The Bois de Boulogne, home to the Fondation Louis Vuitton (inset)

A YEAR IN
PARIS

JANUARY

△ **Fête des Rois** (6 Jan). Feast on galettes des rois (a puff pastry cake) to celebrate the Epiphany.
Prix d'Amérique (end Jan). World-famous trotting race, first held in 1920.

FEBRUARY

△ **Chinese New Year** (early Feb). Parades and street festivals in Chinatown.
Salon International d'Agriculture (end Feb–early Mar). One of the world's largest farming fairs.

MAY

Shakespeare Garden Festival (throughout until Oct). Plays performed in Bois du Boulogne.
Nuit Européenne des Musées (mid-May). Museums open for one spring evening.
Taste of Paris (mid-May). Four-day food festival at the Grand Palais.
△ **Roland-Garros** (end May–early Jun). French Open tennis tournament.
Le Printemps des Rues (end May). Art and performance festival in east Paris.

JUNE

Fête de la Musique (21 Jun). All-day celebration of music, with many free events across the city.
Les Grandes Eaux-Nocturnes (mid-Jun–mid-Sep). Music and light show in Versailles gardens.
△ **Gay Pride** (end Jun). Lively parade and festivities.
International Paris Air Show (end Jun). One of the oldest and largest air shows in the world.
Fête du Cinema (end Jun–early Jul). Four-day film festival with discounted tickets.
Paris Jazz Festival (end-Jun–end Jul). A celebration of jazz music held in the Park Floral de Paris.

SEPTEMBER

Jazz à La Villette (mid-Sep). Programme of jazz-related music, films and exhibitions.
Journées du Patrimoine (mid-Sep). Historical buildings open their doors to the public.
△ **La Parisienne** (mid-Sep). A running race just for women.
Techno Parade (end Sep). Electronic music festival.

OCTOBER

Nuit Blanche (1st Sat). All-night art installations.
Prix de l'Arc de Triomphe (1st Sun). Renowned flat race at the Hippodrome de Longchamp.
△ **Mondial de l'Automobile** (1st fortnight, alternate years). Commercial motor show.
Foire International d'Art Contemporain (FIAC) (end Oct). Modern and contemporary art fair.
BNP Paribas Masters (end Oct–early Nov). Prestigious indoor tennis tournament.

APRIL

Easter *(4 Apr)*. Religious services plus delicious chocolates galore.

△ **Paris Marathon** *(early Apr)*. A lengthy run through the streets of Paris.

Foire de Paris *(Apr–May)*. Lifestyle, leisure, fashion and food at an enormous trade fair.

MARCH

Printemps du Cinema *(late Mar)*. Discounted tickets available for films shown citywide.

Festival des Arts Martiaux *(late Mar)*. Martial arts fair.

△ **Foire du Trône** *(Mar–May)*. Funfair held in Bois de Vincennes with hundreds of rides and attractions.

JULY

Festival du Cinéma en Pleine Air *(mid-Jul–mid-Aug)*. Outdoor cinema in La Villette.

△ **Paris Plages** *(Jul–Aug)*. The seaside comes to the Seine.

Paris Quartier d'Été *(mid-Jul–early Aug)*. Citywide dance, music, theatre and ballet.

Bastille Day *(14 Jul)*. Fireworks and festivities.

Tour de France *(end Jul)*. The world's greatest cycle race arrives in Paris.

AUGUST

Festival Classique au Vert *(mid-Aug–early Sep)*. Classical music in the Parc Floral.

△ **Rock en Seine** *(end Aug)*. Major international rock music festival.

NOVEMBER

△ **Beaujolais Nouveau** *(3rd Thu)*. Celebrations to mark the arrival of a new vintage wine on Parisian shelves.

Salon des Vins des Vignerons Indépendants *(end Nov–early Dec)*. Independent festival for wine lovers and winegrowers.

DECEMBER

Christmas illuminations *(until Jan)*. Paris lights up to celebrate Christmas.

Nautic *(early to mid-Dec)*. International boat show presenting the latest from the seas.

△ **New Year's Eve** *(31 Dec)*. Light shows at the Arc de Triomphe bring in the new year.

A BRIEF
HISTORY

1

For over 2,000 years, Paris has survived endless invasions, wars and plagues that have tested the spirits of its citizens. The seat of power for world leaders such as Louis XIV and Napoleon, and the backdrop for events including revolution and Nazi invasion, Paris has endured – and with style.

From Roman Outpost to Capital City

The first permanent settlers, the Parisii, landed here around 2,500 years ago – though artifacts show that others were here before them. In 52 BCE, Rome conquered the Parisii, creating an outpost called Lutetia. By the fall of the Roman Empire in the 3rd century CE, Paris was on the rise. Clovis I, King of the Franks, made the city his kingdom's capital in 508 and, despite outbreaks of plague and English occupation hammering at the city's morale over the following centuries, art and culture flourished. Notre-Dame rose from Île de la Cité and the University of Paris became a centre for European education.

1 A medieval map of Paris ↑

2 The Sorbonne, seat of the University of Paris, in 1550

3 The Hundred Years' War between France and England

4 Revolutionaries storming the Bastille

Timeline of events

508

Clovis I, King of the Franks, establishes Paris as the capital of his kingdom, which becomes France

987

Hugh Capet, forbearer of all future kings of France, rules the Kingdom of Franks

1240

Church bells are regulated by clocks for the first time, facilitating the regulation of work hours in Paris

1429

Joan of Arc fails to retake Paris from English control and is burned at the stake one year later

A Cultural Centre

By the 1500s, the Italian Renaissance had arrived in Paris by way of the Medici family of Florence, and the city began to shine. Despite severe religious wars, exacerbated by the Protestant faith of King Henri IV, culture thrived with new foods, fashions and even ballet. The Louvre became a royal palace and the nobility constructed mansions in the Marais. The French monarchs made Paris a world capital, epitomized by Louis XIV's opulent château and gardens at Versailles.

Revolution

In the 1700s the Enlightenment blossomed in Paris while the monarchy shrivelled. Famine and excessive spending at Versailles, as well as near-constant war, led to a call to arms. The French Revolution put a turbulent end to divine right as citizens stormed the Bastille prison on 14 July 1789. In 1793, Louis XVI and Marie-Antoinette both met their ends at Place de la Concorde, subjected to the guillotine. Parisians shook their city – and country – to the core, and a new government strove to regain order in a country divided by various ideologies.

FIRSTS IN PARIS

1348 Bubonic Plague first arrives
1660 Coffee first arrives from the East
1728 First street signs are erected
1827 First giraffe arrives in Paris, a gift from the ruler of Egypt
1907 First woman gets a taxi licence in Paris
1986 First Paris Marathon takes place
2014 Anne Hidalgo, first female mayor, is elected

1528
François I returns the monarchy to Paris after a century-long hiatus

1546
Work starts on the new Louvre palace and the first stone quay is built along the Seine

1572
St Bartholomew's Day Massacre ends with some 2,000 Protestants dead in Paris, following the wedding of future King Henri IV and Marguerite de Valois

1671
Louis XIV moves the entire royal court to Versailles

1789
French Revolution dethrones Louis XVI and Marie-Antoinette from Versailles

1

2

The Napoleonic Era

The rise to power of military leader Napoleon Bonaparte saw France's influence spread throughout its newly created Empire. The Bourbon kings briefly returned to power after Napoleon's downfall, before giving way to Louis-Napoleon Bonaparte, known as Napoleon III, who pursued France's Second Empire in his great-uncle's tradition. During the latter half of the 1800s, he charged administrator Baron Haussmann with modernizing Paris, creating the sweeping boulevards that define the city. By 1860, towns such as Montmartre and Belleville had been incorporated into Paris, establishing the present-day city limits.

The Belle Époque

The end of the brief and bloody Paris Commune of 1871, in which the citizens of Paris rose up against the French government, marked the emergence of the new Third Republic, which flourished during the belle époque (beautiful age) of the late 19th and early 20th centuries. The Eiffel Tower soared over Paris in 1889 and in 1900 the Metro opened. Paris truly was a glittering city at the cutting edge of art and technology.

↑ Louis-Napoleon Bonaparte, Emperor Napoleon III

Timeline continued

1804
Napoleon crowns himself Emperor of France

1853
Baron Haussmann's renovations of Paris begin

1871
The Bloody Week sees up to 10,000 French citizens killed at the hands of the army during the Paris Commune uprising

1941
The first Jewish Parisians are arrested by occupying forces

1944
Paris is liberated from Nazi occupation

Occupation and Recovery

In 1940, during World War II, the republic fell to Nazi Germany. Parisians survived the Occupation – albeit emerging beaten and subdued – and the city slowly recuperated. In 1968, student protests threatened to upturn the government, but the unrest quickly subsided. A series of ambitious architectural projects began at this time, and by the turn of the millennium, Paris was a world-class city with modernization firmly in its sights. The Vélib' bike service changed the way Parisians travel, and cars were banned from the riverbanks, creating new green spaces.

Paris Today

A model city, Paris embraces innovation while retaining its traditional elements. The city was shaken in 2015 by the Charlie Hebdo and Bataclan terrorist attacks, but it refuses to be cowed. Its revolutionary spirit continues to thrive, through the *gilets jaunes* protests that began in 2018 and the Black Lives Matter demonstrations of 2020. With an increasingly engaged citizenry and a future-facing mayor now in her second term, Paris affirms its status as a global, outward-looking city.

1. The Champ-de-Mars and Eiffel Tower during the Exposition Universelle of 1900

2. Students marching during the protests of 1968

3. The Vélib' bike scheme, launched in 2007

4. A streetside memorial following the Charlie Hebdo attacks

1961–62
Often-deadly protests are held by Algerians in Paris over the French-Algerian War

1968
Student riots and worker strikes take place in the Latin Quarter

1977
Jacques Chirac is installed as the first elected mayor of Paris since 1871

2019
Notre-Dame suffers a terrible fire, destroying its roof and spire

2024
Paris is set to host the Summer Olympic Games

EXPERIENCE

The stunning stained-glass windows of Sainte-Chapelle

ÎLE DE LA CITÉ AND ÎLE ST-LOUIS

The history of Paris started on the Île de la Cité, an island formed by two meanders of the Seine. Inhabited by the Parisii Gauls from the 3rd century BCE and taken over in 52 BCE by Caesar's Romans, the Île de la Cité was the birthplace of river commerce, and in medieval times it became a centre of political and religious power. Some imposing evidence of this power can still be seen in the Conciergerie, a medieval palace-turned-prison, and in Notre-Dame, the island's world-famous Gothic cathedral. The huddles of tiny houses and narrow streets that once characterized the island were swept away by the spacious thoroughfares built in the 19th century, but there are still charming snippets of another time around the romantic Square du Vert-Galant and the venerable Place Dauphine.

At the island's eastern end, the Pont St-Louis connects it to the smaller Île St-Louis. This former swampy pastureland was transformed into an elegant 17th-century residential area, with picturesque tree-lined quays. More recently, it has been home to rich artists and actors.

ÎLE DE LA CITÉ AND ÎLE ST-LOUIS

Must Sees

1. Notre-Dame
2. Sainte-Chapelle

Experience More

3. Mémorial des Martyrs de la Déportation
4. Conciergerie
5. Crypte Archéologique
6. Hôtel Dieu
7. Marché aux Fleurs Reine Elizabeth II
8. Palais de Justice
9. Place Dauphine
10. Pont Neuf
11. Square du Vert-Galant
12. St-Louis-en-l'Île

Eat

1. Berthillon

Stay

2. Paris Perfect Flat Place Dauphine
3. Saint-Louis en l'Isle
4. Hôtel du Jeu de Paume

Centre Georges Pompidou

RUE RAMBUTEAU

L

Archives Nationales

RUE DES FRANCS BOURGEOIS

M

6

ÎLE DE LA CITÉ AND ÎLE ST-LOUIS

RUE DU RENARD

RUE DU TEMPLE

RUE STE-CROIX

RUE DES BLANCS MANTEAUX

ARCHIVES

RUE VIEILLE DU TEMPLE

RUE DE LA BRETONNERIE

RUE LA VERRERIE

M Hôtel de Ville

RUE DE LOBAU

Hôtel de Ville

i

PLACE ST-GERVAIS

RUE FRANÇOIS MIRON

RUE DE RIVOLI

RUE DU ROI DE SICILE

RUE DES ROSIERS

RUE PAVÉE

MARAIS

Musée Cognacq-Jay

Musée Carnavalet

RUE DES FRANCS BOURGEOIS

Hôtel de Lamoignon

7

St-Paul **M**

Maison Européenne de la Photographie

Hôtel de Sully

RUE ST-ANTOINE

QUAI DE L'HÔTEL DE VILLE

RUE DE L'HÔTEL DE VILLE

Quai de l'Hôtel de Ville

Mémorial de la Shoah

RUE CHARLEMAGNE

St-Paul-St-Louis

RUE SAINT-PAUL

Pont-Marie **M**

AUX FLEURS

Pont Louis Philippe

THE MARAIS
p84

QUAI DES CELESTINS

RUE DU PETIT MUSC

RUE DU BELLAY

QUAI DE BOURBON

Pont Marie

BOULEVARD HENRI IV

Pont St-Louis

③

RUE LE REGRATTIER

RUE BUDE

RUE ST LOUIS

④

Île St-Louis

RUE POULLETIER

QUAI D'ANJOU

SQUARE H GALLI

8

Square de l'Île de France

QUAI D'ORLEANS

①

RUE DES DEUX PONTS

RUE SAINT LOUIS EN L'ILE

⑫

M Sully Morland

3 Mémorial des Martyrs de la Déportation

Musée Adam Mickiewicz

St-Louis-en-l'Île

Pavillon de l'Arsenal

QUAI DE LA TOURNELLE

QUAI DE BETHUNE

Pont de la Tournelle

Square Barye

Préfecture de Paris

RUE PONTOISE

LATIN QUARTER
p248

Pont de Sully

QUAI HENRI IV

BLVD ST-GERMAIN

BOULEVARD MORLAND

RUE CARDINAL LEMOINE

RUE DES FOSSES SAINT-BERNARD

Institut du Monde Arabe

QUAI SAINT-BERNARD

La Seine

RUE DU

RUE JUSSIEU

Université Pierre et Marie Curie

SQUARE TINO ROSSI

9

PLACE JUSSIEU

M Jussieu

| 0 metres | | 250 |
| 0 yards | | 250 |

N

L

M

1 NOTRE-DAME

📍K8 🏛 Parvis Notre-Dame 75004 - Pl Jean-Paul II Ⓜ Cité 🚌21, 38, 47, 58, 70, 72, 81, 82
🚇Notre-Dame 🕐Until further notice 🌐notredamedeparis.fr

No other building is more associated with the history of Paris than Notre-Dame (Our Lady). The "heart" of the country, both geographically and spiritually, the cathedral rises majestically at the eastern end of the Île de la Cité. A Gothic masterpiece, it was severely damaged by fire in 2019 – including the loss of its spire – and is currently closed to visitors while reconstruction is carried out.

Notre-Dame was built on the site of a Roman temple. After Pope Alexander III laid the first stone in 1163, an army of architects and craftsmen toiled for 170 years to realize Bishop Maurice de Sully's magnificent design. At the time it was finished, in about 1334, it was 130 m (430 ft) long and featured flying buttresses, a large transept, a deep choir and 69-m- (228-ft-) high towers.

Within the cathedral's hallowed walls, kings and emperors were crowned and royal Crusaders were blessed. But Notre-Dame was also the scene of turmoil. Revolutionaries ransacked it, banished religion, changed it into a temple to the Cult of Reason, and then used it as a wine store. Napoleon restored religion in 1804 and architect Viollet-le-Duc later restored the building to its former glory. Tragedy struck again in 2019, however, when a devastating fire engulfed the roof of the cathedral. Following a flood of high-profile donations, French President Emmanuel Macron vowed to rebuild Notre-Dame in time for the Paris 2024 Olympics.

> After Pope Alexander III laid the foundation stone in 1163, an army of architects and craftsmen toiled for 170 years to realize Bishop Maurice de Sully's magnificent design.

↑ Jean Ravy's spectacular flying buttresses, with a span of 15 m (50 ft), at the east end of the cathedral

↑ The cathedral's legendary gargoyles (chimères), hiding behind a large upper gallery between the towers

Timeline

1163 ▲ Foundation stone laid by Pope Alexander III

1708 ▲ Choir remodelled by Louis XIV, fulfilling his father's promise to honour the Virgin

1793 ▲ Revolutionaries loot the cathedral and rename it the Temple of Reason

2019 ▲ The cathedral's roof and spire are destroyed by a catastrophic fire

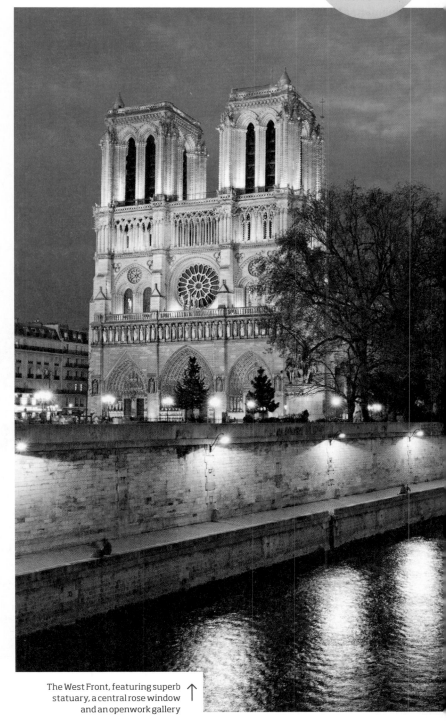

The West Front, featuring superb
statuary, a central rose window
and an openwork gallery ↑

Rebuilding Notre-Dame

Restoration work inside the cathedral means that visitors can't currently enter. The church, however, still plays a part in daily life, and its main bell rang to mark the death of former president Jacques Chirac in 2019. While architects focus on stabilizing the structure and cleaning up the mess, city planners are looking forward to working on the roof and spire. The government has set an ambitious goal to have the cathedral restored to its former glory – including a faithful reconstruction of the original spire – by 2024.

The spire was completely destroyed during the fire in 2019.

Galerie des Chimères

South tower

Portal of the Virgin

West rose window

Transept

The King's Gallery

↑ Cross-section illustration of how Notre-Dame looked before the fire

387

steps up the north tower lead to the famous gargoyles.

Flying buttresses

South rose window

Treasury

① A 14th-century screen enclosed the chancel, offering canons at prayer peace from noisy congregations.

② Behind the high altar is Nicolas Coustou's *Pietà*, standing on a gilded base.

③ Only the north window retains its 13th-century stained glass.

A MEDIEVAL ROMANCE

The 12th-century romance between the monk Pierre Abélard and the young Héloïse began in the cloisters of Notre-Dame. Abélard was hired as a tutor to the 17-year-old niece of a canon, and a love affair soon developed between the teacher and his pupil. In his wrath, Héloïse's uncle had the scholar castrated and Héloïse took refuge in a convent.

SAINTE-CHAPELLE

⬥ J7 ⌂ Blvd du Palais 75001 Ⓜ Cité 🚌 21, 38, 58, 85, 96 to Île de la Cité
🚆 St-Michel Ⓞ Notre-Dame Ⓞ Apr–Sep: 9am–7pm daily; Oct–Mar: 9am–
5pm daily 🚫 1 Jan, 1 May, 25 Dec Ⓦ sainte-chapelle.fr

Ethereal and magical, Sainte-Chapelle has been hailed
as one of the greatest architectural masterpieces
of the Western world. In the Middle Ages, the devout
likened this church to "a gateway to heaven". Today,
no visitor can fail to be transported by the blaze
of light created by the 15 magnificent
stained-glass windows.

A Gothic Masterpiece

The chapel was built in 1248 by Louis IX
to house Christ's purported Crown of
Thorns. A Gothic masterpiece, its
stunning stained-glass windows – the
oldest extant in Paris – are separated
by narrow columns that soar 15 m
(50 ft) to the star-studded, vaulted
roof. The windows portray over
1,000 biblical scenes, from Genesis
right through to the Crucifixion, in a
kaleidoscope of red, gold, green, blue
and mauve. Servants and commoners
worshipped in the Lower Chapel, while
the Upper Chapel was reserved for the
use of the king and the royal family.

Spire

Crown of
Thorns
decoration

Rose
window

Main portal

Lower Chapel

↑ The rose window,
telling the story of
the Apocalypse

Did You Know?

The spire is 75m (245 ft) high. It was erected in 1853 after four previous spires burned down.

Angel

Upper Chapel

↑ Cross-section illustration of Sainte-Chapelle

1 The Lower Chapel is not as light and lofty as the Upper Chapel, but is still magnificent.

2 The windows of the Upper Chapel contain 600 sq m (6,458 sq ft) of stained glass.

3 Carved stone statues of the Apostles adorn the 12 pillars of the Upper Chapel.

ST LOUIS' RELICS

Louis IX was extremely devout, and was canonized in 1297, not long after his death. In 1239, he acquired the Crown of Thorns from the Emperor of Constantinople and, in 1241, a fragment of Christ's Cross. He built this chapel as a shrine to house them. Louis paid nearly three times more for the relics than for the construction of Sainte-Chapelle. The Crown of Thorns was kept in Notre-Dame and survived the fire.

EXPERIENCE MORE

3

Mémorial des Martyrs de la Déportation

📍 K8 🏠 Sq de l'Île de France 75004 📞 06 14 67 54 98 Ⓜ Cité, St-Paul, Maubert Mutualité, Pont Marie 🚆 St-Michel ⏰ 10am–5pm daily (to 7pm Apr–Sep) 🚫 First Mon of month, 1 Jan, 1 May, 15 Aug, 1 Nov & 25 Dec

The memorial to the 200,000 French men, women and children deported to Nazi concentration camps in World War II is covered with the names of the camps to which they were deported. Earth from these camps has been used to form tombs and the interior walls are decorated with poetry and thousands of glass crystals. At the far end is the tomb dedicated to the Unknown Deportee.

4

Conciergerie

📍 J7 🏠 2 Blvd du Palais 75001 Ⓜ Cité ⏰ 9:30am–6pm daily 🚫 1 May, 25 Dec 🌐 paris-conciergerie.fr

The Conciergerie, part of the larger Palais de Justice (p78), was under the administration of the palace "concierge", the keeper of the king's mansion. When the monarch moved to the Marais (in 1417), the palace remained the seat of royal administration and law; the Conciergerie became a prison, with the "concierge" as its chief gaoler. Henry IV's assassin, Ravaillac, was imprisoned and tortured here.

During the French Revolution, the Conciergerie housed more than 4,000 prisoners, including Marie-Antoinette, who was held in a tiny cell,

and Charlotte Corday, who stabbed Revolutionary leader Marat as he lay in his bath. Ironically, the Revolutionary judges Robespierre and Danton also became "tenants" before being sent in turn to the guillotine.

The Conciergerie has a superb, four-aisled Gothic Salle des Gens d'Armes (Hall of the Men-at-Arms), the dining hall for the castle's 2,000 members of staff. The building, renovated in the

> 💬 **INSIDER TIP**
> ## Ticket Savings
>
> If you plan on visiting both the Conciergerie and Sainte-Chapelle on the same day, you can save money by buying a combined ticket.

The old Conciergerie prison, with its medieval turreted towers, overlooking the River Seine ↑

The Marché aux Fleurs, with its wonderful variety of seasonal and exotic flowers and plants

> During the French Revolution, the Conciergerie housed more than 4,000 prisoners, including Marie-Antoinette, who was held in a tiny cell.

19th century, retains the 14th-century clock on the Tour de l'Horloge (Clock Tower). It is the city's oldest public clock and is still operating.

⑤ Crypte Archéologique

📍K8 🏛7 Parvis Notre-Dame – Pl Jean-Paul II 75004 Ⓜ Cité, St-Michel ⏰10am–6pm Tue–Sun ❌1 Jan, 1 May, 8 May, 25 Dec & religious hols 🌐crypte.paris.fr

Situated on the main square (the *parvis*) in front of Notre-Dame and stretching 120 m (393 ft) underground, the Crypte Archéologique exhibits the remains of foundations and walls that predate the cathedral by several hundred years. The foundations of Paris's oldest rampart, dating from the 3rd century BCE, are displayed, as are the medieval foundations of the Hôtel Dieu. Interactive touchscreens help to bring the exhibits to life. Within the crypt are also traces of a hypocaust, a sophisticated underground heating system used for heating ancient Roman thermal baths.

⑥ Hôtel Dieu

📍K7 🏛1 Parvis Notre-Dame – Pl Jean-Paul II 75004 📞01 42 34 82 34 Ⓜ Cité

On the north side of the Parvis Notre-Dame is the Hôtel Dieu, the city's oldest hospital, dating back to the 12th century. The original building stretched across the island to both banks of the river, but was demolished to make way for one of Baron Haussmann's urban-planning schemes. It was rehoused on the site of an old orphanage in 1878. Though it remains a hospital, it's possible to step inside and have a look at its tranquil courtyard garden. It was nearby, at the Préfecture de la Police *(p80)*, in 1944, that the Paris police courageously resisted the German army; the battle is commemorated by a monument on Cour du 19-Août, within the Préfecture.

EAT

Berthillon
Parisians flock to this ice-cream parlour for its unusual flavours.

📍L8 🏛29–31 Rue St-Louis-en-l'Île 75004 ❌Mon, Tue 🌐berthillon.fr

€€€

⑦ Marché aux Fleurs Reine Elizabeth II

📍K7 🏛Pl Louis-Lépine 75004 Ⓜ Cité ⏰9:30am–7pm Mon-Sat

The year-round flower market adds colour and scent to an area otherwise dominated by administrative buildings. It is the most famous and, unfortunately, one of the last remaining flower markets in the city of Paris, its attractive iron pavilions harbouring both seasonal flowers and a wide range of specialist varieties such as orchids. The popular Marché aux Oiseaux, an animal and bird market, used to be held here every Sunday but closed in 2022.

** 8**

Palais de Justice

▣ J7 **🏛** 4–10 Blvd du Palais 75001 (main entrance by the Cour de Mai, 10 Blvd du Palais) **Ⓜ** Cité **🕐** 9am–6pm Mon-Fri **W** cours-appel.justice.fr/paris

The monumental block of buildings stretching the entire width of the Île de la Cité was formerly the home of the central law courts, most of which have now moved into brand-new premises in the Clichy-Batignolles quarter in the 17th arrondissement. The site, occupied since Roman times, was the seat of royal power until Charles V moved the court to the Hôtel St-Paul in the Marais during the 14th century. In April 1793, the Revolutionary Tribunal began dispensing justice from the Première Chambre, but this court eventually degenerated during Robespierre's Reign of Terror. Plans are afoot to open up more of the site to the public.

9

Place Dauphine

▣ J7 **🏛** 75001 (enter by Rue Henri-Robert) **Ⓜ** Pont Neuf, Cité

Southeast of Pont Neuf is this ancient square, laid out in 1607 by Henri IV and named after the Dauphin, the future Louis XIII. It is actually triangular in shape and lined with cafés, wine bars and restaurants. In the middle is a park with trees and benches. No 14 is one of the few buildings to have avoided any subsequent restoration. This haven of 17th-century charm is popular with *pétanque* (boules) players.

→

The tranquil Square du Vert-Galant, at the extreme point of the Île de la Cité

** 10**

Pont Neuf

▣ J7 **🏛** Quai de la Mégisserie and Quai des Grands Augustins 75001 **Ⓜ** Pont Neuf, Cité

Despite its name (New Bridge), this is the oldest of the existing bridges in Paris and has been immortalized by major literary and artistic figures since it was built. The first stone was laid by Henri III in 1578, but it was Henri IV who inaugurated it and gave it its name in 1607. His statue stands in the central section.

The bridge, which was the widest of its kind in Paris, has 12 arches and spans 275 m (912 ft). The first stone bridge in the city to be built without houses and with pavements for pedestrians, it heralded a new era in the relationship between the Île de la Cité and the river.

From its very beginning, the Pont Neuf has had heavy traffic, and it has undergone many renovations and repairs over the centuries.

11

Square du Vert-Galant

▣ J7 **🏛** Île de la Cité 75001 **Ⓜ** Pont Neuf, Cité

One of the most magical spots in Paris, this peaceful, tree-lined garden bears the nickname of Henri IV, "*vert-galant*". This eccentric monarch did much to beautify Paris in the early 17th century, and his popularity has lasted right up to this day. From here, there are splendid views of the Louvre and the Right Bank of the river, where Henri was assassinated in 1610. This is also the point from which the Vedettes du Pont Neuf pleasure boats depart.

Did You Know?

Henri IV's nickname, *vert-galant*, means "old flirt". The king was infamous for his womanizing.

→ The ornate interior of the Baroque church of St-Louis-en-l'Île

12

St-Louis-en-l'Île

📍L8 🏠19 Rue St-Louis-en-l'Île 75004 📞01 46 34 11 60 Ⓜ️Pont Marie 🕐10am–12:30pm & 3–5:30pm Mon-Sat; mass 7pm Mon-Fri, 6:30pm Sat & 11am Sun

The construction of this church began in 1664 from plans by the royal architect Louis Le Vau, who lived on the island. It was completed and consecrated in 1726. Among its outstanding exterior features are the 1741 iron clock at the entrance and the pierced iron spire.

The interior, in the Baroque style, is richly decorated with gilding and marble. There is a statue of St Louis holding a Crusader's sword. A plaque in the north aisle bears the inscription "in grateful memory of St Louis in whose honour the City of St Louis, Missouri, USA is named". The church is also twinned with Carthage cathedral in Tunisia, where St Louis is buried.

A SHORT WALK
ÎLE DE LA CITÉ

Distance 1.5 km (1 mile) **Nearest Metro** Cité
Time 15 minutes

The origins of Paris are here on the Île de la Cité, the boat-shaped island on the Seine first inhabited over 2,000 years ago by Celtic tribes. There is no older place in Paris, and remains of the first buildings are housed in the archaeological crypt under the square in front of Notre-Dame. A stroll in this part of the city takes you from one Parisian icon – the great medieval cathedral – to another: the Gothic masterpiece that is Sainte-Chapelle.

A grisly antechamber to the guillotine, the Conciergerie prison was much used in the Revolution (p76).

The colourful, lively Marché aux Fleurs Reine Elizabeth II is one of Paris's few remaining flower markets (p77).

The Cour du Mai is the impressive main courtyard of the Palais de Justice.

START

A jewel of Gothic architecture, Sainte-Chapelle is one of the most magical sights in Paris, noted for the magnificence of its stained glass (p74).

The Quai des Orfèvres owes its name to the goldsmiths (orfèvres) who frequented the area from medieval times onwards.

With its ancient towers lining the quays, the Palais de Justice has a history that extends back over 16 centuries (p78).

The Préfecture de Police was the scene of intense battles during World War II.

PONT AU CHANGE

QUAI DE LA CORSE

RUE DE LUTÈCE

BLVD DU PALAIS

QUAI DES ORFÈVRES

PONT ST-MICHEL

QUAI DU MARCHÉ NEUF

RUE DE LA CITÉ

PETIT PONT

Deep under the square, in the Crypte Archéologique, lie the remains of houses from 2,000 years ago (p77).

← A riverside view of the Conciergerie, a former prison

Patrons sitting outside one of the delightful cafés on the quaint Rue Chanoinesse

Locator Map
For more detail see p68

Did You Know?

In ancient times the island was used as a river crossing between northern and southern Gaul.

Once an orphanage, the Hôtel Dieu is now a city hospital (p77).

Point Zéro is the point from which all distances are measured in France.

Rue Chanoinesse has many charming old restaurants, cafés and shops.

The quaint streets of the Ancien Cloître quarter were once home to medieval clergymen and students.

Notre-Dame cathedral suffered a devastating fire in 2019 that destroyed its spire (p70).

The Square Jean XXIII is a peaceful square close to the river.

The Statue of Charlemagne commemorates the King of the Franks, who was crowned emperor in 800. He united all the Christian peoples of the West.

A LONG WALK
ÎLE ST-LOUIS

Distance 2 km (1 mile) **Walking time** 40 minutes
Nearest metro Pont Marie

The tiny Île St-Louis has been an exclusive residential enclave since the 17th century and is a lovely place for a stroll. This route passes along the picturesque tree-lined quais from Pont Louis-Philippe to Quai d'Anjou, before penetrating into the heart of the island along the Rue St-Louis-en-l'Île. The quiet streets here are a haven of chic cafés, restaurants, art galleries and boutiques, and are lined with elegant *hôtels particuliers* that infuse the area with a powerful sense of period.

*From the **corner of the Quai d'Orléans and the Rue Jean du Bellay**, there are fine views of the Panthéon's dome and Notre-Dame.*

*Opposite the Pont St-Louis, on the corner of Rue Jean du Bellay, is **Le Flore en l'Île**, the smartest café-cum-tea salon on the island.*

Hôtel Chernizot *is one of the few 18th-century hôtels particuliers on the island, with a superb Rococo balcony resting on leering gargoyles.*

*The former Polish library, founded in 1838, now houses the **Société Historique et Littéraire Polonaise**, focusing on the life of Polish poet Adam Mickiewicz.*

Looking along the Seine from the bank of the Île St-Louis

ÎLE DE LA CITÉ
AND ÎLE ST-LOUIS

Île St-
Loius

Locator Map
For more detail see p68

A statue in the
leafy grounds of
Square Barye,
at the island's
eastern tip

*Starting at Pont Marie Metro
station, walk down **Quai des
Celestins and Quai de l'Hôtel
de Ville**, lined with bookstands.*

*End the walk by crossing the
17th-century **Pont Marie** to the
Pont Marie Metro on the other side.*

**START/
FINISH**

Pont Marie Ⓜ

*Rue St-Louis-en-l'Île abounds in small,
chic, bistro-style restaurants with
pleasantly old-fashioned interiors;
at No 31 is the original **Berthillon**
ice cream parlour (p77).*

Pont
Marie

*At the corner of Rue Poulletier and
Rue St-Louis-en-l'Île, is the church
of **St-Louis-en-l'Île** (p79), with its
unusual tower, projecting clock, and
carved main door.*

Berthillon

*The most famous house on the island
is the **Hôtel Lambert**, at the eastern
end of Rue St-Louis-en-l'Île.*

Plaque
Marie Curie

St-Louis-
en-l'Île

Hôtel
Lambert

Hôtel
Richelieu

*The **Hôtel Richelieu** at No 18 Quai
de Béthune is one of the island's most
beautiful houses. It features a fine
garden that has retained its original
Classical blind arcades.*

La Seine

Square
Barye

*Square Barye, a shady
public garden at the east
point of the island, has fine
views of the river.*

Pont de
Sully

*The riverbanks
are joined by the
late-19th-century
Pont de Sully.*

*The Nobel-laureate Marie Curie
lived at **No 36 Quai de Béthune**.*

THE MARAIS

This district was little more than a muddy swamp until Henri IV built the Place Royale (now Place des Vosges) in 1605. But its position of prestige as a royal residence was soon swept away by the Revolution, which saw the Marais all but abandoned, before later descending into an architectural wasteland. Towards the end of the 19th century, a large number of Jewish settlers from Eastern Europe moved to the neighbourhood, establishing the Jewish Quarter around Rue des Rosiers. Beginning in the 1960s, sensitive restoration brought the Marais' historic buildings to life again; some of Paris's most popular museums are now housed in its elegant mansions, while the main streets and narrow passageways bustle with trendy restaurants, bars and chic boutiques. A hot spot for eclectic art galleries, the Marais is also the heart of the Parisian LGBTQ+ community.

THE MARAIS

Must Sees
1 Musée Picasso Paris
2 Pompidou Centre

Experience More
3 Musée Cognacq-Jay
4 Place des Vosges
5 Maison de Victor Hugo
6 Rue des Rosiers
7 Pavillon de l'Arsenal
8 St-Paul-St-Louis
9 Maison Européenne de la Photographie
10 Mémorial de la Shoah
11 Hôtel de Ville
12 La Cuisine Paris
13 Enceinte de Philippe August
14 Hôtel de Guénégaud
(Musée de la Chasse et de la Nature)
15 Musée d'Art et d'Histoire du Judaïsme
16 Musée Carnavalet

Eat
1 L'Ambassade d'Auvergne
2 L'As du Fallafel

Stay
3 Hôtel Jules et Jim
4 Hôtel de la Bretonnerie
5 Le Pavillon de la Reine

Shop
6 Meert
7 Edwart Chocolatier
8 Village St-Paul

❶ 🎨 ♿ 📽️ 🛍️

MUSÉE PICASSO PARIS

📍M6 🏠 Hôtel Salé, 5 Rue de Thorigny 75003 Ⓜ St-Sébastien Froissart, St-Paul, Chemin Vert 🚌 29, 69, 75, 96 to St-Paul, Bastille, Pl des Vosges 🕐 10:30am–6pm Tue–Fri; 9:30am–6pm Sat & Sun, advance booking recommended 🔒 1 Jan, 1 May, 25 Dec 🌐 museepicassoparis.fr

The Musée Picasso Paris holds the world's largest Picasso collection. Comprising over 5,000 works and tens of thousands of archived pieces, it offers an unparalleled insight into the artist's creative process.

↑ *Head of a Woman* (1931)

A visitor contemplating ↑ Picasso's *Femmes à leur Toilette* (1938)

Spanish-born Pablo Picasso lived most of his life in France. Upon his death in 1973, the French state inherited many of his works in lieu of death duties. It used them to establish the Musée Picasso Paris, which opened in 1985. The museum is housed in a large 17th-century mansion, the Hôtel Salé, which was built in 1656 for Aubert de Fontenay, a salt-tax collector (*salé* means "salty"). The original character of the mansion has been preserved, and large sculptures adorn the garden and courtyard. Reopened in 2014 following a five-year renovation, the museum holds works spanning a full range of media – paintings, sculptures, ceramics, drawings and etchings – covering all of Picasso's creative periods. Be sure not to miss Picasso's own collection of paintings on the second floor.

↑ The Hôtel Salé, considered to be one of the most exquisite historic houses in the Marais

PICASSO IN FRANCE

Born in Malaga, Spain, Picasso first visited Paris in 1900. He moved to the city in 1904, before later settling in the south of France. After 1934, Picasso never returned to his homeland due to his rejection of Franco's regime. However, throughout his life in France he used Spanish themes in his art, such as the bull (often in the form of a minotaur) and the guitar, which he associated with his Andalusian childhood.

↑ *The Kiss* (1969), one of many works concerned with the theme of the couple painted by Picasso during his later years

② ⊘ ⓂᎩ ▭ 🛍

POMPIDOU
CENTRE

📍K6 🏛️Pl Georges Pompidou Ⓜ️Rambuteau, Châtelet, Hôtel de Ville
🚌29, 38, 47, 75 🕐MNAM & temp exhibitions: 11am–9pm Wed–Mon
(to 11pm Thu); library: noon–10pm Wed–Mon (from 10am Sat,
Sun & pub hols); Atelier Brancusi: 2–6pm Wed–Mon 🗓️1 May
🌐centrepompidou.fr

Home to the Musée National d'Art Moderne, with over 120,000 works of art
by more than 5,000 artists, the Pompidou holds Europe's largest collection of modern and contemporary art. Looking like a building turned
inside out, its exterior is as eye-catching as the works on display within.

Blue: air
conditioning

Did You Know?

The Pompidou Centre's
collection was originally
housed in the Palais
de Tokyo (p229).

← *With the Black Arc* (1912) by Vassily Kandinsky

← *Le Rhinocéros* (1999) by Xavier Veilhan

Museum Guide

The "historical" collections bring together the great artistic movements of the first half of the 20th century, from Fauvism to Abstract Expressionism. A rich collection of Cubist sculptures is displayed, as well as examples of the great masters of the 20th century. Matisse, Picasso, Braque, Duchamp, Kandinsky, Léger, Miró, Giacometti and Dubuffet command large areas at the heart of the collection, which also shows the groups and the movements on which the history of modern art is based, or by which it has been affected, including Dada, Abstract Art and Informal.

The contemporary art section occupies the fourth floor. The collection includes works by leading French artists of the second half of the 20th century: Louise Bourgeois, Pierre Soulages, Jean-Pierre Raynaud, François

Morellet and Bertrand Lavier. The display is organized around a central aisle from which the rooms lead off. Certain areas have been designated to bring together different disciplines around a theme, such as minimalist painting or conceptual art, rather than a school or movement, while other rooms are artist-specific. Design, digital art and architecture are also covered, and major pieces by international artists are woven throughout the exhibition spaces. A graphic arts exhibition room and a video area complete the collection.

↑ The escalator overlooking the piazza

Red: elevators and escalators

Green: water

Yellow: electricity

← The distinctive exterior of the Pompidou, with service pipes that are colour-coded according to their various functions

BRANCUSI'S STUDIO

The Atelier Brancusi, on the piazza, is a reconstruction of the workshop of the Romanian-born artist Constantin Brancusi (1876–1957), who lived and worked in Paris from 1904. He bequeathed his entire collection of works to the French state on condition that his workshop be rebuilt as it was on the day he died.

EXPERIENCE MORE

 Musée Cognacq-Jay

📍M7 🏛Hôtel Donon, 8 Rue Elzévir 75003 Ⓜ St-Paul, Chemin Vert 🕐10am-6pm Tue-Sun 📅1 Jan, Easter Mon, 1 May, 1 Jun, 25 Dec 🌐museecognacqjay.paris.fr

This small, fine collection of 18th-century French works of art and furniture was formed by Ernest Cognacq and his wife, Marie-Louise Jay, founder of the Art Deco La Samaritaine, on the Quai du Louvre, which was once Paris's largest department store. The collection was bequeathed to the city and is now housed here in the Hôtel Donon, an elegant building dating from 1575 with an 18th-century façade and wood-panelled rooms.

 Place des Vosges

📍M7 📮75003, 75004 Ⓜ Bastille, St-Paul

This square is considered among the most beautiful in the world by Parisians and visitors alike. Its impressive symmetry – 36 houses, nine on each side, of brick and stone, with deep slate roofs and dormer windows over arcades – is still intact after 400 years. It has been the scene of many historic events over the centuries. A three-day tournament was held here to celebrate the marriage of Louis XIII to Anne of Austria in 1615. Cardinal Richelieu, pillar of the monarchy, stayed here in 1615; the famous literary hostess Madame de

 INSIDER TIP
Marais Mansions

Many of the former mansion houses in the Marais are open to the public; just walk through any doors that you see open.

Sévigné was born here in 1626; and the writer Victor Hugo lived here for 16 years. The arcades surrounding the square are full of art galleries and upmarket fashion boutiques and often ring out with the sound of buskers playing classical music or jazz, while at the centre of the *place* is a lovely formal garden with fountains and sandpits, popular with young families.

EAT

L'Ambassade d'Auvergne
Enjoy food from the Auvergne region in central France, with an emphasis on seasonal produce and hearty meat dishes.

📍K6 📮22 Rue du Grenier-St-Lazare 75003 🌐ambassade-auvergne.fr

€€€

L'As du Fallafel
The best falafel wraps in Paris, if the queues at this bustling local favourite are any indication.

📍L7 📮34 Rue des Rosiers 75004 📞01 48 87 63 60

€€€

A room decorated in Chinese style, in the Maison de Victor Hugo ↑

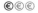

5
Maison de Victor Hugo

M7 **6 Pl des Vosges
75004** **Bastille, Chemin
Vert** **10am–6pm Tue–Sun**
**maisonsvictorhugo.
paris.fr**

The French poet, dramatist
and novelist lived on the
second floor of the former
Hôtel Rohan-Guéménée
from 1832 to 1848. It was
here that Victor Hugo wrote
most of *Les Misérables* and
completed many other
famous works. The museum
inside displays reconstruc-
tions of the rooms in which
the writer lived, his vivid
pen-and-ink drawings and
caricatures, and books and
mementos from the crucially
important periods in his life,
from his childhood to his exile
from France between 1852 and
1870. It also holds temporary
ticketed exhibitions.

6
Rue des Rosiers

L7 **75004**
St-Paul, Chemin Vert

The Jewish quarter in and
around this street is one of
the most colourful areas of
Paris. The street's name refers
to the rose bushes within
the old city wall. A Jewish
community first settled here
in the 13th century, with a
second wave of immigration
occurring in the 19th century
from Russia, Poland and
Central Europe. Sephardic
Jews arrived from North
Africa in the 1950s and 1960s.
Some 165 students were
deported from the Jewish
boys' school nearby at 10 Rue
des Hospitalières-St-Gervais
in World War II. *"N'oubliez pas"*
(Lest we forget) is engraved
on the wall. Today, this area
contains synagogues, bakeries
and kosher restaurants.

7
Pavillon de l'Arsenal

M8 **21 Blvd Morland
75004** **Sully Morland,
Bastille** **11am–7pm
Tue–Sun** **1 Jan**
pavillon-arsenal.com

Dedicated to architecture
and urbanism, the Pavillon
de l'Arsenal houses a large
number of fascinating
exhibitions throughout the
year that illustrate the
architectural evolution of
Paris. Using films, models
and panoramic images,
it explores how Paris was built
over the centuries, as well as
looking at future plans for
the city. Though the building
dates back to 1879, inside the
space feels very modern.
Regular activities are held for
children, and on weekends
free tours are provided by
architecture students (in
French only).

Paris's imposing town hall (Hôtel de Ville), with its elaborate façade ↑

8

St-Paul-St-Louis

📍 M7 🏠 99 Rue St-Antoine 75004 📞 01 42 72 30 32 Ⓜ St-Paul
🕐 8am–8pm daily

A Jesuit church, St-Paul–St-Louis is an important symbol of the influence that the Jesuits held from 1627, when Louis XIII laid the first stone, to 1762, when they were expelled from France. The Gesù church in Rome served as the model for the nave, while the 60-m-(180-ft-) high dome was the forerunner of those of the Invalides (p206) and the Sorbonne (p255). Most of the church's treasures were removed during periods of turmoil, but Delacroix's masterpiece *Christ in the Garden of Olives* can still be seen. The church sometimes hosts concerts. It is on one of the main streets of the Marais, but can also be approached by the Passage St-Paul.

9

Maison Européenne de la Photographie

📍 L7 🏠 5-7 Rue de Fourcy 75004 Ⓜ St-Paul, Pont Marie 🕐 11am–8pm Wed–Fri, 10am–8pm Sat & Sun
🚫 1 Jan, 1 May, 25 Dec
🌐 mep-fr.org

Located in the 18th-century Hôtel Hénault de Cantobre, a former private home, the Maison Européenne de la Photographie (MEP) hosts some of the best exhibitions of contemporary photography in the whole of Europe. The centre organizes cutting-edge shows alongside retrospectives on major photographers, and since opening its doors in 1996, it has hosted displays by such celebrated photographers as Elliott Erwitt, Don McCullin, Annie Leibovitz, Robert Doisneau and Henri Cartier-Bresson. The MEP's extensive permanent collection on the history of photography is a must-see for anyone interested in exploring this medium.

THE MANSIONS OF THE MARAIS

In the 1500s, noblemen and women began building sumptuous residences in the newly drained marshlands called the Marais. Many of these mansions have now been restored as museums, such as the Musée Carnavalet (p97) and Musée Cognacq-Jay (p92).

DOOR DETAIL

SHOP

Meert
This elegant branch of the 18th-century Lillois patisserie is known for its fine vanilla-cream *gaufres* (waffles).

📍 M7 🏠 16 Rue Elzévir 75003 🌐 meert.fr

Edwart Chocolatier
Gourmet chocolates with unusual flavours such as curry praline and Oolong tea are the star products at this sleek boutique.

📍 L7 🏠 17 Rue Vieille du Temple 75004 🌐 edwart.fr

Village St-Paul
These interlocking courtyards house all sorts of antique, interior-design, art and curiosity shops, as well as occasional flea markets.

📍 M8 🏠 Off Rue St-Paul 75004 🌐 levillagesaint paul.com

Mémorial de la Shoah

📍 L7 🏠 17 Rue Geoffroy-l'Asnier 75004 Ⓜ Pont Marie, St-Paul ⏰ 10am–6pm Sun-Fri (to 10pm Thu); multimedia & reading rooms: 10am–5:30pm Sun-Fri (to 7:30pm Thu) 🚫 Public & Jewish hols 🌐 memorialdelashoah.org

The eternal flame burning in the crypt here is the memorial to the unknown Jewish martyrs of the Holocaust. Its striking feature is a large cylinder that bears the names of the concentration camps where Jewish victims of the Holocaust died. In 2005, a stone wall engraved with the names of 76,000 Jews – 11,000 of them children – who were deported from France to the Nazi death camps, was put up here. Various drawings, letters and artifacts from the camps are also on display, as well as photos of deportees. Every other Sunday at 3pm, free guided tours take place in English.

Hôtel de Ville

📍 K7 🏠 Pl de l'Hôtel de Ville 75004 (visitor entrance 29 Rue de Rivoli, exhibitions entrance 5 Rue de Lobau) Ⓜ Hôtel de Ville ⏰ Hours vary for temporary exhibitions 🚫 Public hols, official functions 🌐 paris.fr

Home of the city council, the town hall is a 19th-century reconstruction of the original building erected between 1533 and 1628, which was burned down during the Paris Commune of 1871 (p62). It is highly ornate, with elaborate stonework, turrets and statues overlooking a pedestrianized square whose fountains are lit up at night.

The square was once the main site for hangings, burnings and other gruesome executions. It was here that Ravaillac, Henri IV's assassin, was quartered alive in 1610, his body ripped to pieces by four strong horses.

Inside, a notable feature is the long Salle des Fêtes (ballroom), with adjoining salons devoted to science, literature and the arts. The impressive staircase, the decorated ceilings with their chandeliers, and the statues and caryatids all add to the air of ceremony and pomp. While these parts are mostly closed to the public (except during some of the Journées du Patrimoine in September), certain annexes are used for free, acclaimed temporary exhibitions on various themes related to Paris.

Artworks on display in the Musée d'Art et d'Histoire du Judaïsme →

 (12)

La Cuisine Paris

◉ L7 ⌂ 80 Quai de l'Hôtel de Ville 75004 Ⓜ St-Paul Ⓦ lacuisineparis.com

With Paris having so many restaurants and bakeries, few visitors stop to think about learning to make their own French-inspired dishes. La Cuisine offers a variety of cooking classes run by real French cooks, who teach you how to make classic savoury dishes as well as sweet pastries in a slick kitchen boasting views over the Seine. English-speaking instructors demonstrate the techniques behind buttery croissants and crusty baguettes, and demystify many of France's most iconic dishes, such as fluffy soufflés and perfectly prepared crêpes. Some of the classes offered even combine a market visit with a cooking class where you prepare a

whole lunch. After rolling up their sleeves for a few hours, La Cuisine students walk away with either a full belly or a package of flaky, buttery, or otherwise decadent pastries. The school also offers culinary walking tours of the Marais and nearby neighbourhoods for visitors wanting to discover local shops and flavours. Classes and tours are open to all ages and levels of experience.

---

(13)

Enceinte de Philippe Auguste

◉ L7 ⌂ 13 Rue Charlemagne 75004 Ⓜ St-Paul, Sully Morland

Dating back to 1190, these fortifications are the remains of Paris's oldest wall. King Philippe Auguste built the wall around Paris to protect the city from attacks while he was away fighting in the Crusades.

A hallmark of the wall was a fortress where the Louvre now stands; its remnants are visible today in the museum's lower levels. The section here in the Marais, however, hides in plain sight. It is still possible to see the large tower, the Tour Montgomery, that formed part of the gates through which everyone had to pass in order to enter the city. The wall was an effective means of regulating trade, allowing the king to levy taxes on imports such as wine and furs, as well as many other goods.

---

 (14)

Hôtel de Guénégaud (Musée de la Chasse et de la Nature)

◉ L6 ⌂ 62 Rue des Archives 75003 Ⓜ Hôtel de Ville Ⓦ chassenature.org

The celebrated architect François Mansart built this mansion in the mid-17th century for Henri de Guénégaud des Brosses, who was Secretary of State and Keeper of the Seals. Since 1967, it has housed the Musée de la Chasse et de la Nature (Nature and Hunting Museum), which features a collection of 5,000 works that are classified as

---

RIVERBANK WALK

After the success of the Left Bank renovation, Berges de Seine, Paris City Hall decided to tackle the Right Bank. In 2017, the two banks were joined as the Parc Rives de Seine, which passes through the Marais and offers a pleasant waterfront stroll. Citizens embraced the change, already acquainted with the car-free zone during the annual Paris Plages beach festival. Now, the festive atmosphere lasts all year long, with bars and cafés lining the promenade.

"national treasures" by the Museum of Culture. A reflection on man's relationship with animals and wild spaces, the museum's exhibits include a fine collection of hunting weapons, stuffed animals and objets d'art. There are also drawings and paintings by Oudry, Vernet and Rubens (including *Diane and her Nymphs Preparing to Hunt*).

 15

Musée d'Art et d'Histoire du Judaïsme

📍L6 🏠Hôtel de St-Aignan, 71 Rue du Temple 75003 Ⓜ Rambuteau 🕐11am-6pm Tue-Fri (to 9pm Wed), 10am-7pm Sat & Sun 🚫1 Jan, 1 May, Rosh Hashanah & Yom Kippur 🌐mahj.org

Housed in an elegant Marais mansion, this is one of the world's leading museums on Judaism and the largest in France. It commemorates the culture of French, Sephardic (Spain, Portugal, North Africa), Ashkenazi (Germany and Eastern Europe), Italian and Dutch Jewry from medieval times to the present. There has been a sizeable Jewish community in France since Roman times, and some of the world's greatest Jewish scholars were French. Much exquisite craftsmanship is displayed, with elaborate silverware and Torah covers. There are also archaeological artifacts, historical documents, photographs, paintings and cartoons.

 16

Musée Carnavalet

📍M7 🏠23 Rue de Sévigné 75003 Ⓜ St-Paul, Chemin Vert 🕐11am-6pm Tue-Fri 🚫1 Jan, 1 May, 24 Dec 🌐carnavalet.paris.fr

Situated inside two adjoining mansions, this museum is dedicated to the history of Paris. It has a range of child-friendly displays and digital innovations that introduce the fascinating collection. The Hôtel Carnavalet, which was built as a town house in 1548, was transformed in the mid-17th century by architect François Mansart, while the neighbouring 17th-century Hôtel Le Peletier de St-Fargeau features superb early-20th-century interiors. In both, entire rooms are lavishly decorated with gilded wood panelling, furniture and objets d'art, including paintings and sculptures of prominent personalities, and engravings showing Paris being built. One of the most engaging parts of the museum is a section covering the French Revolution.

STAY

Hôtel Jules et Jim
Well-located and modern, it's popular with LGBTQ+ travellers.

📍L6 🏠11 Rue des Gravilliers 75003 🌐hoteljulesetjim.com

€€€

Hôtel de la Bretonnerie
With old-world décor and wooden beams, this is a comfortable and welcoming place.

📍L7 🏠22 Rue Ste-Croix de la Bretonnerie 75004 🌐hotelparismarais bretonnerie.com

€€€

Le Pavillon de la Reine
This sumptuous hotel is an experience fit for the royals who would have lived on this square.

📍M7 🏠28 Place des Vosges 75003 🌐pavillon-de-la-reine.com

€€€

> **After rolling up their sleeves for a few hours, La Cuisine students walk away with either a full belly or a package of flaky, buttery, or otherwise decadent pastries.**

↑ The handsome Renaissance Musée Carnavalet

A SHORT WALK
THE MARAIS

Distance 1.5 km (1 mile) **Nearest Metro**
St-Paul **Time** 20 minutes

Once an area of marshland as its name suggests
(*marais* means swamp), the Marais grew steadily in
importance from the 14th century, by virtue of its
proximity to the Louvre, the preferred residence of
Charles V. Its heyday was in the 17th century, when
it became the fashionable area for the monied
classes. They built many grand mansions (*hôtels
particuliers*) that still dot the Marais today – some
of these *hôtels particuliers* have been restored and
turned into museums. Once again fashionable
with the affluent, the neighbourhood is home
to designer boutiques, trendy restaurants,
art galleries and cafés.

*The Hôtel Salé is the setting
for the Musée Picasso Paris.
It boasts the largest collection
of Picassos in the world, many of
which came from Picasso's own
collection after his death (p88).*

START

RUE BARBETTE

RUE ELZÉVIR

RUE PAYENNE

RU...

RUE DES FRANCS...

RUE DES HOSPITALIÈRES
ST-GERVAIS

*The centuries-old Rue
des Francs-Bourgeois
is lined with intriguing
buildings and
trendy shops.*

RUE DES ROSIERS

*The smell of hot pastrami and
challah wafts from restaurants
and bakeries on Rue des Rosiers,
the heart of the Jewish area (p93).*

RUE PAVÉE

RUE MALHER

*Discover the exquisite
collection of 18th-century
paintings and furniture
at the Musée
Cognacq-Jay (p92).*

*Behind the ornate
doorway of the fine
Hôtel de Lamoignon is
Paris's historical library.*

Walking along the
shopping street of Rue
des Francs-Bourgeois

Locator Map
For more detail see p86

↑ The interior courtyard of the
Musée Carnavalet, housed in
two adjoining mansions

Did You Know?

It took Victor Hugo
nearly two decades to
write *Les Misérables*.

*The Hôtel Le Peletier de St-Fargeau
adjoins the Hôtel Carnavalet to form
the Musée Carnavalet (p97).*

*The statue of Louis XIV in
Roman dress by Coysevox
is in the courtyard of the
Hôtel Carnavalet, home to
the Musée Carnavalet.*

DU PARC ROYAL

SÉVIGNÉ

RUE DE BÉARN

RUE DE TURENNE

RUE DE BOURGEOIS

RUE DE

| 0 metres | 100 |
| 0 yards | 100 |

N
↑

*Once the site of jousting
and tournaments, the
historic Place des Vosges,
in the very heart of the
Marais, is a square of
perfect symmetry (p92).*

Author of Les
Misérables, *Victor
Hugo lived at No 6
Place des Vosges.
The Maison de
Victor Hugo is now
a museum of his life
and work (p93).*

RUE DE BIRAGUE

◉ FINISH

*The Hôtel de Sully
was built for a
notorious gambler.*

BASTILLE AND OBERKAMPF

East of the Marais, Bastille and Oberkampf were once Parisian *faubourgs*, or suburbs, well outside the main city wall in the Middle Ages. Furniture-makers inhabited the area around Bastille, capitalizing on wood delivered at the nearby docks, while Oberkampf was a working-class neighbourhood filled with artisans, including leather-makers. Where the Opéra National de Paris Bastille stands today, Parisians once gaped at the mighty Bastille – an imposing medieval prison fortress and symbol of royal repression, which famously met its demise in 1789 during the French Revolution. Throughout the 19th century, this largely working-class neighbourhood grew into one of Paris's most densely populated districts. In 1840, the Colonne de Juillet rose in Place de la Bastille, joined some 150 years later by the modern Opéra. Many of the artisans disappeared during this time, but an energetic nightlife grew up in their wake, fuelled by the culturally diverse and generally younger populations living here.

RÉPUBLIQUE AND CANAL ST-MARTIN
p114

THE MARAIS
p84

BASTILLE AND OBERKAMPF

Edith Piaf Museum 6

Ménilmontant M

Parmentier M

Rue St-Maur 6 5

RUE OBERKAMPF

AVENUE DE LA RÉPUBLIQUE

RUE DES BLUETS

BLVD DE MÉNILMONTANT

AVENUE GAMBETTA

Oberkampf M

Filles du Calvaire M

Rue Oberkampf 9

BLVD R LENOIR

RUE DE LA FOLIE MÉRICOURT

RUE OBERKAMPF

RUE TERNAUX

RUE PARMENTIER

RUE ST-MAUR

RUE DES BLUETS

Père Lachaise M

Cimetière du Père-Lachaise

RUE JP TIMBAUD

BLVD DES FILLES DU CALVAIRE

St-Sébastien Froissart M 8

Merci 11

RUE ST-SEBASTIEN

SQUARE RICHARD LENOIR

St-Ambroise M

RUE ST-AMBROISE

LACHARRIERE

RUE ST-MAUR

RUE SERVAN

RUE DU CHEMIN VERT

RUE OMER TALON

RUE DE LA FOLIE REGNAULT

Philippe Auguste M

RUE PELEE

Richard Lenoir M

ALLÉE VERTE

BOULEVARD VOLTAIRE

RUE PARMENTIER

RUE CAMILLE DESMOULINS

DURANTI

RUE SERVAN

RUE MERLIN

BLVD DE MÉNILMONTANT

BLVD

RUE AMELOT

Chemin Vert M

RUE AMELOT

RUE RICHARD LENOIR

SQUARE BREGUET SABIN

Bréguet Sabin M

RUE BREGUET

RUE SEDAINE

RUE POPINCOURT

Voltaire M

PLACE LEON BLUM

RUE DE LA ROQUETTE

LA ROQUETTE

RUE MERCOEUR

RUE DE BELFORT

RUE LEON FROT

BLVD DE CHARONNE

BLVD BEAUMARCHAIS

RUE DES TOURNELLES

RUE RICHARD

Rue de la Roquette 4 2 5

DE LA ROQUETTE

RUE KELLER

AVENUE LEDRU ROLLIN

RUE BASFROI

RUE GODEFROY CAVAIGNAC

RUE RICHARD LENOIR

CHARONNE

Charonne M

RUE DE CHARONNE

AVE PHILIPPE AUGUSTE

Cour Damoye 10 7

RUE DAVAL

RUE DE LAPPE

Place de la Bastille 1

Bastille M

Passage du Cheval Blanc 10

Port de l'Arsenal

Opéra National de Paris Bastille 2

Ledru-Rollin M

RUE DU FAUBOURG ST-ANTOINE

PGE DE LA MAIN D'OR

RUE TROUSSEAU

DE

RUE FAIDHERBE

RUE CHANZY

Rue des Boulets M

BOULEVARD VOLTAIRE

RUE ST-BERNARD

RUE DU DAHOMEY

BLVD BOURDON

BLVD DE LA BASTILLE

RUE DE LYON

RUE DE CHARENTON

RUE DE COTTE

RUE D'ALIGRE

RUE DE PRAGUE

Coulée Verte René-Dumont 3

RUE LACUEE

RUE JULES CESAR

RUE E. CASTELAR

Marché d'Aligre 4

RUE DE CITEAUX

Faidherbe-Chaligny M

RUE DU FAUBOURG ST-ANTOINE

RUE DE REUILLY

Bassin de l'Arsenal 7

AVENUE LEDRU ROLLIN

AVENUE DAUMESNIL

RUE TRAVERSIERE

RUE BECCARIA

RUE DE CHARENTON

RUE DE CHARENTON

RUE CROZATIER

BOULEVARD DIDEROT

Quai de la Rapée M

RUE PARROT

RUE DE LYON

RUE ABEL

RUE MALTE

PLACE H FRENAY

Reuilly-Diderot M

PLACE MAZAS

BLVD. DIDEROT

Gare de Lyon RER M 4

RUE H.

RUE BOUTON

PLACE RUTEBEUF

AVENUE DAUMESNIL

Pont d'Austerlitz

Quai de la Rapée

Gare de Lyon 8 i

RUE DE BERCY

Montgallet M

QUAI DE LA RAPEE

RUE VAN GOGH

RUE DE BERCY

AVENUE DAUMESNIL

QUAI D'AUSTERLITZ

La Seine

Pont C de Gaulle

RUE DE LA RAPEE

RUE VILLIOT

RUE DE BERCY

AVENUE DAUMESNIL

REUILLY

PONT DE LA RAPEE

BERCY

Bercy M

BLVD DE REUILLY

Paris-Bercy - Bourgogne - Pays d'Auvergne

Dugommier M

JARDIN DES PLANTES AND PLACE D'ITALIE
p262

Pont de Bercy

AccorHotels Arena

Bercy 12

Parc de Bercy

BLVD DE BERCY

Quai de la Gare M

0 metres		400
0 yards		400

N

❶

PLACE DE LA BASTILLE

🄿 N8 🄰 Place de la Bastille 75004 Ⓜ Bastille 🚌 29, 69, 76, 86, 87, 91

This busy square was the scene of one of the most important events in French history – the storming of the Bastille on 14 July 1789. Little trace of the infamous prison remains, and today the square is a hub for nightlife and cultural events such as concerts.

↑ The Marché Bastille on nearby Boulevard Richard Lenoir

At the centre of the large square that marks the site of the prison is the Colonne de Juillet. Topped by the elegant, gilded statue of the winged "genius of liberty", this column of hollow bronze reaches 50.5 m (166 ft) into the sky. It is a memorial to those who died in the street battles of July 1830 that led to the overthrow of the monarch. The crypt contains the remains of 504 victims of the violent fighting and others who died in the 1848 revolution.

Place de la Bastille was once the border between central Paris and the eastern working-class areas (faubourgs). Gentrification, however, is well under way. Just east of the Opéra Bastille is the starting point of the Coulée Verte René-Dumont (p106), an elevated walking trail built on a disused railway line, while the creation of a vast pedestrian plaza around the column, connected to the Bassin de l'Arsenal marina (p108), transformed the square in 2020.

←

The Opéra National de Paris Bastille (p106), designed by Carlos Ott

THE FRENCH REVOLUTION

In 1789, most Parisians were living in squalor and poverty. Rising inflation and opposition to Louis XVI culminated in the storming of the Bastille, the king's prison; the Republic was founded three years later. However, the Terror soon followed, when those suspected of betraying the Revolution were executed without trial: more than 60,000 people lost their lives.

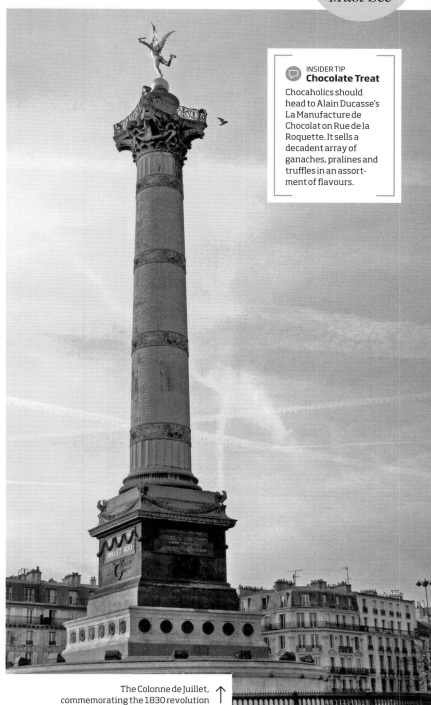

INSIDER TIP
Chocolate Treat

Chocaholics should head to Alain Ducasse's La Manufacture de Chocolat on Rue de la Roquette. It sells a decadent array of ganaches, pralines and truffles in an assortment of flavours.

The Colonne de Juillet, commemorating the 1830 revolution that saw the fall of King Charles X

EXPERIENCE MORE

Opéra National de Paris Bastille

📍 N8 📌 120 Rue de Lyon 75012 Ⓜ Bastille 🌐 operadeparis.fr

The controversial "people's opera" was officially opened on 14 July 1989 to coincide with the bicentennial celebrations of the storming of the Bastille. Carlos Ott's imposing building is a notable break with 19th-century opera-house design, epitomized by Charles Garnier's opulent Opéra in the heart of the city (p172). The Bastille opera house is a massive, modern, curved, glass building. The main auditorium seats an audience of 2,700; its design is functional and modern, the black upholstered seats contrasting with the granite of the walls and the impressive glass ceiling. With its five moveable stages, this opera house is certainly a masterpiece of technological wizardry and it's well worth seeing a performance here; the website has full details of what's on and also has information about guided tours (in French).

❸ Coulée Verte René-Dumont

📍 P9 📌 Ave Daumesnil 75012 Ⓜ Bastille 🕐 8am-dusk Mon-Fri, 9am-dusk Sat & Sun

This former elevated railway hosts Paris's most exclusive verdant walkway. Rising up to 10 m (33 ft) above the streets, the promenade is planted with many varieties of flowers and trees, stretches for about 5 km (3 miles) between the Opéra Bastille and the Périphérique city boundary to the east.

The original railway closed in 1969 but the city preserved the structure and opened the Coulée Verte René-Dumont (also known as the Promenade Plantée) in 1993, serving as a model for urban renewal that has been replicated around the world. The topography varies from planted gardens and larger parks to narrow walkways snaking between apartment buildings. A stroll or jog along the Coulée Verte René-Dumont is a delightful traffic-free experience, with epic views of the city. Underneath the red-brick railway arches by the opera house, the Viaduc des Arts houses artisan and craft shops and fashion boutiques. All along the promenade, staircases lead down to street level, where cafés and bakeries are rarely far away for a quick pick-me-up while exploring Paris's eastern extremities in bucolic bliss.

(p172)

Did You Know?

Remnants of the walls of the Bastille prison can be seen in the Bastille Metro.

❹ Marché d'Aligre

📍 P8 📌 Place d'Aligre 75012 Ⓜ Ledru-Rollin 🕐 7:30am-1:30pm Tue-Fri, 7:30am-2:30pm Sat & Sun (indoor market 9am-1pm & 4-7:30pm Tue-Fri, 9am-1pm & 3:30-7:30pm Sat, 9am-1:30pm Sun)

On most mornings, this lively and good-value market offers one of the most colourful sights in Paris. French, Arab and African traders hawk fruit, vegetables, flowers, clothing,

> A stroll or jog along the Coulée Verte René-Dumont is a delightful traffic-free experience, with epic views of the city.

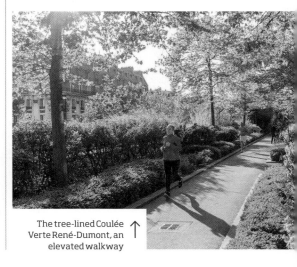

The tree-lined Coulée Verte René-Dumont, an elevated walkway ↑

Busy Rue de la Roquette with its lively cafés and restaurants ↑

bric-a-brac and second-hand books on the streets, while the adjoining covered market, the Marché Beauvau, offers fruit, vegetables, a great selection of cheese, charcuterie and olive oils, plus many intriguing international delicacies.

The Marché d'Aligre is where old and new Paris meet. Here, the established community of this old artisan quarter coexists with a more recently established group of hip urban professionals, lured here by the transformation of the nearby Bastille area. Some parts of the indoor market have been renovated following a fire in 2015.

⑤

Rue de la Roquette

🔲 N7 Ⓜ Bastille, Voltaire

This bustling street, lined with bars, cafés and restaurants, stretches from the Opéra Bastille towards Père Lachaise Cemetery (p130). At No 17 stands the house of Symbolist poet Paul Verlaine, a 19th-century regular in the neighbourhood. At No 70, a 19th-century fountain once brought water from the canal into the densely populated district. The five stone slabs in the road where the street meets Rue de la Croix Faubin are an eerie reminder of a much darker history. They are the foundations of the guillotine where inmates of the Prison de la Roquette met their fate, usually in front of a crowd of onlookers. Around 200 executions were carried out between 1851 and 1899, while some 4,000 women, members of the French Resistance, were incarcerated in the prison in 1944. The former entrance can still be seen across the street, on Square de la Roquette. Rue de la Roquette and the surrounding area, particularly cobbled Rue de Lappe, with its numerous bars, gets pretty animated at night.

EAT

Bofinger
This classic 19th-century brasserie serves up Alsatian fare in a glitzy setting.

🔲 M7 🏠 5 Rue de la Bastille 75004 bofingerparis.com

€€€

Café de l'Industrie
Simple food and a funky setting make this a neighbourhood favourite.

🔲 N7 🏠 16 Rue St-Sabin 75011 cafedelindustrie paris.fr

€€€

Septime
Innovative cuisine and a relaxed atmosphere combine for perfect Michelin-star dining.

🔲 P8 🏠 80 Rue de Charonne 75011 🕒 Sat & Sun septime-charonne.fr

€€€

→

Memorabilia, paintings and artifacts in the small Edith Piaf Museum

6

Edith Piaf Museum

⊙P5 **⌂**5 Rue Crespin du Gast 75011 **☎**01 43 55 52 72 **Ⓜ**Ménilmontant **⊙**By appt 1–6pm Mon–Wed **⊗**Jun & Sep

Legend has it that singer Edith Piaf was born in the street in nearby Belleville (p132). Historians debate that story, but she did actually live in this tiny apartment, now a museum dedicated to the singer's legacy. It is privately owned by a fan who has curated a collection of memorabilia and personal artifacts that belonged to the chanteuse. Just 1.42 m (4 ft 8 inches) tall and known as the "Little Sparrow", she possessed a voice that was anything but small, echoing across concert halls worldwide. Buried in nearby Père Lachaise Cemetery (p130), Piaf is today best known for songs such as "La Vie en Rose". An engaging collection of souvenirs, prints and Piaf's signature black dresses are on display. Entry to the museum is by appointment only. A charming, intimate experience, it should appeal to both die-hard fans and visitors with just a casual interest.

7

Bassin de l'Arsenal

⊙M9 **⌂**5 Quai de la Rapée **Ⓜ**Bastille

Between Place de la Bastille and the Seine, this pleasure-boat arena hides below street level. A lock joins it to the River Seine. The location of a weapons storehouse since the 16th century, the arsenal eventually fell into disuse as revolutionaries removed the Bastille fortress, stone by stone. Nowadays, the tiny marina hosts private watercraft and is also the starting point for tour cruises along the Canal St-Martin (p118). Find a spot to relax on the lawn of the pretty canalside garden where, on warm evenings, Parisians picnic along the traffic-free waterfront. Two bridges crossing the water offer picture-postcard views of the Colonne de Juillet in Place de la Bastille.

8

Gare de Lyon

⊙N9 **⌂**Place Louis-Armand 75012 **Ⓜ**Gare de Lyon **🖥**Le Train Bleu: le-train-bleu.com

Built for the 1900 Exposition Universelle, this station is

DRINK

Moonshiner
This 1920s-inspired speakeasy hides behind a pizzeria. It can be crowded, but serves great cocktails.

⊙N7 **⌂**5 Rue Sedaine 75011 **☎**09 50 73 12 99

La Fine Mousse
It's all about craft beer here, with up-and-coming local brews on tap. They also offer tasting workshops.

⊙P5 **⌂**6 Ave Jean Aicard 75011 **🖥**lafinemousse.fr

Le Perchoir
Clink glasses and feast on light fare from this rooftop bar with a 360-degree view of the city.

⊙P5 **⌂**14 Rue Crespin du Gast 75011 **🖥**leperchoir.fr

With high-end restaurants, gourmet coffee shops, craft beer and spicy Mexican fare, Rue Oberkampf caters to all sorts of flavours and fancies.

INSIDER TIP
Chambelland

Chambelland, at 14 Rue Ternaux, just off Rue Oberkampf, is one of the few gluten-free bakeries in Paris, serving delicious bread, biscuits and pastries.

the third busiest in France, with about 110 million annual passengers. It welcomes trains from throughout France, as well as Italy, Switzerland and other international destinations. In the summer months you'll notice many sun-kissed travellers returning from the Côte d'Azur, as this station serves Nice and other southern French destinations. On the exterior of the station looms the iconic clock tower, reminiscent of the UK Parliament's Big Ben tower. Inside the Gare de Lyon is the illustrious restaurant Le Train Bleu, a glitzy dining experience that has been in operation for over a century. The ornate dining rooms are decorated with gilded carvings, mouldings and chandeliers, as well as 41 paintings representing French cities or regions by prominent French artists including François Flameng and Henri Gervex. Even if you're not catching a train to some sun-soaked destination, it's worth a visit to the station to sip a glass of wine amid the restaurant's sumptuous décor.

Rue Oberkampf

◉ M6 Ⓜ Oberkampf, Parmentier

Rue Oberkampf stretches from the Upper Marais all the way to Ménilmontant, with most of the action happening around Metros Parmentier and Oberkampf. Dating back to the 1500s, the street gained its name in the 19th century from the German-born industrialist Christophe-Philippe Oberkampf, who contributed to the manufacturing of painted French cloth (toile). Today, the area is anything but old-fashioned. With high-end restaurants, gourmet coffee shops, craft beer and spicy Mexican fare, Rue Oberkampf caters to all sorts of flavours and fancies in its many bars and eateries. The street becomes especially lively at night, with younger Parisians congregating at watering holes like Café Charbon or Le Quartier Général. There are few tourist attractions here. It's all about local colour – literally, too, if you keep an eye out for the vibrant street art covering the walls and even the chimney stacks. Spend an evening or afternoon hopping from venue to venue in search of the perfect fit.

The opulent interior of Le Train Bleu restaurant, inside the Gare de Lyon

10

Cour Damoye and Passage du Cheval Blanc

🔲N7 Ⓜ Bastille, Voltaire, Bréguet Sabin

Amid the bustle of Place de la Bastille, there are tiny enclaves of calm hidden in two historic passages, the Cour Damoye and the Passage du Cheval Blanc. Most people walk right by their entrances without daring to enter, but they are public walkways. This area has been a centre of carpentry and French furniture design since the time of the Middle Ages. Its location near a port on the Seine that dealt with wood and timber made it popular with craftsmen, and many high-end artisans producing fine furnishings can still be found in the district.

The late-18th-century Cour Damoye is today largely

↓ The bold architecture of Bercy, a former wine-trading district

residential, with a few small businesses still functioning, but remnants of its former artisan workshops are visible in the façades.

The Passage du Cheval Blanc, just off Rue de la Roquette, is named after the sign of a horse that once adorned the entrance. Offering a peaceful respite from the busy Rue du Faubourg St-Antoine, its small labyrinth of cobbled courtyards, named after the months of the year (Cour de Janvier etc), hide architecture companies and apartments, with wooden beams still visible in some buildings. The Cité Parchappe spills you back out onto the main road.

FURNITURE-MAKING DISTRICT

Close to the former docks at Quai de la Rapée, this district east of the Place de la Bastille served to stock lumber, leading to its renown as a centre for furniture- and cabinet-making and their related trades. The craftsmen even caught the eye of Louis XIV, and his Minister of Finances, Colbert, established the royal mirror factory here. Today, there are still antique sellers, cabinet-makers and craftsmen dotted around Rue du Faubourg St-Antoine, especially on Le Passage du Chantier.

11

Merci

🔲M6 🏠111 Boulevard Beaumarchais 75003 Ⓜ St-Sébastien Froissart 🕐10:30am-7:30pm Mon-Thu (to 8pm Fri & Sat), 11am-7pm Sun 🌐merci-merci.com

Paris has grand department stores and luxury boutiques aplenty, but around Bastille, Merci is the place for retail therapy. A concept store housed in an old wallpaper factory, it opened in 2009 and curates the best in fashion and design. Homewares, clothing and kitchen products are housed under a glass atrium, spread across multiple floors. It has none of the glitz or brand names of big-brother department stores like Printemps or Le Bon Marché. Instead, it reflects the neighbourhood's character, featuring independent designers and local brands. If you're not interested in swiping your cards on trendy accessories, you could join the locals at Merci's popular restaurant and two cafés. The Used Book Café, set among towering shelves of literature, is especially appealing for afternoon tea or coffee. Fresh salads, egg dishes and *tartines* are all on the menu. The shop also houses temporary exhibitions and pop-up events that manage to keep it fresh and exciting.

Bercy

P11 **75012** **Bercy, Cour St-Émilion**

This former wine-trading quarter east of the city centre, with its once-grim warehouses, pavilions and slum housing, is now a modern district. An automatic Metro line (Line 14) links it to the heart of the city. The centrepiece is the pyramidal landmark Accor Arena, which hosts sports events, operas and rock concerts.

Other architecturally adventurous buildings dominate Bercy, notably Chemetov's gigantic building for the Ministry of Finance, and Frank Gehry's American Center. This houses the Cinémathèque Française, a wonderful cinema museum that hosts frequent retrospectives of famous directors.

At the foot of these structures, the imaginatively designed 14-ha (35-acre) Parc de Bercy provides a welcome green space for this part of the city.

Former wine stores and cellars along Cours St-Émilion have been restored as bars, restaurants and shops, and one of the warehouses now contains the Musée des Arts Forains (Fairground Museum), open for private tours only.

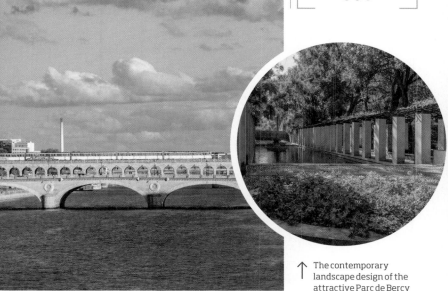

↑ The contemporary landscape design of the attractive Parc de Bercy

A LONG WALK
FAUBOURG ST-ANTOINE

Distance 4.5 km (3 miles) **Walking time** 90 minutes **Nearest metro** Bastille

In the east of the city, moments away from the bustle of the Bastille, lies the peaceful Faubourg St-Antoine district, traditionally a working-class neighbourhood full of furniture designers, carpenters and artisans. Their fascinating legacy can still be seen on this stroll through the district, which takes in Paris's pleasure-boat port, the artisan area around the Viaduc des Arts – a former viaduct with arts and crafts studios nestling in the arches – and the tree-lined Coulée Verte René-Dumont.

*The walk begins at busy **Place de la Bastille** (p104), site of the infamous prison that was stormed during the Revolution in 1789.*

*Pause to admire the modern architecture of the **Opéra National de Paris Bastille** (p106) before ending the walk at Bastille Metro.*

PLACE DE LA BASTILLE

START ▶ **FINISH**

Ⓜ **Bastille**

Port de l'Arsenal 🚊

RUE DU FAUBOURG

Opéra National de Paris Bastille

RUE DE CHARENTON

Ledru-Rollin Ⓜ

RUE DE LYON

Viaduc des Arts

Ateliers du Temps Passé

RUE DE PRAGUE

RUE LACUÉE

de l'Arsenal

RUE DE

Viaduc Café

Bassin

BLVD DE LA BASTILLE

RUE JULES CÉSAR

AVE DAUMESNIL

RUE TRAVERSIÈRE

Ⓜ **Quai de la Rapée**

AVENUE LEDRU ROLLIN

RUE PARROT

DIDEROT

BOULEVARD

PLACE H FRENAY

🚉 RER Ⓜ **Gare de Lyon**

*The lawns of the **Port de l'Arsenal garden** are perfect for a picnic, and the children's play areas are well stocked with rocking chairs, slides and climbing frames.*

*The **Bassin de l'Arsenal** (p108) was inaugurated in 1983 to provide a harbour for pleasure craft. Today, it's a pretty spot full of yachts, dinghies and Parisians out for a stroll.*

*Built in 1859 as a railroad track, the Paris Viaduct was restored and revamped in 1994 as the **Viaduc des Arts**, with 50 shops and studios in its archways.*

*The **Atelier du Temps Passé** at No 3 is a restorer of paintings.*

*For refreshment, stop at **Le Viaduc** brasserie at No 43, which serves simple meals and hearty salads to the area's hip creatives.*

← Boats line up along the river at the Bassin de l'Arsenal marina

↑ Strolling along the Coulée Verte René-Dumont, a park built on a former railway line

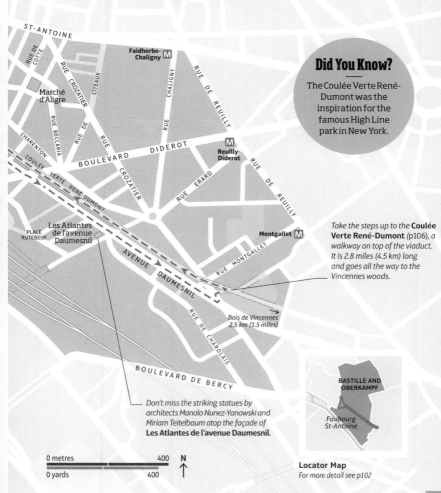

ST-ANTOINE

RUE DE COTTE

RUE CROZATIER

CITEAUX

Faidherbe-Chaligny Ⓜ

RUE CHALIGNY

RUE DE REUILLY

Marché d'Aligre

RUE BECCARIA

RUE DE

RUE

CHARENTON

BOULEVARD   DIDEROT

COULÉE VERTE RENÉ-DUMONT

RUE CROZATIER

Reuilly-Diderot Ⓜ

RUE ERARD

RUE DE REUILLY

Montgallet Ⓜ

PLACE RUTEBEUF

Les Atlantes de l'avenue Daumesnil

AVENUE DAUMESNIL

RUE MONTGALLET

Bois de Vincennes 2.5 km (1.5 miles)

RUE DE CHAROLAIS

BOULEVARD DE BERCY

Don't miss the striking statues by architects Manolo Nunez-Yanowski and Miriam Teitelbaum atop the façade of **Les Atlantes de l'avenue Daumesnil**.

Did You Know?

The Coulée Verte René-Dumont was the inspiration for the famous High Line park in New York.

Take the steps up to the **Coulée Verte René-Dumont** (p106), *a walkway on top of the viaduct. It is 2.8 miles (4.5 km) long and goes all the way to the Vincennes woods.*

BASTILLE AND OBERKAMPF

Faubourg St-Antoine

0 metres   400

0 yards   400

N ↑

Locator Map
For more detail see p102

RÉPUBLIQUE AND CANAL ST-MARTIN

Lying beyond central Paris, this area was once farmland. The Knights Templar established their European headquarters here during the medieval period, at which time it was also home to a community of lepers. In the 17th century, King Henri IV built a hospital for plague victims, while the 18th century saw a new wall envelop these districts within the city limits. Following industrialization of the area in the 19th century, thanks to Napoleon's canal, the neighbourhood became largely working class. It suffered from dereliction in the 20th century, although strong African communities grew up here, especially around Chateau d'Eau. In the 1990s, a class of bohemian-bourgeois Parisians – known as *bobos* – began to gentrify the district. Place de la République, totally redesigned in 2013, now welcomes street fairs and public demonstrations.

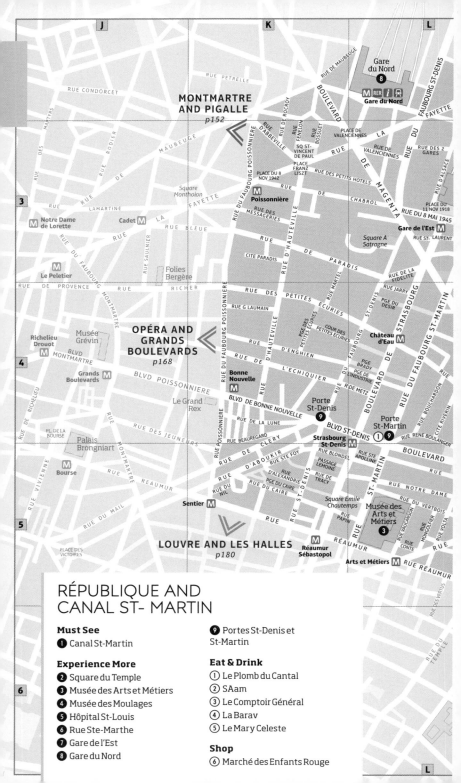

MONTMARTRE
AND PIGALLE
p152

OPÉRA AND
GRANDS
BOULEVARDS
p168

LOUVRE AND LES HALLES
p180

RÉPUBLIQUE AND CANAL ST- MARTIN

Must See

① Canal St-Martin

Experience More

② Square du Temple
③ Musée des Arts et Métiers
④ Musée des Moulages
⑤ Hôpital St-Louis
⑥ Rue Ste-Marthe
⑦ Gare de l'Est
⑧ Gare du Nord

⑨ Portes St-Denis et St-Martin

Eat & Drink

① Le Plomb du Cantal
② SAam
③ Le Comptoir Général
④ La Barav
⑤ Le Mary Celeste

Shop

⑥ Marché des Enfants Rouge

CANAL ST-MARTIN

M4 Jacques Bonsergent, Goncourt, République 26, 46, 75

Dating back to the time of Napoleon, this 4.5-km (2¾-mile) waterway flows through one of Paris's trendiest districts. Colourful shops and cafés line its banks, where locals spend weekends picnicking or cycling along the waterfront.

Stretching between the Seine in the south and the Bassin de la Villette in the north, the Canal St-Martin opened in 1825 as a means of bringing fresh water to Paris's polluted city centre. However, in the late 19th century part of the canal was covered to make way for new roadways, and within a few decades the canal and the boats that worked upon it had become obsolete. City officials almost drained and filled the entire waterway in the 1970s, but by the turn of the millennium it had became a popular location for wealthy young Parisians to buy and renovate properties. This once-derelict district is now one of the Right Bank's most desirable areas, a culturally mixed neighbourhood where Paris's hipsters mingle among families and international arrivals.

 INSIDER TIP
Canalside Eats

Order a snack or a meal to take away from one of the many casual eateries nearby – choices range from Taiwanese to Mexican – then find a spot along the canal.

DRINK

Here are the best coffee shops around the canal.

Ten Belles
M4 10 Rue de la Grange aux Belles 75010 tenbelles.com

Holybelly
L4 5 & 19 Rue Lucien Sampaix 75010 holybellycafe.com

Caoua Coffee Stop
M4 98 Quai de Jemmapes 75010 09 50 73 47 17

Radiodays
M4 15 Rue Alibert 75010 radiodays.cafe

DonAntónia
M4 8 Rue de la Grange aux Belles 75010 01 42 45 72 06

1 Cafés and restaurants populate the neighbourhood around the canal.

2 A selection of treats is sold at the bakery Du Pain et des Idées on Rue Yves Toudic.

3 The Canal St-Martin is punctuated by romantic bridges, including two swing ones.

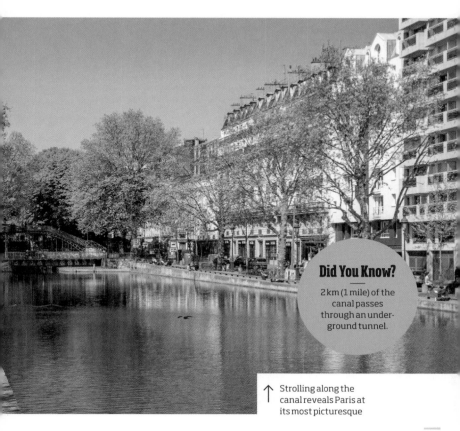

Did You Know?

2 km (1 mile) of the canal passes through an underground tunnel.

↑ Strolling along the canal reveals Paris at its most picturesque

EXPERIENCE MORE

2

Square du Temple

◎L5 🏠75003
Ⓜ Temple, République

A quiet and pleasant square today, this was once a fortified centre of the medieval Knights Templar. A state within a state, the area contained a palace, a church and shops behind high walls and a drawbridge, making it a haven for those who were seeking to escape from royal jurisdiction. Louis XVI and Marie-Antoinette were held in the Temple fortress after their arrest in 1792. The king set out from here for his execution by guillotine.

Did You Know?

The Square du Temple contains 70 species of trees, including an 18-m- (59-ft-) tall Turkish hazel.

3

Musée des Arts et Métiers

◎L5 🏠60 Rue Réaumur 75003 Ⓜ Arts et Métiers
🕐10am–6pm Tue–Sun (to 9pm Fri) 🚫1 Jan, 1 May & 25 Dec 🌐arts-et-metiers.net

Housed within the old Abbey of St-Martin-des-Champs, the Arts and Crafts Museum was founded in 1794. After major renovations in the 1990s it reopened in 2000 as an excellent museum of science and industry displaying 5,000 items (it has 75,000 additional artifacts in storage that are available to academics and researchers). The museum explores the theme of ingenuity in the worlds of invention and manufacturing, covering such topics as textiles, photography and machines. Among the most entertaining displays are those of musical clocks, mechanical musical instruments and automata (mechanical figures). One of these figures, the "Joueuse de Tympanon", is said to represent Marie-Antoinette.

4

Musée des Moulages

◎M4 🏠1 Ave Claude Vellefaux 75010 📞01 42 49 49 86 Ⓜ Goncourt, Colonel Fabien 🕐By appt 9am–4:30pm Mon–Fri

Housed inside the Hôpital St-Louis, this museum boasts 4,807 wax moulds of horrific skin diseases of the 1800s. Dr Lallier of the Hôpital St-Louis hired Jules Baretta, a wax-fruit maker, to create models of real diseases to teach students about things

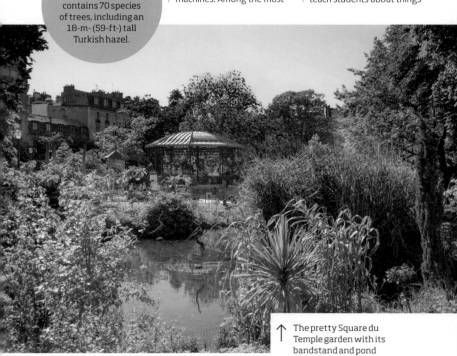

↑ The pretty Square du Temple garden with its bandstand and pond

↑ A plane on display at the Museé des Arts et Métiers, housed in a former church

SHOP

Marché des Enfants Rouges

This market, founded in 1628, on Rue de Bretagne is full of food stalls and international cuisine, and is usually packed at lunchtime.

⬤ M6 ⬤ 39 Rue de Bretagne 75003
⬤ Mon

such as syphilis and elephantiasis. Baretta would spend time with patients in the hospital, carefully using plaster of Paris to create his moulds. He would then paint them in great detail, even adding hair to keep them realistic. While many of the faces and body parts are unsettling in their realism, they are true works of art. Cyclopoid babies, various stages of then-fatal syphilis, and all sorts of abnormal skin growths are as fascinating as they are gruesome. The collection is an enlightening look into how far medicine has come in the past 150 years, to a time before the discovery of antibiotics that could cure

many of these diseases. Today, few students visit the antiquated learning tools, so the museum is often empty. Call ahead to arrange an appointment, and purchase tickets within the modern hospital's register, adjacent to the original structure.

---

⑤ Hôpital St-Louis

⬤ M4 ⬤ 1 Ave Claude Vellefaux 75010
Ⓜ Goncourt, Colonel Fabien

Built by order of King Henri IV in 1607 and completed after his death, this hospital originally served the growing number of plague victims at the time. Patients crowded into the rooms surrounding the square courtyard, reminiscent of Place des Vosges in the Marais (p92), and constructed by the same architect. Most would never see the sky again except for a rare stroll through that grassy courtyard. Conditions in the hospital worsened over time, but eventually

the plague passed. The building later served as a dermatology hospital and a prison for nuns during the French Revolution. Today, modern facilities next to the 17th-century buildings still function as a hospital. A small adjacent chapel – built for local farmers and not for plague victims – was used for King Henri IV's funeral in 1610. The main courtyard is open to the public and is an almost hauntingly calm respite in the heart of Paris. One of its wings is home to the Musée des Moulages, a museum dedicated to skin diseases.

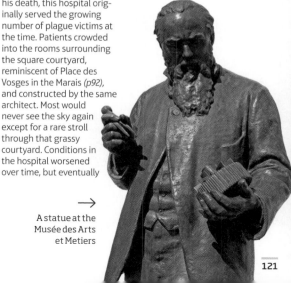

→ A statue at the Musée des Arts et Metiers

The Gare de l'Est, lit up at night

6

Rue Ste-Marthe

🚇 N4 🏠 75010
Ⓜ Goncourt, Belleville

Just north of the Hôpital St-Louis, this little street feels more like a walk through some southern provincial French town than central Paris. Colourful doors and façades contrast with the often grey Parisian skies. Each one opens up to an artist's studio, a workshop, a quirky restaurant, or some oddball boutique. There is little historical significance in these former workers' quarters, but the area is a unique slice of Parisian life. Look for olives in the independent grocery, try some Vietnamese food, or spend an evening with a glass of wine and charcuterie at any

of the local bars here. Tourists rarely make it this far, stopping instead at the Canal St-Martin. A walk along Rue Sainte-Marthe, however, is a very Parisian experience.

  7

Gare de l'Est

🚇 L3 🏠 Place du 11 Novembre 1918 75010
Ⓜ Gare de l'Est

Whether travelling to Germany or just passing through the neighbourhood, visitors should take a moment to marvel at one of Paris's oldest train stations. Opened in 1849, it had doubled in size by 1931 after several renovations. Statues atop the façade represent Strasbourg and Verdun, two of the

 HIDDEN GEM
Marché St-Quentin

The 19th-century covered market Marché St-Quentin on Boulevard de Magenta makes a handy stop for last-minute cheese and wine before you board a train from the Gare de l'Est or Gare du Nord.

original destinations served by the station. In 1883, the very first Orient Express departed from Gare de l'Est for Istanbul. Inside the main hall, a massive painting by American artist Albert Herter depicts French troops leaving the station for the Front during World War I in 1914. German forces transformed an underground air-raid shelter into a wartime bunker during World War II, which is still preserved under the station, though it is not open to visitors.

← Statues adorning the imposing façade of the Gare du Nord station

8 Gare du Nord

L2 | **18 Rue de Dunkerque 75010** | **Gare du Nord**

Opened in 1864, this train station is best known today as the hub for the Eurostar to London, as well as services to Brussels and Amsterdam. This massive station is Europe's busiest, with over 200 million passengers per year. The imposing façade is dotted with sculptures representing other European capitals, including Berlin and London. The soaring iron structure inside creates a romantic departure hall, and has been used as a film location for several movies. Inside the station, a new wave of cafés and restaurants is reinventing the travelling experience, as well as the surrounding neighbourhood. The station is undergoing further refurbishments in preparation for the 2024 Olympic Games.

9 Portes St-Denis et St-Martin

K4, L4 | **Blvds St-Denis & St-Martin 75010** | **Strasbourg-St-Denis**

These imposing gates give access to the two ancient and important thoroughfares whose names they bear, running across Paris in a north–south direction. They once marked the entrance to the city. The Porte St-Denis is 23 m (76 ft) high and was built in 1672 by François Blondel. It is decorated with figures by Louis XIV's sculptor, François Girardon. The gates commemorate the victories of the king's armies in Flanders and the Rhine that year. Porte St-Martin is 17 m (56 ft) tall and was built in 1674 by Pierre Bullet, a student of Blondel. It celebrates the capture of Besançon and the defeat of the Triple Alliance of Spain, Holland and Germany.

EAT & DRINK

Le Plomb du Cantal
A local establishment serving well-prepared, no-frills, traditional French food.

L4 | **4 Bvld St-Denis 75010** | **leplombducantal.fr**

€€€

SAam
Korean street food pairs with rice wine, sake and daily juices at this hip, fun eatery.

M4 | **59 bis Rue de Lancry 75010** | **09 83 50 84 94**

€€€

Le Comptoir Général
This quirky venue hosts events and has a bar popular during the evenings and on Sunday afternoons.

M4 | **80 Quai de Jemmapes 75010** | **lecomptoir general.com**

La Barav
This popular wine bar fills up with locals sharing bottles and cheese plates.

M5 | **6 Rue Charles-François Dupuis 75003** | **lebarav.fr**

Le Mary Celeste
Go for cocktails, stay for the small plates, and then have more cocktails.

M6 | **1 Rue Commines 75003** | **lemaryceleste.com**

↓ The impressive interior of Gare de l'Est

BELLEVILLE AND MÉNILMONTANT

Belleville and Ménilmontant are two of the newest
districts to have been incorporated into the city.
Various religious orders called the area home in
the Middle Ages, and the land was cultivated by
monks. Belleville was famous as a wine-growing
suburb of Paris, with vineyards covering the hilly
district. Both districts were beyond the tax reaches
of the city, and in the 18th century Ménilmontant
became popular with the working classes, who
would drink cheaply at watering holes called
guinguettes. After city planners removed the wall
circling Paris in 1860, the two areas were absorbed
into the 20 arrondissements, and much of the
farmland and vineyards gave way to new homes.
The districts became militant hotbeds during the
1871 Paris Commune, when clashes with the army
erupted in the streets. Throughout the 20th
century, the area attracted immigrants fleeing
persecution, including Jewish people from Europe
and inhabitants of former French colonies in North
Africa. A bustling Chinese community added to
the multicultural fabric of the districts, where
lower rent continues to attract many artists
and migrants today.

BELLEVILLE AND MÉNILMONTANT

Must See
① Cimetière du Père Lachaise

Experience More
② Parc de Belleville
③ Rue de Belleville
④ Rue Dénoyez
⑤ Marché de Belleville
⑥ La Maroquinerie
⑦ Notre-Dame-de-la-Croix
⑧ La Bellevilloise
⑨ Église Saint-Jean-Baptiste
⑩ Quartier Jourdain
⑪ Regard Saint-Martin
⑫ La Campagne à Paris

Eat
① Ama Siam
② Ravioli Nord-Est
③ Le Baratin

Drink
④ Aux Folies
⑤ Le Barbouquin
⑥ Café Chéri(e)
⑦ Le Cave de Belleville

Stay
⑧ Mama Shelter

R

S

T

RUE DE CRIME

RUE DES SOLITAIRES

Place des Fêtes M

RUE HENRI RIBIÈRE

RUE DE ROMAINVILLE

3

BELLEVILLE AND MÉNILMONTANT

Télégraphe M

RUE DE BELLEVILLE

RUE DE BELLEVILLE

RUE DU BORREGO

RUE DU TÉLÉGRAPHE

RUE HAXO

BOULEVARD

Quartier Jourdain
❿

RUE LEVERT

RUE FRÉDÉRICK LEMAÎTRE

RUE DU SOLEIL

RUE PIXÉRÉCOURT

PLACE DES GRANDES RIGOLES

RUE OLIVIER MÉTRA

RUE DES RIGOLES

RUE DES

RUE SAINT-FARGEAU

Adrienne Bolland

MORTIER

4

Regard St-Martin ⓫

RUE DE L'EST

RUE DE LA DUÉE

RUE PELLEPORT

RUE SAINT-FARGEAU

AVENUE GAMBETTA

RUE HAXO

Saint-Fargeau M

RUE DES CASCADES

RUE DE L'ERMITAGE

PYRÉNÉES

RUE DE MÉNILMONTANT

RUE DE

RUE H. JAKUBOWICZ

RUE DE LA CHINE

RUE DU SURMELIN

RUE DE LA JUSTICE

BLVD

❻ La Maroquinerie
❽ La Bellevilloise

RUE JULIEN

RUE BOYER

RUE DES PYRÉNÉES

RUE D'ANNAM

RUE ORFILA

Pelleport M

RUE DU

RUE A. PENAUD

RUE ÉTIENNE MAREY

MORTIER

5

RUE DE LA BIDASSOA

RUE SORBIER

PLACE HENRI MATISSE

RUE SOLEILLET

RUE ORFILA

RUE DU CAMBODGE

AVENUE GAMBETTA

RUE DE LA CHINE

Square Édouard-Vaillant

Hôpital Tenon

RUE PELLEPORT

RUE DE LA PY

RUE D. MONTIBŒUFS

RUE DU CAPITAINE FERBER

RUE P. STRAUSS

Séverine

❿ La Campagne à Paris

PLACE SULLY LOMBARD

RUE DES PARTANTS

RUE ROBINEAU

PLACE MARTIN NADAUD

Gambetta M

RUE BELGRAND

Porte de Bagnolet M

AVENUE GAMBETTA

RUE DES RONDEAUX

RUE RAMUS

RUE DES

RUE STENDHAL

RUE DES PRAIRIES

RUE LISFRANC

RUE DES PRAIRIES

RUE PELLEPORT

RUE DE LA PY

RUE DE BAGNOLET

Porte de Bagnolet

BOULEVARD

Cimetière du Père Lachaise
❶

RUE DES PYRÉNÉES

PLACE ST-BLAISE

RUE DES BALKANS

RUE VITRUVE

DAVOUT

6

RUE DU REPOS

⑧

RUE SAINT-

RUE VITRUVE

Marie de Miribel

BLVD DE CHARONNE

Philippe Auguste M

RUE LIGNER

RUE DE BAGNOLET

RUE DE BAGNOLET

RUE DES PYRÉNÉES

RUE VITRUVE

RUE DU CLOS

7

RUE DE BAGNOLET

RUE DE LA RÉUNION

RUE MONTE CRISTO

Alexandre Dumas M

0 metres 250
0 yards 250

N ↑

R

S

T

1 Ⓜ

CIMETIÈRE DU PÈRE LACHAISE

📍 R6 🏠 Blvd de Ménilmontant, 75020 Ⓜ Père Lachaise, Alexandre Dumas 🚌 26, 60, 61, 64, 69 to Pl Gambetta 🕐 8am-5:30pm daily (from 8:30am Sat, 9am Sun; mid-Mar-Oct: to 6pm)

This is the most visited cemetery in the world. It contains over 70,000 graves, including the tombs of numerous famous figures, such as the writer Honoré de Balzac, the composer Frédéric Chopin, the singer Jim Morrison and the actor Yves Montand.

Paris's most prestigious cemetery is set on a wooded hill overlooking the city. The land was once owned by Père de la Chaise, Louis XIV's confessor, but it was bought in 1803 by order of Napoleon to create a new cemetery. Père Lachaise, the first cemetery in France with a crematorium, became so popular that it was expanded six times during the 19th century.

Today the cemetery is a place of pilgrimage for rock fans, who come from around the world to see the grave of Jim Morrison of The Doors. With its moss-grown tombs and ancient trees, as well as striking funerary sculpture, Père Lachaise is an atmospheric and rather romantic place for a stroll.

Did You Know?

The remains of Molière were transferred here in 1817 to add historic glamour to the new cemetery.

→
A visitor strolling along a leafy lane at the fascinating Cimetière du Père Lachaise

← Théodore Géricault's tomb, with a depiction of *The Raft of the Medusa*

MUR DES FÉDÉRÉS

Following France's defeat in the Franco-Prussian War in 1871, a left-wing group revolted, setting up the Paris Commune. After 72 days, government troops marched on the city and in a week of brutal street fighting, much of the city was burned and thousands were killed. Mur des Fédérés in Père Lachaise is where the last Communard rebels were shot by government forces.

Notable Residents

Allan Kardec

▶ Kardec was the founder of a 19th-century spiritual cult, which still has a strong following. His tomb is perpetually covered in pilgrims' flowers.

George Rodenbach

The monument to this 19th-century poet depicts him rising out of his tomb with a rose in the hand of his outstretched arm.

Oscar Wilde

◀ The Irish dramatist, aesthete and great wit was exiled from virtuous Britain to die of drink and dissipation in Paris in 1900. American-British artist Jacob Epstein sculpted his tomb.

Marcel Proust

The French novelist brilliantly chronicled the belle époque in *Remembrance of Things Past*.

Sarah Bernhardt

▶ The great French tragedienne, who died in 1923 aged 78, was once the most famous actress in the world.

Edith Piaf

Known as the "Little Sparrow" because of her size, Piaf was the 20th century's greatest French popular singer. In her tragic voice, she sang of the sorrows and woes of the Parisian working class.

Jim Morrison

▶ The Doors' lead singer died in Paris in 1971. The circumstances of his death are still a mystery.

EXPERIENCE MORE

2

Parc de Belleville

Q4 **47 Rue des Couronnes 75020** **Couronnes, Belleville** **Oct-May: 8am-dusk; Jun-Sep: 7am-dusk**

It has less of the manicured appeal of some of Paris's other parks, but the Parc de Belleville has views that no other green space can boast. This steep garden offers unparalleled panoramas of Paris, including the Eiffel Tower and Notre-Dame. The hill was originally settled by religious orders, who purchased parcels of land and planted vines. *Guinguettes* popped up in the Middle Ages, the outdoor pubs or beer gardens of their day. It was here that Parisians drank "*piquette*", a young wine from the area, which today is also French slang for bad wine. Eventually windmills dominated the landscape, owing to the park's altitude.

The park is a welcome green space in densely populated east Paris. Between the patches of exquisitely maintained flowerbeds are stairs and pathways crisscrossed by waterways and trestles. There is even a waterfall that trickles 100 m (328 ft) from the top of the grounds to the bottom. In a throwback to Belleville's winemaking past, 140 grapevines grow on the slopes, and the grapes are harvested each year.

3

Rue de Belleville

P4 **75020** **Belleville, Pyrénées, Jourdain**

The main street of the former Belleville village, Rue de Belleville cuts through the district from Belleville Metro station. The street used to be the location of the old wall that separated Paris from its suburbs. Belleville gets its name from a deformation of the French words *belle vue*, or "beautiful view" – the reason for which becomes apparent when you look downhill from the street towards where the Eiffel Tower rises up in the distance. The stretch between the Metro stations Belleville and Pyrénées is the most interesting. At No 72, a plaque commemorates the birth in 1915 of Edith Piaf, who, according to popular legend, was born here on the steps. Over the past decades, many ethnic restaurants and East Asian shops have sprung up along the street as immigrants have moved into the area, and all sorts of exciting and inexpensive food items can be found here. Restaurants serve a variety of dumplings, pork-filled *bao* and *banh mi* sandwiches that are worth the hike up the hilly street. Cafés are far from fussy affairs, serving inexpensive wine and beer in the old working-class Belleville tradition.

Did You Know?

At 108 m (354 ft), Parc de Belleville is the highest park in Paris.

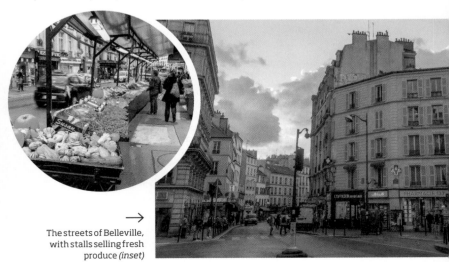

→ The streets of Belleville, with stalls selling fresh produce *(inset)*

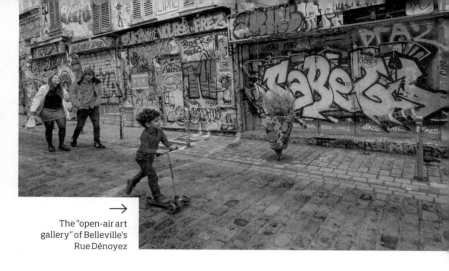

→

The "open-air art gallery" of Belleville's Rue Dénoyez

 4 (☐)

Rue Dénoyez

◉ P4 🏠 75020
Ⓜ Belleville

Throughout Paris, street artists take advantage of any surface they can. In Rue Dénoyez, however, it seems as if the city actively encourages it. This narrow street, tucked away off Rue de Belleville and formerly rather run down, is essentially an outdoor contemporary art gallery where street artists constantly leave their mark. It is named after a local family

who ran a popular dance hall in the 1830s, but today it is all about street art, reflecting the lively, bohemian spirit of the neighbourhood. On any given day, someone will be out there, spray-painting their newest mural on one of the walls. The buildings are mostly artists' studios – some will let you in if you are lucky – but the real draw is the colourful and daring works on the walls. In recent years, some of the

studios have been replaced by more modern social housing, but the artistic spirit of Rue Dénoyez remains. Parisians still gather at the end of the street at Aux Folies, a bar known for its cheap drinks and a sea of plastic chairs spilling onto the sidewalk, while at the other end of the street Le Barbouquin is a great place to relax with a drink and a book from one of its groaning shelves.

DRINK

Aux Folies

Plastic chairs all over the terrace give this a homey feel, reinforced by cheap drinks and loud locals.

◉ P4 🏠 8 Rue de
Belleville 75020
☎ 06 28 55 89 40

Le Barbouquin

This cosy café - part coffee shop, part bar and part bookshop/library - is an ideal chill-out spot. It also hosts regular music nights.

◉ P4 🏠 1 Rue Dénoyez
75020 ☎ 09 84 32 13 21

Café Chéri(e)

This dive bar attracts a hip local crowd. On weekends, DJs play electro, rock, hip-hop, funk and indie sets.

◉ N3 🏠 44 Boulevard
de la Villette 75019
☎ 09 53 05 93 36

Le Cave de Belleville

Sample natural wines over a plate of cheese and cured meat at this chic wine bar in Belleville.

◉ P4 🏠 51 Rue de Belleville
75019 ☎ 01 40 34 12 95

The ever-popular La Maroquinerie rock, pop and world music venue ↑

 ⑤

Marché de Belleville

📍P4 🏠Blvd de Belleville 75020 Ⓜ Belleville 🕐Tues & Fri 7am-1:30pm

Every Tuesday and Friday morning, the Belleville outdoor market comes alive, stretching from the Belleville Metro station to Couronnes. It dates back to the 19th century, when it was just a little market for the independent commune outside Paris's wall, and is still a popular and inexpensive source of fresh produce for eastern Parisians. The stalls follow the seasons, with clementines in the winter, strawberries in the spring, and the best tomatoes in late summer. Some stalls sell odds and ends such as wine openers, French candy bars

and bags of olives – it's the place to stock up on anything and everything. Vendors yell out prices, pushing the foods that need to go. By the end of the market, they start selling large piles of produce for a euro, so there are true bargains to be had. The locals pile into the crowded market rain or shine, so be prepared to manoeuvre around caddies and Parisians arguing about bruised apples.

 ⑥

La Maroquinerie

📍R5 🏠23 Rue Boyer 75020 Ⓜ Ménilmontant, Gambetta 🌐lamaro quinerie.fr

True music fans will want to visit this former leather workshop turned concert

Did You Know?

The first ever telegraph was communicated from Ménilmontant in 1793.

venue. It's intimate, with a capacity of about 500, and has hosted some big names before they hit success. Bruno Mars and Sam Fender are just some of the acts who have played here. The bohemian-chic venue also has a restaurant with a constantly changing menu of French classics, and a terrace bar for drinking the night away. Book in advance for a wide range of musical productions.

⑦

Notre-Dame-de-la-Croix

📍Q5 🏠3 Place de Ménilmontant 75020 Ⓜ Ménilmontant, Couronnes 🕐8am-7:30pm Tue-Sat, 8:30am-7pm Sun notre damedelacroix.com

Consecrated in 1863 under the reign of Napoleon III, this stunning church looms over Ménilmontant, built as the

---

NIGHTLIFE HOTSPOT

Both Belleville and Ménilmontant have historically been popular drinking locations with a reputation for being cheap and rowdy – labels that locals would defend proudly. Their former position just outside the tax wall meant that drinks were cheaper, so Parisians flocked to the *guinguettes* (taverns) that made these districts popular. Today the area is still known as inexpensive, whether it's for cheap Vietnamese food or drinks at Le Cave de Belleville. Nightlife has evolved from *guinguettes* as well, and popular hotspots such as La Bellevilloise and La Maroquinerie keep the neighbourhood lively at night.

population of the area boomed. Its architecture is an odd mix of Romanesque and Gothic elements, with an enormous tower reaching 78 m (256 ft) high. In terms of size, it's actually the third-largest church in Paris after Notre-Dame and St-Sulpice.

This district was particularly caught up by the Paris Commune of 1871, when Parisians rose up against the government, which had been exiled to Versailles by Prussian forces. During this turbulent time the Communards, as the rebels were known, held meetings in Notre-Dame-de-la-Croix. It was here that they decided to execute the Archbishop, Georges Darboy, who had been taken hostage by the Communards, on 24 May at the prison on Rue de la Roquette (p107).

The church does not stir up much of this stormy history, but instead offers a splendid visit devoid of the tourists crammed into other monuments. Look out for the organ, constructed in two separate parts in order to avoid obstructing the rose window overhead. The church also has two significant artworks: *Christ in Limbo* (1819) by Pierre Delorme and *Christ Curing the Sick* (1827) by Jean-Pierre Granger.

EAT

Ama Siam
Modern Thai food, inspired by the chef's family recipes, is served at this cheery spot.

 P4 49 Rue de Belleville 75019
 Mon & Sun
 amasiam.com

€€€

Ravioli Nord-Est
It's all about the dumplings here – homemade, cheap and delicious.

 N4 11 Rue Civiale 75010 01 75 50 88 03 Wed

€€€

Le Baratin
An institution; go to experience quintessentially meaty French fare.

 Q4 3 Rue Jouye-Rouve 75020
 01 43 49 39 70
 Sun, Mon

€€€

 8

La Bellevilloise

 R5 19 Rue Boyer 75020 Ménilmontant, Gambetta labelle villoise.com

Set up in 1877, this community art centre's original aim was to bring cultural education to less affluent Parisians. This spirit lives on in its numerous events, which include concerts – often jazz or Latin – and art exhibits, as well as freelancer fairs, vintage markets and the occasional jazz brunch. A standout feature is the Halle aux Oliviers, a glass atrium performance area with tables surrounded by an urban jungle of sorts.

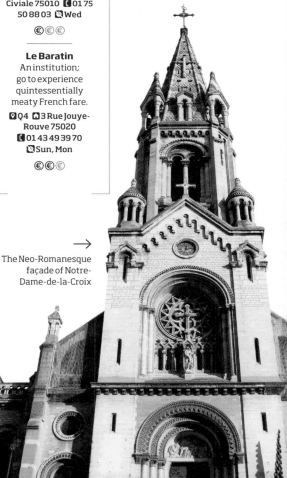

→ The Neo-Romanesque façade of Notre-Dame-de-la-Croix

The soaring Neo-Gothic interior of Église St-Jean-Baptiste ↑

9

Église St-Jean-Baptiste

📍 Q3 🏠 139 Rue de Belleville 75019 Ⓜ Jourdain ⏰ 8:15am-7:45pm daily (9:30am-8:30pm Mon, to 8:30pm Fri) 🌐 sjbb.fr

As far as churches go, the Neo-Gothic St-Jean-Baptiste de Belleville flies under the radar of most people in Paris. Set high above the city in a vibrant district full of shops, it's an exciting find for architecture enthusiasts. Built to

STAY

Mama Shelter
This modern hotel near Père Lachaise offers a comfortable alternative to tourist-laden central Paris.

📍 S6 🏠 109 Rue de Bagnolet 75020 🌐 mamashelter.com

€€€

replace the original church dating back to the 1600s, the current structure was erected between 1854 and 1859. The architect, Jean-Baptiste Antoine Lassus, was a specialist in medieval architecture. He is largely responsible for bringing back Gothic themes in modern structures and participated heavily in the restorations of Notre-Dame and other monuments. Though a master in his craft, Lassus is often overlooked for the more famous Viollet-le-Duc, who lauded this structure after Lassus' death. It was, in fact, Lassus' final project. This church, with its twin bell towers and vaulted ceilings, evokes the grandeur and traditions of churches such as the Sainte-Chapelle *(p74)*.

10

Quartier Jourdain

📍 R4 🏠 75019 & 75020 Ⓜ Jourdain

If you are looking to get away from the crowds but still get a taste of Parisian life, an afternoon wandering the Jourdain quarter is a perfect

Stone carvings, Église St-Jean-Baptiste ↑

start. Sprawling out from the Neo-Gothic St-Jean-Baptiste church, the area has really come into its own. The central square, full of cafés and quintessentially Parisian shops – cheese here, meat there, pastries everywhere – is little visited by tourists; this is one of the rare districts of Paris that still retains a village feel. It might be towards the edge of the city, but it is a quick and easy trip on line 11 of the Metro from Hôtel de Ville in the centre. The nearby Parc des Buttes-Chaumont *(p146)* pairs nicely with a visit to Jourdain, as does a detour to Le Plateau on Rue des Alouettes, an industrial-white exhibition space run by Frac (the Fonds régional d'art contemporain, or regional collection of contemporary art). It displays modern art – including paintings, photography and everything in between – from its 1,600-piece collection. There's also occasional performance art.

Regard St-Martin

R4 **42 Rue des Cascades 75020** **Jourdain, Pyrénées**

This curious little stone building on Rue des Cascades was once vital to ensuring medieval Parisians had clean drinking water. Known as a *regard* – or, essentially, a manhole – it was part of a system to collect rainwater from the hilly area of Belleville and channel it to the fountains of Paris below. The water of the Seine was infamously dirty, polluted by the mix of sewage and chemicals from tanneries flowing into it. These stone structures provided fresh water before the canals were constructed in the 19th century. Renovated in the 17th century (as a plaque in Latin on the building testifies), but dating from the 12th century, the Regard St-Martin still functions, except that nowadays the water makes it no further than the sewers.

La Campagne à Paris

T5 **Rue du Père-Prosper-Enfantin, Rue Irénée Blanc, Rue Mondonville, Rue Jules Siegfried 75020** **Porte de Bagnolet**

This former housing estate is one of the most picturesque parts of Paris, with stone-fronted houses lining the cobbled streets. La Campagne, literally "the countryside", feels exactly like that. A pastor, Sully Lombard, conceived of the development in 1907 for lower-income Parisians. Built on top of an old gypsum quarry and completed well after World War I, the 90-odd houses stood out from the rest of Paris's architecture. Brick façades, creeping ivy and wisteria, and tiny gated gardens full of roses and clematis adorn the two-storey houses. These provincial-looking cobbled streets offer some splendid photo opportunities and are a wonderful oasis of calm away from the bustle of urban Paris.

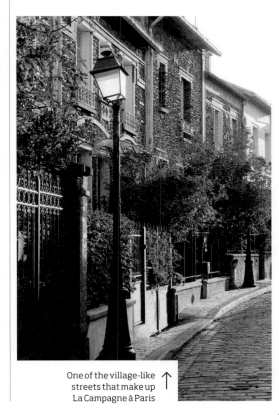

One of the village-like streets that make up La Campagne à Paris ↑

LA VILLETTE

A Gallo-Roman town once stood in this area, which subsequently became home to religious workers at a nearby leper colony. It remained an agricultural hamlet beyond the city wall for many years, but gained attention when Napoleon began his canal project here. The district formally joined Paris in 1859. La Villette is best known for its large 19th-century slaughterhouses, constructed under Napoleon III. The giant halls replaced those in five other locations in Paris, centralizing the city's meat industry. By the 1970s, the slaughterhouses had ceased operations and the mayor decided to revive the area with a new park. Designed in the 1980s, Paris's third-largest green space evokes post-modern and deconstructive concepts, with standout cultural centres including Europe's largest science museum and the Philharmonie de Paris, designed by Jean Nouvel. Outside the park there are theatres and art centres to explore, as well as another of Paris's most iconic green spaces, the Buttes-Chaumont.

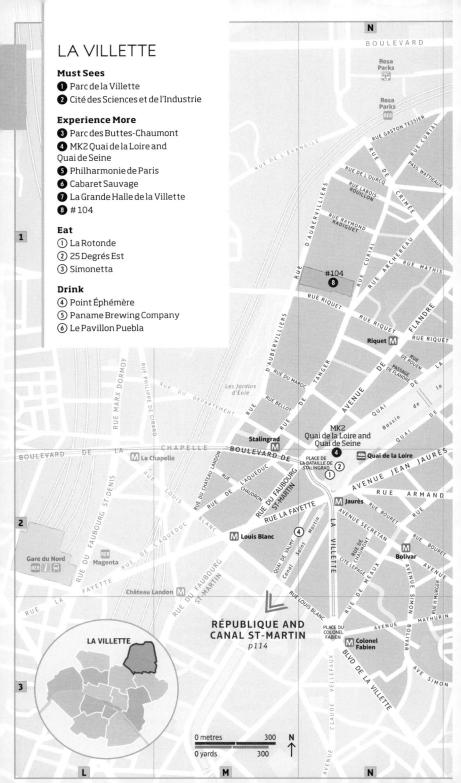

LA VILLETTE

Must Sees
1 Parc de la Villette
2 Cité des Sciences et de l'Industrie

Experience More
3 Parc des Buttes-Chaumont
4 MK2 Quai de la Loire and Quai de Seine
5 Philharmonie de Paris
6 Cabaret Sauvage
7 La Grande Halle de la Villette
8 #104

Eat
① La Rotonde
② 25 Degrés Est
③ Simonetta

Drink
④ Point Éphémère
⑤ Paname Brewing Company
⑥ Le Pavillon Puebla

RÉPUBLIQUE AND
CANAL ST-MARTIN
p114

PARC DE LA VILLETTE

🗺 Q1 🏠 211 Ave Jean Jaurès 75019 Ⓜ Porte de Pantin, Porte de la Villette 🚌 75, 139, 150, 151, 152 🚊 T3b 🕐 Public spaces: 24 hrs daily; gardens: May-Sep: 3-7pm Sat & Sun (Oct-Mar: by reservation only); Jardin des Vents et des Dunes: Apr-Oct: 10am-8pm daily (Nov-Mar: 10am-5pm Wed, Sat & Sun, plus public and school holidays) 🌐 lavillette.com

This inventive urban park offers an appealing combination of nature and modern architecture, containing gardens, playgrounds and a variety of cultural spaces.

Urban Regeneration

Once home to slaughterhouses and a livestock market, this former industrial area has been transformed into a vibrant urban park. Designed by Bernard Tschumi, its vast facilities cover 55 ha (136 acres) of a previously run-down part of the city. The plan was to revive the tradition of parks for meetings and activities, and to stimulate interest in the arts and sciences. Work began in 1984, and the park has grown to include the Cité des Sciences et de l'Industrie – a high-tech hands-on science museum (p144) – a cutting-edge concert hall, an exhibition pavilion, a spherical cinema, a circus and a music centre. Linking them all is the park itself, Paris's third largest, with its follies, walkways, gardens and playgrounds. In the summer, the park holds several festivals, including an open-air film event.

26

jaunty, red modern follies brighten up the park.

OPEN-AIR FILM FESTIVAL

Each summer the park hosts the free Cinéma en Plein Air festival *(p59)*, screening a mix of French and international films in the open air several evenings a week for a month. Deckchairs and blankets are available for hire, and many people bring their own picnic to make an evening of it.

↑ Taking time out in the sunshine in front of one of the cafés in the park

The view from the rooftop of the Philharmonie de Paris concert hall *(p147)* ↓

Le grand récit d

②

CITÉ DES SCIENCES ET DE L'INDUSTRIE

📍 Q1 🏠 30 Ave Corentin Cariou 75019 Ⓜ Porte de la Villette 🚌 75, 139, 150, 152 🚊 T3b 🕐 10am–6pm Tue–Sat, 10am–7pm Sun, advance booking recommended 🚫 1 Jan, 1 May, 25 Dec 🌐 cite-sciences.fr

Located within the Parc de la Villette, the Cité des Sciences et de l'Industrie is an interactive science and technology museum that is hugely popular with families.

The museum occupies the largest of the old Villette slaughterhouses. Architect Adrien Fainsilber has created an imaginative interplay of light, vegetation and water in the high-tech, five-storey building, which soars 40 m (133 ft) high, stretching over 3 ha (7 acres). At the museum's heart is the Explora exhibit, a fascinating guide to the worlds of science and technology. Visitors can take part in computerized games on space, the earth, transport, energy, design and sound. On other levels, there is a children's science city with machines to play and experiment with, a planetarium, a library and shops.

3

greenhouses on the southern façade flood the building with natural light.

l'Univers — entrée

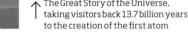

↑ The Great Story of the Universe, taking visitors back 13.7 billion years to the creation of the first atom

↑ The museum building, encircled by a moat and joined to the park via raised walkways

LA GÉODE

Fittingly for a building that looks as if it is from the set of a sci-fi movie, this Adrien Fainsilber-designed sphere was built to house a cinema showing IMAX and 3D films. It is closed for refurbishment, but is well worth admiring from the outside.

← Kids observing plants and insects in the hothouse garden of the children's science city

EXPERIENCE MORE

3

Parc des Buttes-Chaumont

📍 Q2 🏠 Rue Botzaris 75019 (main access from Rue Armand Carrel) Ⓜ Botzaris, Buttes-Chaumont 🕐 Apr & Sep: 7am–9pm; May–Aug: 7am–10pm; Oct–Mar: 7am–8pm daily

For many, this is the most pleasant and unexpected park in the city. The panoramic hilly site was formerly a gallows for the execution of criminals, a lime quarry

---

🔍 HIDDEN GEM
Rosa Bonheur

Named after a 19th-century artist, Rosa Bonheur is a popular *guinguette* in the Parc des Buttes-Chaumont. It's a bucolic spot for a glass of wine and tapas, and on Sunday nights it's a popular LGBTQ+ venue.

---

and a rubbish dump. It was converted in the mid-1860s, one of Napoleon III's many projects to renovate the city. Baron Haussmann worked with the landscape architect/designer Adolphe Alphand, who organized a vast programme to furnish the new pavement-lined avenues with benches and lampposts. Others involved in the creation of this large park were the engineer Darcel and the landscape gardener Barillet-Deschamps. They created a lake and made an island with real and artificial rocks, which they crowned with a Roman-style classical temple (the Temple de la Sibylle, modelled after the Temple of Sybil in Tivoli, Italy). The pair also added a waterfall, streams, and two footbridges to connect the island to the park.

→

The romantic Parc des Buttes-Chaumont

4

MK2 Quai de Loire and Quai de Seine

📍 N2 🏠 7 Quai de la Loire & 14 Quai de la Seine 75019 Ⓜ Stalingrad, Jaurès 🌐 mk2.com

These two cinemas on opposite banks of the canal basin are popular hangouts during the evenings. Neighbouring cafés and bars fill with cinephiles who are waiting to see the latest release. The cinemas screen a large selection of French and international movies that cater to both art-house and blockbuster crowds, sometimes showing

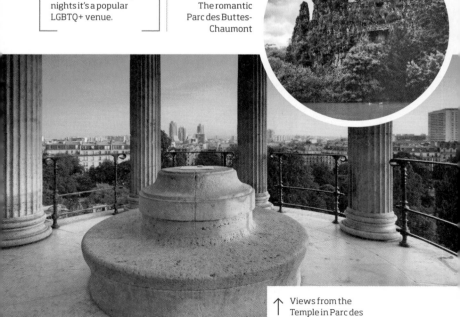

↑ Views from the Temple in Parc des Buttes-Chaumont

The state-of-the-art interior of the Paris Philharmonic concert hall ↑

Hollywood pictures before their US release. When buying a ticket, note which cinema your film is in; if it's on the opposite bank, a water shuttle will carry you across the canal. Bear in mind that international films are shown in VO *(version originale)* or VF *(version française)*. If you don't want to watch a film dubbed into French, buy tickets for the VO version. Afterwards, you could join a game of *pétanque* along the canal, just next to the cinemas, where Parisians while away their evenings.

---

⑤

Philharmonie de Paris

⑨R1 ⬛221 Ave Jean Jaurès 75019 Ⓜ Porte de Pantin ⬛Museum: Noon–6pm Tue–Sun (from 10am Sat & Sun) ⬛Mon ⬛philharmonie deparis.fr

Built in 2015, the futuristic Philharmonie, designed by French architect Jean Nouvel, rises above Parc de la Villette like a silver spaceship. The main concert hall seats up to 3,650 people, depending

on the configuration and the placement of floating balconies. The idea is that spectators are never further than 32 m (105 ft) from the conductor, creating a more immersive, intimate experience. The building went well over budget – more than double the expected €170 million – causing quite a scandal. Still, the hall's inaugural concert, held in honour of the victims of that year's *Charlie Hebdo* attacks, was well attended, with patrons including then-president François Hollande.

The Philharmonie caters mostly to symphonic concerts, but also hosts jazz and world music performances. It houses cultural centres and exhibition halls, as well as smaller concert halls. Visitors can book a concert, pop in for a meal with views over the park, or discover over 1,000 instruments in the museum. The Philharmonie offers guided tours, with bookings available through their website. Smaller-scale concerts are also held at the neighbouring Cité de la Musique, now rechristened Philharmonie 2.

> Built in 2015, the futuristic Philharmonie, designed by French architect Jean Nouvel, rises above Parc de la Villette like a silver spaceship.

EAT

La Rotonde

Part of Paris's last great periphery wall, this lovely classical-style rotonda is now a great stop for a meal or cocktails.

⑨N2 ⬛6–8 Place de la Bataille de Stalingrad 75019 ⬛larotonde stalingrad.com

€€€

---

25 Degrés Est

With a terrace overlooking the canal, this laid-back bar-restaurant attracts sun-seekers in the summer.

⑨N2 ⬛10 Place de la Bataille de Stalingrad 75019 ⬛09 53 27 68 16

€€€

Simonetta

Enjoy excellent Neapolitan-style pizzas on the bustling canalside terrace of this restaurant.

⑨Q1 ⬛32 Quai de la Marne 75019 ⬛simonetta-paris.com

€€€

The rooftop of Jean Nouvel's Philharmonie de Paris

The Fontaine aux Lions in front of La Grande Halle de la Villette ↑

Cabaret Sauvage

R1 **59 Blvd Macdonald 75019** **Porte de la Villette** **cabaret sauvage.com**

On the bank of the canal, just before it leaves Paris's city limits, a curious venue stands all by itself in the Parc de la Villette. Opened in 1997, the Cabaret Sauvage is an entertainment venue unlike any other in Paris. Algerian-born Méziane Azaïche created the space, which welcomes all sorts of up-and-coming and little-known artists. Concerts and shows range from contemporary acrobatic and circus displays to dance and West African musical performances, and international artists such as Redman, Mos Def and Noel Gallagher have played here over the years. Inside the red velour draping, spectators cannot help but be drawn into the Cabaret Sauvage's unique circus-ring atmosphere: there are bevelled mirrors, banquettes and a circular dance floor. Renovations have resulted in improved acoustics, plus a wide terrace for open-air events. A night out at the Cabaret Sauvage is sure to be as memorable as it is individual.

La Grande Halle de la Villette

Q1 **211 Ave Jean Jaurès 75019** **Porte de Pantin** **lavillette.com**

A former slaughterhouse, this massive hall is one of three that were once in this part of La Villette. In the 19th century, Haussmann decided it would be easier to concentrate all of the meat industry in one spot. Eventually, and perhaps unsurprisingly, the area gained the nickname "City of Blood". In the 1980s, the veal hall was destroyed while the sheep hall was

BASSIN DE LA VILLETTE

The Bassin de la Villette hosts activities all year. Join Parisians, both young and old, in a game of *pétanque* on the banks, or try your hand at Mölkky, a Finnish game with wooden pins. The canal is popular with locals for rowing, but visitors can also hit the water by renting a motorboat from the Marin d'Eau Douce. A Paris Plage (beach) is set up here in July and August, and there is swimming and boating. The most popular activity, however, is picnicking. Head here early, especially in the summer, to secure a space along the waterfront.

Inside the red velour draping, spectators cannot help but be drawn into the Cabaret Sauvage's unique circus-ring atmosphere.

deconstructed in hopes of rebuilding it elsewhere. President Mitterrand preserved this iron beauty, used for slaughtering cows for beef, and today it houses an event space. Concerts, plays, exhibitions and other events take place regularly. Drop into the café/restaurant for a coffee or meal; it has an inviting garden area for when the weather is fair.

#104

📍 N1 🏠 5 Rue Curial 75019
Ⓜ Riquet, Stalingrad
🕐 Noon–7pm daily (from 11am Sat & Sun) ⊘ Mon
🌐 104.fr

It might not be obvious upon entering, but this art centre was originally built by the Parisian Archbishop in 1874 for funeral services. It housed a coffin warehouse, stables for horses and shops where individuals could purchase decorations for tombs. Eventually

the hearses of the 20th century disappeared when the public sector lost its monopoly on conducting funeral services. The space, however, underwent a renaissance. The vast hall, with iron beams and a glass roof, was slowly transformed into #104 (or Centquatre-Paris), an artists' residence and exhibition space. The centre is an excellent example of urban renewal in a city skilled at repurposing its historic structures. The mayor inaugurated the space in 2008, and the city still funds the majority of its costs. Today there are performances, concerts and art shows year-round, open to the public. Visitors can see artists at work experimenting with different media. Centquatre-Paris is quickly becoming a major player on the local and international art scene: it has hosted exhibitions dedicated to well-known contemporary artists such as Keith Haring and Krijn de Koning.

DRINK

Point Éphémère
Part concert hall, part drinking venue. There are often special nights with food trucks or other pop-ups.

📍 N2 🏠 200 Quai de Valmy 75010
🌐 pointephemere.org

Paname Brewing Company
Perched on the canal in an old warehouse; local craft beers are the favourite here.

📍 P1 🏠 41 bis Quai de la Loire 75019
🌐 panamebrewing company.com

Le Pavillon Puebla
Nestled in the greenery of Parc des Buttes-Chaumont, this is a peaceful oasis with a mix of Moroccan and modern touches.

📍 P3 🏠 Ave Darcel 75019
🌐 leperchoir.fr

MONTMARTRE AND PIGALLE

Once a separate village outside Paris, Montmartre was formerly a rural district dotted with windmills and vineyards. Following its incorporation into the city limits in 1860, it swiftly transformed into an urban neighbourhood that was popular with the working classes for its low-cost housing. By the end of the 19th century, this bohemian area had a reputation for decadence and free living, which turned it into a magnet for artists, writers and intellectuals. The still-standing Bateau-Lavoir was a shared studio and home to artists such as Matisse, Picasso and Modigliani. Montmartre's reputation for depravity stemmed in large part from its numerous dance halls, among them the infamous Moulin Rouge, said to have been the birthplace of the cancan dance. Although some of the entertainment has taken on a seedier character, Montmartre and Pigalle are still popular nightlife destinations, with numerous lively bars and restaurants.

MONTMARTRE AND PIGALLE

Must See
1. Sacré-Coeur

Experience More
2. St-Pierre de Montmartre
3. Place du Tertre
4. St-Jean l'Evangéliste de Montmartre
5. Place des Abbesses
6. Cimetière de Montmartre
7. Dalí Paris
8. Musée de Montmartre
9. Moulin de la Galette
10. Au Lapin Agile
11. Halle St-Pierre
12. Batignolles
13. Moulin Rouge

14. Musée de la Vie Romantique
15. Rue des Martyrs

Eat
1. Un Zèbre à Montmartre
2. Le Pantruche
3. Restaurant Caillebotte

Stay
4. Hôtel Amour
5. Le Pigalle
6. Hôtel Particulier Montmartre

Shop
7. Maison Arnaud Delmontel
8. Mamiche
9. Popelini
10. Henri Le Roux

OPÉRA AND GRANDS BOULEVARDS
p168

MONTMARTRE

H

Square Léon-Serpollet

RUE VAUVENARGUES
RUE DAMRÉMONT
RUE ORDENER
RUE DUHESME
RUE MARCADET
RUE FRANCŒUR
RUE DUHESME
RUE LAMARCK
RUE LAMARCK

J

Jules Joffrin Ⓜ
RUE DU MONT CENIS
RUE ORDENER
RUE EUGÈNE SUE
RUE DE CLIGNANCOURT
RUE RAMEY

K

Marcadet-Poissonniers Ⓜ
BLVD ORNANO
BLVD BARBÈS
RUE DES POISSONNIERS

1

Lamarck-Caulaincourt Ⓜ
RUE CAULAINCOURT
RUE LAMARCK
RUE CUSTINE
Cimetière St-Vincent
RUE BACHELET
RUE NICOLET
RUE LAMARCK
RUE RAMEY
RUE POULET
Château Rouge Ⓜ
PLACE DU CHÂTEAU ROUGE
RUE MYRHA

MONTMARTRE
AVENUE JUNOT ⑥
Ⓐ⑩ **Au Lapin Agile**
RUE BÉCQUEREL
RUE ST-VINCENT
RUE FEUTRIER
RUE MULLER
RUE CHRISTIANI
RUE DES POISSONNIERS
RUE MYRHA

⑨ **Moulin de la Galette**
Musée de Montmartre ⑧
RUE CORTOT
RUE DU MONT CENIS
RUE FEUTRIER
RUE DE LA GOUTTE D'OR

RUE LEPIC
RUE THOLOZÉ
RUE NORVINS
RUE DE SAULES
RUE ST-RUSTIQUE
Sacré-Cœur ①
RUE LAMARCK
RUE ANDRÉ DEL SARTE
RUE DE SOFIA

① RUE JOSEPH DE MAISTRE
RUE DURANTIN
Dalí Paris ⑦
PLACE DU MARAIS
② **St-Pierre de Montmartre**
RUE CARD GUIBERT
③
Place du Tertre
RUE BERTHE
RUE GABRIELLE
Square Louise Michel
RUE RONSARD
RUE P PICARD

RUE VERON
RUE GARREAU
RUE DES ABBESSES
RUE A BARSACQ
RUE CHAPPE
RUE FOYATIER
⑪ **Halle St-Pierre**
RUE P PICARD
RUE BELHOMME

RUE CONSTANCE
RUE R PLANQUETTE
Square J Rictus
RUE DES TROIS FRÈRES
RUE DE LA VIEUVILLE
Abbesses Ⓜ
④ ⑤ **Place des Abbesses**
RUE TARDIEU
D'ORSEL

Ⓜ **Blanche**
St-Jean l'Evangéliste de Montmartre
RUE A
RUE HOUDON
RUE DES MARTYRS
PLACE C DULLIN
BLVD DE LA CHAPELLE

CLICHY
RUE G PILON
RUE ANTOINE
RUE DANCOURT
RUE D'ORSEL
RUE SEVESTE
RUE BRIQUET
RUE DE GÉRANDO
RUE DU DELTA
BOULEVARD DE MAGENTA

RUE FONTAINE
RUE FROMENTIN
RUE DUPERRÉ
PLACE PIGALLE
Ⓜ **Pigalle**
BOULEVARD DE ROCHECHOUART
Anvers Ⓜ
Square d'Anvers
RUE D'ANVERS
RUE STEINKERQUE
DUNKERQUE
Barbès Rochechouart Ⓜ
BOULEVARD DE LA CHAPELLE

2

⑤ RUE FROCHOT
RUE VICTOR MASSÉ
Musée de la Vie Romantique ⑭
RUE CHAPTAL
RUE PIGALLE
RUE V LEDUC
RUE LALLIER
RUE BOCHART
AVENUE TRUDAINE
RUE DE SAÔNE
RUE RODIER
RUE TURGOT
RUE PÉTRELLE
PLACE DE ROUBAIX

② **Rue des Martyrs** ⑮
④ ⑦
⑨
RUE H MONNIER
RUE DE NAVARIN
RUE CLAUZEL
RUE CONDORCET
RUE DE LA TOUR D'AUVERGNE
⑧
CONDORCET
RUE DE ROLROY
RUE DU FAUBOURG POISSONNIÈRE

Ⓜ **St-Georges**
RUE LAFERRIÈRE
RUE BRUYÈRE
RUE NOTRE DAME DE LORETTE
RUE H MONNIER
RUE DES MARTYRS
RUE MILTON
⑩
RUE MANUEL
RUE DE L'AGENT BAILLY
RUE RODIER
RUE MAUBEUGE
RUE DE CHANTILLY
RUE PIERRE SÉMARD
RUE DU FAUBOURG POISSONNIÈRE

3

RUE D'AUMALE
RUE DE LA ROCHEFOUCAULD
Musée Gustave Moreau
RUE CHORON
RUE HIPPOLYTE LEBAS
③
RUE LAMARTINE
Cadet Ⓜ
RUE DE BELLEFOND
Square Montholon
RUE DE
LA
FAYETTE

RÉPUBLIQUE AND CANAL ST-MARTIN
p114

Ⓜ **Trinité**
RUE ST LAZARE
RUE GEORGES
RUE DE CHATEAUDUN
Ⓜ **Notre Dame de Lorette**
RUE DU FAUBOURG MONTMARTRE
RUE DE PROVENCE
RUE RICHER

Ⓜ **Chaussée d'Antin**
RUE TAITBOUT
RUE LAFFITTE
RUE LE PELETIER
Le Peletier Ⓜ
RUE DE PROVENCE
RUE DE PROVENCE

BOULEVARD HAUSSMANN
Richelieu Drouot Ⓜ

4

BLVD DES ITALIENS

0 metres 250
0 yards 250
N ↑

MONTMARTRE AND PIGALLE

H   J   K

① ✏️ 🛍️

SACRÉ-COEUR

⊙ J1 **🏠 35 Rue du Chevalier-de-la-Barre 75018** **Ⓜ Abbesses (then take funicular to the steps of the Sacré-Coeur), Anvers, Barbès-Rochechouart, Lamarck-Caulaincourt** **🚌 30, 31, 40, 80, 85** **🕐 6:30am–10:30pm daily; dome: Oct-Feb: 10:30am–5:30pm daily; Mar-May: 10:30am–7pm daily; Jun-Sep: 10:30am–8:30pm daily** **🌐 sacre-coeur-montmartre.com**

Situated atop the hill of Montmartre, the spectacular white basilica of the Sacré-Coeur watches over Paris from the city's highest point. It stands as a memorial to the 58,000 French soldiers killed during the Franco-Prussian War.

Six months after the outbreak of the Franco-Prussian War in 1870, two Catholic businessmen made a private religious vow to build a church dedicated to the Sacred Heart of Christ, as penance for France's sins. The two men, Alexandre Legentil and Hubert Rohault de Fleury, lived to see Paris saved from invasion despite the war and a lengthy siege – and were able to witness the start of work on the Sacré-Coeur basilica. The project was taken up by Archbishop Guibert of Paris and construction began in 1875 to Paul Abadie's designs, which were inspired by the Romano-Byzantine church of St-Front in Périgueux. The basilica was completed in 1914, but its consecration was forestalled by World War I until 1919, when France was victorious.

THE SIEGE OF PARIS

Prussia invaded France in 1870. During the four-month siege of Paris, instigated by the Prusso-German statesman Otto von Bismarck, hungry Parisians were forced to eat the city's horses and other animals.

Spiral staircase

Ovoid dome

Bell tower

Statue of Christ

Equestrian statues

Main entrance

↑ The 83-m- (272-ft-) high basilica

Crypt vaults

PICTURE PERFECT
The Basilica and the City

The best view of the Sacré-Coeur is from the gardens below, but for a 360-degree panorama of the city, climb the 300 steps to the top of the basilica dome.

↑ The beautiful basilica, crowned by its elegant ovoid dome

EXPERIENCE MORE

② St-Pierre de Montmartre

📍 J1 🏠 2 Rue du Mont-Cenis 75018 Ⓜ Abbesses
🕐 8am–7pm daily (to 6pm Fri) 🌐 saintpierrede montmartre.net

Situated in the shadow of the Sacré-Coeur basilica, St-Pierre de Montmartre is all that remains of the great Benedictine Abbey of Montmartre, which was founded in 1133 by Louis VI and his wife, Adelaide of Savoy, who – as its first abbess – is buried here. Inside the church are four marble columns supposedly from a Roman temple which once stood on the site. The vaulted choir dates from

The church of St-Pierre de Montmartre ↓

the 12th century, the nave was remodelled in the 15th century and the west front in the 18th. During the Revolution, the abbess was executed by guillotine, and the church fell into disuse. St-Pierre was reconsecrated in 1908. Gothic-style stained-glass windows replace those destroyed by a bomb in World War II. The tiny cemetery opens to the public only once a year, on 1 November.

---

③ Place du Tertre

📍 J1 🏠 75018 Ⓜ Abbesses

Tertre means "hillock", or mound, and this picturesque square is the highest point in Paris at 130 m (430 ft).

It was once the site of the abbey gallows but is associated with artists, who began exhibiting paintings here in the 19th century. It is lined with colourful restaurants – La Mère Catherine dates back to 1793. In summer, the restaurant terraces spill out into the centre of the square. The house at No 21 was formerly the home of the irreverent "Free Commune", founded in 1920 to perpetuate the bohemian spirit of the area. The Old Montmartre information office is now here.

---

④ St-Jean l'Évangéliste de Montmartre

📍 H2 🏠 19 Rue des Abbesses 75018
Ⓜ Abbesses 🕐 9am–7pm Mon-Sat; 9:30am-6pm Sun (to 7pm summer)
🌐 saintjeandemont martre.com

Designed by Anatole de Baudot and completed in 1904, this church was, controversially, the first to be built from reinforced concrete. The flower motifs on the interior are typical of the Art Nouveau style, while its interlocking arches suggest Islamic architecture. The red-brick facing has earned it the nickname St-Jean-des-Briques.

---

⑤ Place des Abbesses

📍 H2 🏠 75018 Ⓜ Abbesses

This is one of Paris's most picturesque squares. It is sandwiched between the rather dubious attractions of Place Pigalle, with its strip clubs, and Place du Tertre, which is usually mobbed by tourists. Be sure not to miss the Abbesses Metro station

The charming Place du Tertre with its many restaurants

with its unusual green wrought-iron arches and amber lights. Designed by the architect Hector Guimard, it is one of the few surviving original Art Nouveau stations.

6

Cimetière de Montmartre

 G1 🏠 20 Ave Rachel 75018 📞 01 53 42 36 30 Ⓜ Place de Clichy, Blanche 🕐 8am–6pm Mon–Fri, 8:30am–6pm Sat, 9am–6pm Sun (to 5:30pm winter)

This has been the resting place for many artistic luminaries since the beginning of the 19th century. The composers Hector Berlioz and Jacques Offenbach (who wrote the famous cancan tune) are buried here, alongside many other celebrities, such as La Goulue (stage name of Louise Weber, the cancan's first star performer and Toulouse-Lautrec's model), the painter Edgar Degas, writer Alexandre

Dumas, German poet Heinrich Heine, Russian dancer Vaslav Nijinsky and film director François Truffaut. Cimetière de Montmartre is an evocative, atmospheric place, conveying some of the heated energy and artistic creativity of the area a century ago.

To the east, close to Square Roland Dorgelès, is the often overlooked **Cimetière St-Vincent**. Here lie more of the great artistic names of the district, including Swiss composer Arthur Honegger and writer Marcel Aymé. Most notable of all is the grave of the French painter Maurice Utrillo, one of the few famous Montmartre artists actually born in the area and many of whose works afford some of the most enduring images of the district.

Cimetière St-Vincent

🏠 6 Rue Lucien-Gaulard 75018 📞 01 46 06 29 78 Ⓜ Lamarck-Caulaincourt 🕐 8am–6pm Mon–Fri, 8:30am–6pm Sat, 9am–6pm Sun (to 5:30pm winter)

> Cimetière de Montmartre is an evocative, atmospheric place, conveying some of the heated energy and artistic creativity of the area a century ago.

EAT

Un Zèbre à Montmartre
This is a great go-to for a lunchtime *croque monsieur* or an evening steak tartare.

 H1 🏠 38 Rue Lepic 75018 🌐 zebreamontmartre.fr

€€€

Le Pantruche
A handwritten menu is always a good sign; here they serve French classics with fun twists.

🗺 J2 🏠 3 Rue Victor Massé 75009 🕐 Sat, Sun 🌐 lapantruchoise.com/ lepantruche

€€€

Restaurant Caillebotte
This bustling little bistro, owned by the team behind Le Pantruche *(above)*, serves fresh, modern dishes.

🗺 J3 🏠 8 Rue Hippolyte Lebas 75009 🕐 Sun 🌐 lapantruchoise.com/ caillebotte

€€€

The Moulin de la Galette, one of two windmills that can still be seen in Montmartre

STAY

Hôtel Amour
Lively and contemporary, but always with a romantic undertone.

◊ J2 **⌂** 8 Rue de Navarin 75009 **Ⓦ** hotelamourparis.fr

€€€

Le Pigalle
Rooms are decorated with a tasteful play on the former red light district surroundings. Great breakfast and restaurant downstairs.

◊ H2 **⌂** 9 Rue Frochot 75009 **Ⓦ** lepigalle.paris

€€€

Hôtel Particulier Montmartre
Suites in this 19th-century mansion are ideally located for exploring the Montmartre and Pigalle districts.

◊ H1 **⌂** 23 Ave Junot 75018 **Ⓦ** hotel particulier.com

€€€

7

Dalí Paris

◊ J1 **⌂** 11 Rue Poulbot 75018 **Ⓜ** Abbesses **◷** 10am–6pm daily **◷** 24 & 25 Dec **Ⓦ** daliparis.com

A permanent exhibition of more than 300 works by the prolific painter and sculptor Salvador Dalí is displayed at this small but substantial space in the heart of Montmartre. Through this impressive private collection – France's largest – of Dalí's Surrealist paintings, sculptures, engravings, objects and furniture, the dramatic character of the 20th-century Catalan genius comes to light. This fascinating museum also houses a commercial art gallery.

8

Musée de Montmartre

◊ J1 **⌂** 12 Rue Cortot 75018 **Ⓜ** Abbesses, Anvers **◷** 10am–7pm daily **Ⓦ** museede montmartre.fr

During the 17th century, this charming home belonged to the actor Rosimond (Claude de la Rose), a member of Molière's theatre company. From 1875, the big white house, undoubtedly the finest in Montmartre, provided living and studio space for artists, including Maurice Utrillo and his mother Suzanne Valadon,

a former acrobat and model who became a talented painter, as well as Raoul Dufy and Auguste Renoir.

The museum recounts the history of Montmartre through artifacts, drawings and photographs. It is particularly rich in memorabilia of bohemian life, and has a reconstruction of the Café de l'Abreuvoir, Utrillo's favourite watering hole. Valdon's studio-apartment was renovated and opened to the public in 2014, as was the Hôtel Demarne, which stages temporary exhibitions on Montmartre themes.

9

Moulin de la Galette

◊ H1 **⌂** T-junction at Rue Tholozé and Rue Lepic 75018 **Ⓜ** Lamarck-Caulaincourt, Abbesses

Once, some 14 windmills dotted the Montmartre skyline and were used for grinding wheat and pressing grapes. Today, only two remain, both on Rue Lepic: the Radet, now above a restaurant confusingly named Moulin de la Galette, and the reconstructed Moulin de la Galette, originally built in 1622 and formerly known as the Blute-fin. One of its mill owners, Debray, was supposedly crucified on one of the windmill's sails during the 1814 Siege of Paris. He had been trying to repulse the invading Cossacks. At the end of the 19th century, both mills became famous dance halls providing inspiration for many artists, notably Pierre-Auguste Renoir and Vincent van Gogh.

Rue Lepic runs steeply uphill from Montmartre's central shopping area. The Impressionist painter Armand Guillaumin once lived on the first floor of No 54. Van Gogh inhabited its third floor, and painted the view from there.

Au Lapin Agile

📍J1 🏠22 Rue des Saules 75018 Ⓜ️Lamarck-Caulaincourt 🕐9pm–1am Tue & Thu–Sat 🌐au-lapin-agile.com

The former Cabaret des Assassins derived its current name from a sign painted by the humorist André Gill. His picture of a rabbit escaping from a cooking pot (Le Lapin à Gill) is a pun on his own name. The club enjoyed popularity with intellectuals and artists at the start of the 20th century. Here in 1911, the novelist

Roland Dorgelès and a group of other regulars staged one of the modern art world's most celebrated hoaxes, with the help of the café owner's donkey, Lolo. A paintbrush was tied to Lolo's tail, and the resulting daub was shown to critical acclaim at the Salon des Indépendants, under the enlightening title Sunset over the Adriatic, before the joke was revealed.

In 1903, the premises were bought by the cabaret entrepreneur Aristide Bruand (painted in a series of posters by Toulouse-Lautrec). Years later, the cabaret venue manages to retain much of its original atmosphere.

Halle St-Pierre

📍J1 🏠2 Rue Ronsard 75018 Ⓜ️Anvers 🕐11am–6pm Mon–Fri, 11am–7pm Sat, noon–6pm Sun 🕐1 Jan, 1 May, 14 July, 15 Aug, Sat & Sun in Aug, 25 Dec 🌐halle saintpierre.org

In 1945, the French painter Jean Dubuffet developed the concept of Art Brut (Outsider

or Marginal Art) to describe works created outside the boundaries of "official" culture, often by psychiatric patients, prisoners and children. The Halle St-Pierre, at the foot of the Butte, is a museum and gallery devoted to these "raw" art forms. It also hosts avant-garde theatre and musical productions, holds regular literary evenings and debates and runs children's workshops. In addition to temporary exhibitions, the permanent collection includes more than 500 works of Naïve art collected by the publisher Max Fourny in the 1970s. There is also a specialist bookshop and café.

↑ Suzanne Valadon's studio-apartment at the Musée de Montmartre

The stunning view from the Sacré-Coeur in Montmartre

12 Batignolles

F1 **75017** **M** Place de Clichy, Rome, Brochant

Formerly used as a royal hunting ground, this neighbourhood in the 17th arrondissement of northwestern Paris later grew into a small hamlet. Although it officially became part of the city in the second half of the 19th century, it still feels like a small French village inside cosmopolitan Paris. In the 19th century, the area had a lively cultural vibe and counted among its residents the painter Edouard Manet and his fellow artists (who became known as the Groupe des Batignolles), the writer Émile Zola and, later, the Belgian singer Jacques Brel.

The lovely church of Ste-Marie des Batignolles sits in the heart of the neighbourhood. While Batignolles has a calm, community feel, it also has a slightly urban atmosphere, with a good mix of well-frequented bars, stylish boutiques and restaurants. It was one of the first areas in Paris to label its up-and-coming class of residents *bobos*, a short-hand term for "bourgeois bohemians".

Two markets are held in the area: the organic Marché Biologique des Batignolles on Boulevard des Batignolles and the covered market on Rue Lemercier, which dates back to 1846. At weekends, families converge on the area's several parks, the two largest being the Square des Batignolles and

the Parc Clichy-Batignolles – Martin-Luther-King, which features playgrounds, duck ponds, a skate park and running trails. The district has undergone substantial development in recent years, and there are modern flats, shops and office buildings, including the new Paris law courts.

---

13 Moulin Rouge

H2 **82 Blvd de Clichy 75018** **M** Blanche **Dinner: 7pm; shows: 9pm and 11pm daily** **W** moulinrouge.fr

Built in 1885, the Moulin Rouge was turned into a dance hall as early as 1900. The cancan originated in Montparnasse, in the polka gardens of the Rue de la Grande-Chaumière, but it will always be associated with the Moulin Rouge, where the wild and colourful dance shows were immortalized in the posters and drawings of Henri de Toulouse-Lautrec. The high-kicking routines of famous "Doriss girls" such as Yvette Guilbert and Jane Avril continue today in a glittering,

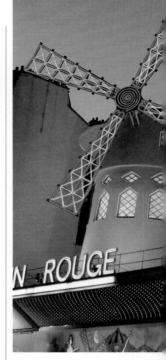

The Moulin Rouge, an iconic symbol of Parisian nightlife ↑

Las Vegas-style revue that includes sophisticated light shows and displays of magic.

---

14 Musée de la Vie Romantique

H2 **16 Rue Chaptal 75009** **M** Blanche, Pigalle **10am–6pm Tue–Sun, advance booking recommended** **Public hols** **W** museevie romantique.paris.fr

This quaint, tiny 19th-century house was once home to Ary Scheffer, the portrait painter of the monarch during the Bourbon Restoration. Here, the artist welcomed great cultural icons of the mid-19th century, including Eugène Delacroix and Charles Dickens. Now a museum, the house displays 19th-century paintings, and

---

MONTMARTRE'S WINDMILLS

Windmills were common in Montmartre in the late 19th century, when the area was still essentially a village. As the city began to consume the local farmland, proprietors turned their nearly defunct windmills into entertainment venues such as the Moulin de la Galette *(p160)*. The most famous windmill, the Moulin Rouge, pays homage to these parties, though it was never actually a functional windmill itself.

SHOP

Maison Arnaud Delmontel

Come for exquisite bread and pastries from this award-winning bakery.

📍 J2 🏠 39 Rue des Martyrs 🌐 arnaud-delmontel.com

Mamiche

A friendly boulangerie with a fabulous chocolate babka.

📍 J2 🏠 45 Rue Condorcet 🌐 mamiche.fr

Popelini

Cream-filled choux and nothing else – well, what else is there?

📍 J3 🏠 44 Rue des Martyrs 📞 01 42 81 35 79

Henri Le Roux

Salted-butter caramels and chocolate fill this boutique.

📍 J3 🏠 24 Rue des Martyrs 🌐 chocolatleroux.com

artifacts that belonged to celebrated author George Sand, as well as her lover Frédéric Chopin. Sand was a prolific writer and critic of the populist uprising known as the Commune. She also famously wore men's clothes in public and smoked tobacco, unlike most women of the time. The museum has a lovely garden café.

15

Rue des Martyrs

📍 J2 🏠 75009
Ⓜ Pigalle

This quintessentially Parisian street owes its name to Saint Denis, who was martyred nearby. Rue des Martyrs retains much of the local, market-street vibe that has been lost in many similar locations in Paris. The street is full of

tried-and-tested destinations adored by Parisians and visitors alike: pastry shops, restaurants, cafés, and even a boutique dedicated to salted-butter caramel. A few recognizable brands pop up here and there, but overall the street is one of the most individual and fashionable in Paris.

The pretty garden café at the Musée de la Vie Romantique ↑

A SHORT WALK
MONTMARTRE

Distance 1.5 km (1 mile) **Nearest Metro** Abbesses
Time 20 minutes

The steep hill of Montmartre has proved a draw for Parisians and visitors for centuries. Artists Théodore Géricault and Camille Corot came here at the start of the 19th century, and in the 20th century Maurice Utrillo immortalized the streets in his works. Today, this picturesque district, which in places still preserves the atmosphere of pre-War Paris, is a perfect place to wander. A stop at the Place du Tertre is recommended: admire the works of street artists and relax with a coffee and pastry before heading back down the hill.

Clos Montmartre is one of the last surviving vineyards in Paris. The grape harvest is celebrated over five days in early October.

Metro Lamarck Caulaincourt

RUE ST-VINCENT

RUE DE L'ABREUVOIR

RUE DES SAULES

RUE CORTOT

RUE ST-RUSTIQUE

RUE NORVINS

RUE LEPIC

PL J B CLEMENT

RUE POULBOT

RUE DE LA MIRE

RUE RAVIGNAN

RUE GABRIELLE

RUE BERTHE

RUE DREVET

RUE DES TROIS FRÈRES

Au Lapin Agile, a rustic café and cabaret, was a popular meeting point for artists including Picasso (p161).

Musée de Montmartre (p160) features the work of artists who lived in the area. The museum has three beautiful gardens, created in memory of painter Auguste Renoir, who lived here for two years.

Dalí Paris is France's only permanent collection of the Surrealist master's sculptures, paintings and graphic works (p160).

The bustling Place du Tertre is the tourist centre of Montmartre and is full of portraitists and other easel artists (p158). Cafés and bars surround the square.

↑ Admiring the works of street artists in the lively Place du Tertre

0 metres   100
0 yards   100

N ↑

La Mère Catherine was a favourite eating place of Russian Cossacks in 1814. They would bang on the table and shout "Bistro!" (Russian for "quick") – hence the Paris bistro was born.

St-Pierre de Montmartre was transformed into a "Temple of Reason" during the Revolution (p158).

Locator Map
For more detail see p154

↑ The beautiful Sacré-Coeur, illuminated at sunrise

The Romano-Byzantine Sacré-Coeur, started in the 1870s and completed in 1914, is a highlight of the area (p156).

Halle St-Pierre hosts exhibitions of Art Brut and Naïve Art (p161).

Did You Know?

Montmartre's name is ascribed to local martyrs tortured in around AD 250: *mons martyrium.*

RUE DU MONT CENIS
RUE DU CHEVALIER
RUE DU CARDINAL GUIBERT
RUE LAMARCK
RUE PAUL ALBERT
PL DU PARVAIS DU SACRÉ-COEUR
RUE AZAIS
RUE ST-ELEUTHERE
RUE DU CARDINAL DUBOIS
SQ LOUISE-MICHEL
RUE CH NODIER
RUE CHAPPE
PL ST-PIERRE
START
RUE TARDIEU
RUE DE STEINKERQUE
FINISH

The funiculaire, or cable railway, at the end of Rue Foyatier, takes you to the foot of the basilica of Sacré-Coeur. Metro tickets are valid on it.

Square Louise-Michel lies below the parvis (forecourt) of Sacré-Coeur. It is laid out on the side of the hill in a series of descending terraces with lawns, shrubs, trees and flower beds.

OPÉRA AND GRANDS BOULEVARDS

Known for its elegant avenues and the Opéra Garnier, this area was an important focus of Baron Haussmann's renovation of Paris in the 19th century. The crowded streets of the medieval city were demolished to make way for a series of Grands Boulevards – Madeleine, Capucines, Italiens and Montmartre – wide avenues flanked by imposing stone buildings with intricate wrought-iron balconies. Many glass-roofed shopping arcades were also constructed around this time, followed by the Printemps and Galeries Lafayette department stores, which firmly established the area's reputation as a major shopping destination. It also became a popular entertainment district, with venues including the dazzling Opéra National de Paris Garnier, and in 1895 the Lumière brothers held the world's first public film show at the Grand Café on Boulevard des Capucines. Today the area is more of a business hub, but night-time revellers will still find a host of clubs and theatres to enjoy.

OPÉRA AND GRANDS BOULEVARDS

Must See

1. Opéra National de Paris Garnier

Experience More

2. La Madeleine
3. Place de la Madeleine
4. Église de la Ste-Trinité
5. Théâtre Mogador
6. Galeries Lafayette
7. Chapelle Expiatoire
8. Église St-Augustin
9. Gare St-Lazare
10. Printemps
11. Musée Grevin
12. Le Grand Rex

Eat & Drink

① La Petite Régalade
② Chartier
③ Harry's New York Bar

Stay

④ Chouchou Hôtel
⑤ Hôtel Chopin
⑥ Hôtel Parister

① ✏️ Ⓜ️ 🛍️ 🍴

OPÉRA NATIONAL DE PARIS GARNIER

📍H4 🏠Pl de l'Opéra 75009 Ⓜ️Opéra 🕙10am–5pm daily, box office hours: 10am–6:30pm Mon–Sat & 1 hr before performances (to 2:30pm on days of matinée performances & public hols) 📅1 Jan, 1 May, 25 Dec 🌐operadeparis.fr

Sometimes compared to a giant wedding cake, this palatial opera house with its ornate interior is a sumptuous setting in which to enjoy a ballet or opera.

The building was designed by Charles Garnier for Napoleon III; construction started in 1862 and finished in 1875 after interruptions from the Prussian War and 1871 uprising. Its unique appearance is due to a mixture of materials (including stone, marble and bronze) and styles, ranging from classical to Baroque, with columns, friezes and sculptures on the exterior.

Behind the flat-topped foyer, the cupola sits above the auditorium, while the triangular pediment that rises up behind the cupola marks the front of the stage. Don't miss the magnificent Grand Staircase, made of white marble with a balustrade of red and green marble, and the Grand Foyer, its domed ceiling covered with mosaics. The five-tiered auditorium is a riot of red velvet, plaster cherubs and gold leaf. The false ceiling was painted by Marc Chagall in 1964.

Operas are performed both here and at the Opéra National de Paris Bastille *(p106)*, but the ballet predominantly remains here.

> **The five-tiered auditorium is a riot of red velvet, plaster cherubs and gold leaf.**

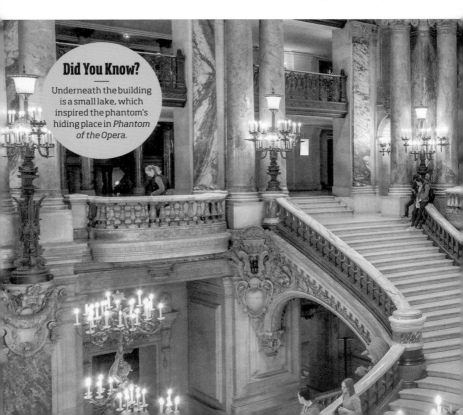

Did You Know?

Underneath the building is a small lake, which inspired the phantom's hiding place in *Phantom of the Opera*.

1

2

3

① The lavish façade is adorned with marble friezes and statuary.

② The auditorium, which can accommodate 2,054 spectators, was designed so that the audience can see and be seen.

③ The ceiling of the Grand Foyer is decorated with paintings by Paul Baudry.

↑ The Grand Staircase, an awe-inspiring welcome to the building

EXPERIENCE MORE

 La Madeleine

📍 G4 🏛 Pl de la Madeleine 75008 Ⓜ Madeleine
🕐 9:30am–7pm daily
🌐 eglise-lamadeleine.com

This church, dedicated to Mary Magdalene, is one of the best-known buildings in Paris because of its prominent location and great size. It stands facing south to Place de la Concorde and is the architectural counterpoint of the Palais Bourbon (home of the French Parliament) across the river. It was started in 1764 but construction halted with the onset of the Revolution in 1789. After the battle of Jena (Iéna) in 1806, Napoleon decided to build a temple dedicated to military glory and he commissioned Pierre Vignon to design it. The church was finished in 1842.

A colonnade of Corinthian columns encircles the building and supports a sculptured frieze. The bas-reliefs on the bronze doors by Henri de Triqueti show the Ten Commandments. The interior is decorated with marble and gilt, and has some fine sculpture, notably François Rude's *Baptism of Christ*. The church has a rich musical tradition; Gabriel Fauré and Camille Saint-Saëns were both organists here. Concerts, especially choral and organ recitals, take place regularly.

Since the funeral of French music icon Johnny Hallyday was held here in 2017, the church has become a shrine to his fans.

Did You Know?

The flower market at Place de la Madeleine has sold colourful bouquets since the early 1800s.

③ Place de la Madeleine

📍 F4 🏛 75008 Ⓜ Madeleine
🕐 Flower market: 9am–8pm Mon–Sat

The Place de la Madeleine was created at the same time as the Madeleine church. This square is lined with many upmarket restaurants, cafés and speciality

> Inside the Église de la Ste-Trinité, each chapel reveals rich paintings and decorations celebrating saints.

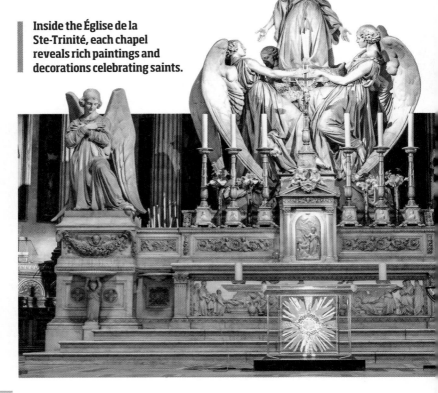

food shops, including Maille at No 6, famous for its mustards. The large house at No 9 Boulevard Malesherbes, just off Place Madeleine, is where Marcel Proust spent his childhood. To the east of La Madeleine are a small flower market and some excellently preserved 19th-century Art Nouveau public toilets.

 Église de la Ste-Trinité

📍G3 🏠Place d'Estienne d'Orves 75009 🚇Trinité-d'Estienne d'Orves 🕐7:15am-7:15pm Mon-Fri, 10am-7:30pm Sat, 10am-8:15pm Sun 🌐latriniteparis.com

Inspired by Renaissance-era Italian churches, this 19th-century masterpiece was consecrated in 1913. The church, often referred to simply as La Trinité, is the monumental centrepiece of the busy Place d'Estienne d'Orves intersection, created by Baron Haussmann. As part of his grand project to

redesign Paris, Haussmann moved the church a few hundred metres from its original location. The church is beautifully decorated with a large belfry. Inside, each chapel reveals a rich series of paintings and decorations celebrating saints such as local favourites Geneviève and Vincent de Paul.

  Théâtre Mogador

📍G3 🏠25 Rue de Mogador 75009 🚇Trinité-d'Estienne d'Orves 🌐theatremogador.com

The Théâtre Mogador was built by London theatre mogul Alfred Butt. It was inaugurated in 1919 by future American president Franklin Delano Roosevelt. Numerous politicians were in town to negotiate the Treaty of Versailles after World War I, so taking in a show must have seemed like a good idea. It once hosted operettas and Sergei Diaghilev's Ballets Russes, but has also staged classic musicals such as *Hello, Dolly!* and *Les Misérables*. Now, this majestic three-tier theatre produces mostly big-budget Broadway shows in French, such as *The Lion KIng* and *The Producers*.

   Galeries Lafayette

📍H4 🏠40 Blvd Haussmann 75009 🚇Chaussée d'Antin-Lafayette 🕐1am-8:30pm daily (11am-8pm Sun) 🌐haussmann. galerieslafayette.com

Dating back to 1893, this store is a Parisian icon and an essential stop on any

←

The ornate high altar of the Église de la Madeleine

visit to the city. The massive complex includes men's and women's fashion, a homewares department and a gourmet food hall. At Christmas, a massive tree fills the Art Nouveau cupola, while the windows tell whimsical holiday stories popular with kids. Anyone can take the escalator to the rooftop terrace, where spectacular views of the city await. The store can become a madhouse during the biannual sales, the *soldes*, but it's all part of the Galeries Lafayette experience.

EAT & DRINK

La Petite Régalade

The chef offers an innovative take on *la pascade*, a crêpe-like dish filled with gourmet ingredients.

📍G4 🏠14 Rue Daunou 75002 🕐Sun 🌐lapetite regalade.com

€€€

Chartier

This old workers' canteen is still a budget favourite for French classics.

📍J4 🏠7 Rue du Faubourg Montmartre 75009 🌐bouillon-chartier.com.

€€€

Harry's New York Bar

Birthplace of the Bloody Mary – and other cocktails – it's tradition to make a stop here *(p178)*.

📍H4 🏠5 Rue Daunou 75002 🌐harrysbar.fr

THE VICTIMS OF THE GUILLOTINE

Along with Louis XVI and Marie-Antoinette, numerous other famous figures were buried where the Chapelle Expiatoire now stands. Among them were Murat's murderer Charlotte Corday, writer and feminist Olympe de Gouges, Louis XV's mistress Jeanne du Barry and Madame Roland.

Chapelle Expiatoire

🛈 F4 🚪 29 Rue Pasquier 75008 Ⓜ St-Augustin 📞 01 42 65 35 80 🕒 Apr– Sep: 10am–12:30pm & 1:30–6:30pm Tue-Sat; Oct-Mar: 10am–12:30pm & 1:30–5pm 🌐 chapelle-expiatoire-paris.fr

King Louis XVIII dedicated this chapel in 1816 to the memory of his brother King Louis XVI and sister-in-law Marie-Antoinette. The pair were buried in a cemetery here after being guillotined nearby at Place de la Concorde (p222). The mass grave, known as the Madeleine Cemetery, was one of four to hold the remains of guillotine victims. Marie-Antoinette and Louis XVI were moved to the Basilica of St-Denis (p305) in the 19th century. The chapel merely hints at this turbulent history with a modest Neo-Classical

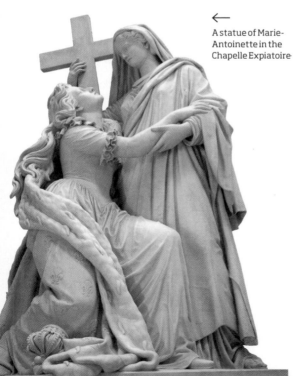

← A statue of Marie-Antoinette in the Chapelle Expiatoire

memorial. The tiny garden contains cenotaphs to those who were buried here, including victims of the fire-works disaster at Marie and Louis's wedding in 1770.

⑧

Église St-Augustin

🛈 F3 🚪 8 Ave César Caire 75008 Ⓜ St-Augustin 🕒 8:30am–7pm Mon–Fri, 9am–12:30pm & 2:30–7:30pm Sat, 8:30am–12:30pm & 4:30–8pm Sun 🌐 saintaugustin.net

This church is located in one of Paris's most exclusive neighbourhoods. Designed by Victor Baltard, the architect of Les Halles, and completed in 1868 at the intersection of sweeping new boulevards, the building initially drew criticism for its oversized dome and curious red turret. Large quan-tities of metal were used in the church's construction, and its cast iron framework provides a decorative feature of the interior, complete with iron angels at the tops of the pillars.

⑨

Gare St-Lazare

🛈 G3 🚪 13 Rue d'Amsterdam 75008 Ⓜ Gare Saint-Lazare

One of Europe's busiest train stations, the Gare St-Lazare is probably the most celebrated in art. Opened in 1837, it sends trains to Normandy, including to the station closest to Giverny, where Claude Monet painted his famous water lilies. The artist was just one of many 19th-century painters to immortalize the Saint-Lazare station in his works. Renowned painters Caillebotte and Manet also lived near the station, and their depictions of it hang in galleries around the world. The station has a shopping mall and a number of restaurants.

A rooftop view of the Art Nouveau Printemps department store

Printemps

📍G4 🏠64 Blvd Haussmann 75009 Ⓜ Havre Caumartin, Haussmann St-Lazare 🕙10am–8pm Mon–Sat, 11am–8pm Sun Ⓦ printemps.com

A stunning Art Nouveau palace dedicated to shopping, the Printemps department store dates back to 1865. High fashion fills the floors, and it feels slightly more elegant and refined than neighbouring Galeries Lafayette. The restaurant under the massive stained-glass dome is a resplendent spot for lunch, while the rooftop café offers great views of the Sacré-Coeur.

Musée Grévin

📍J4 🏠10 Blvd Montmartre 75009 Ⓜ Grands Boulevards 🕙10am–6pm Mon–Fri, 9:30am–7pm Sat, Sun & during school hols Ⓦ grevin-paris.com

This waxworks museum was founded in 1882 and is now a Paris landmark, on a par with Madame Tussauds in London.

It contains tableaux of vivid historical scenes (such as Napoleon's war council), the Palais des Mirages (a giant walk-in kaleidoscope) and the Cabinet Fantastique, which features regular conjuring shows given by a live magician. Famous figures from the worlds of art, sport and politics are also on show, with new celebrities constantly replacing faded and forgotten stars.

Le Grand Rex

📍K4 🏠1 Blvd Poissonnière 75002 Ⓜ Bonne Nouvelle Ⓦ legrandrex.com

A national monument, as well as an innovative example of Art Deco architecture, Le Grand Rex, built in 1932, was long touted as Europe's most opulent cinema, hosting many red-carpet events. One of the largest of its kind in Europe, the Grand Rex is a fading but beautiful symbol of the history of cinema. The auditorium has a starred ceiling and a huge screen. Every December since 1954, the cinema has hosted the Féerie des Eaux, a family-film event featuring an on-stage water show.

STAY

Chouchou Hôtel
Some of the chic rooms at this stylish hotel have views of the Opéra National de Paris Garnier.

📍H4 🏠1 Rue du Helder 75009 Ⓦ chouchouhotel.com

€€€

Hôtel Chopin
Hidden away in a 19th-century covered *passage*, this well-located hotel has charm in spades.

📍J4 🏠46 Passage Jouffroy 75009 Ⓦ hotelchopin-paris-opera.com

€€€

Hôtel Parister
Quiet and calm with contemporary décor, this is a wonderful retreat. The hotel has a swimming pool and a lovely restaurant and cocktail bar.

📍J3 🏠19 Rue Saulnier 75009 Ⓦ hotelparister.com

€€€

A SHORT WALK
OPÉRA

Distance 1.5 km (1 mile) **Nearest Metro** Madeleine
Time 15 minutes

It has been said that if you sit for long enough at the Café de la Paix (opposite the Opéra National de Paris Garnier) the whole world will pass by. During the day, the area is busy with a mix of shoppers, office workers and tourists. A profusion of shops, ranging from the chic, exclusive and expensive to popular department stores, lines the streets. In the evening, when the theatres and cinemas open their doors, the cafés along Boulevard des Capucines are just the place for people-watching.

← The exquisite high altar of La Madeleine

The cafés and restaurants on the west side of the Place de la Madeleine make a good spot for people-watching.

PL DE LA MADELEINE
RUE TRONCHET
RUE VIGNON
RUE GODOT DE MAUROY
RUE CAUMARTIN
RUE EDOUARD VII
RUE

BLVD DE LA MADELEINE
BLVD DES

START
Metro Madeleine

The church of La Madeleine is dedicated to Mary Magdalene and is one of the best-known in Paris (p174).

Did You Know?

George Gershwin is said to have composed *An American in Paris* at Harry's New York Bar.

The opulent Opéra National de Paris Garnier, sometimes described as an enormous wedding cake

Locator Map
For more detail see p170

OPÉRA AND GRANDS BOULEVARDS

Opéra

With a mixture of styles ranging from classical to Baroque, the Opéra National de Paris Garnier of 1875 has come to symbolize the opulence of the Second Empire (p172).

The world of opera is celebrated at the Bibliothèque-Musée de l'Opéra.

Metro Chaussée d'Antin

The Place de l'Opéra was designed by Baron Haussmann and is one of Paris's busiest intersections.

The Café de la Paix maintains its old-fashioned ways and still has its 19th-century decor, designed by Garnier. Their vanilla mille-feuilles are legendary.

Metro Opéra

PL DIAGHILEV

RUE GLUCK

RUE HALEVY

PL J ROUCHE

RUE SCRIBE

AUBER

PL CH GARNIER

RUE

PL DE L'OPERA

M
FINISH

CAPUCINES

RUE DAUNOU

AVE DE L'OPERA

At No 14 Boulevard des Capucines, a plaque tells of the world's first public screening of a movie, by the Lumière brothers in 1895; it took place in the Salon Indien, a room in the Grand Café.

Harry's New York Bar was named after Harry MacElhone, a bartender who bought the bar in 1913. Past regulars have included F Scott Fitzgerald and Ernest Hemingway (p175).

| 0 metres | 100 |
| 0 yards | 100 |

N ↑

LOUVRE AND LES HALLES

Today the heart of the city, this area lay on the outskirts of Paris in the Middle Ages. Its vulnerable position led Philippe Auguste to build a defensive fortress here in 1190, around which grew up a dense urban district. In 1528, François I took up residence in the Louvre, marking the start of centuries of royal redevelopment and the construction of numerous grand buildings and gardens. The area remained affluent following the downfall of the monarchy in 1789, and is still home to many exclusive shops and luxury hotels.

Les Halles, meanwhile, has much more humble origins. For 800 years, the "Belly of Paris" was the site of the central food market in the city. Housed from the late 19th century in 12 magnificent iron-and-glass pavilions designed by Victor Baltard, the market was demolished in 1971 and transformed into a huge underground mall called the Westfield Forum des Halles. Deeply unpopular, it was redeveloped as part of a €1 billion infrastructure project and reopened in 2016.

LOUVRE AND LES HALLES

Must See
1. Musée du Louvre

Experience More
2. Palais-Royal
3. Jardin du Palais-Royal
4. Galerie Vivienne
5. Galerie Colbert
6. Tour Jean Sans Peur
7. St-Eustache
8. Westfield Forum des Halles
9. St-Merry
10. Tour St-Jacques
11. Fontaine des Innocents
12. Jardin des Tuileries
13. Musée de l'Orangerie
14. Galerie Nationale du Jeu de Paume
15. Arc de Triomphe du Carrousel
16. St-Germain l'Auxerrois
17. Place Vendôme
18. Ô Château

Eat
1. Le Grand Colbert
2. Au Pied de Cochon
3. Champeaux

Stay
4. Hotel Regina Louvre
5. Hôtel Thérèse
6. Grand Hôtel du Palais Royal

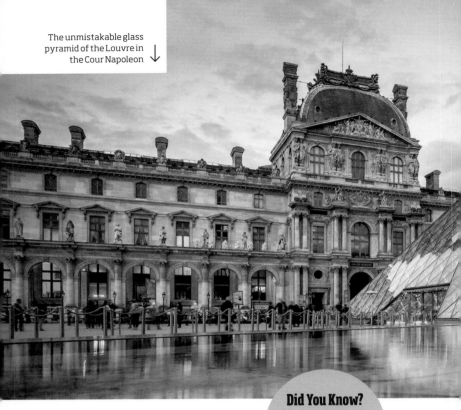

The unmistakable glass pyramid of the Louvre in the Cour Napoleon ↓

❶ 🗝 🅜 🍴 💻 🛍

MUSÉE DU LOUVRE

📍 H6 🏠 Pl du Louvre Ⓜ Palais-Royal-Musée du Louvre 🚌 21, 27, 39, 68, 69, 72, 81, 95 🚆 Châtelet-Les-Halles Ⓞ Louvre 🕘 9am-6pm Wed-Mon (to 9:45pm Fri) 🚫 1 Jan, 1 May, 25 Dec 🌐 louvre.fr

First opened to the public in 1793 after the Revolution, the Louvre contains one of the most important art collections in the world.

Constructed as a fortress in 1190 by King Philippe-Auguste to protect Paris against Viking raids, the Louvre lost its imposing keep during the reign of François I (1514–47), who replaced it with a Renaissance-style building. Thereafter, four centuries of French kings and emperors improved and enlarged it. A glass pyramid designed by I M Pei was added to the main courtyard in 1989, from which all of the galleries can be reached.

The Louvre's treasures can be traced back to the 16th-century collection of François I, who purchased many Italian paintings, including the *Mona Lisa (La Gioconda)*. At the time of Louis XIV's reign (1643–1715) there were a mere 200 works, but donations and purchases augmented the collection and it has been continually enriched ever since.

GALLERY GUIDE

There are eight departments over four floors: Near Eastern antiquities; Egyptian antiquities; Greek, Etruscan and Roman antiquities; Islamic art; sculptures; decorative arts; paintings; and prints and drawings.

1 This sculptural spiral staircase forms part of the modern entrance hall designed by I M Pei.

2 The Marly Horses by Guillaume Coustou once stood near the Place de la Concorde.

3 *The Coronation of Napoleon* by Jacques-Louis David is an impressive 6.2 m (20½ ft) high by 9.8 m (32 ft) wide.

↑ *St Bonaventura's Body Lying in State*
(c 1629) by Francisco de Zurbarán

EUROPEAN PAINTING: 1200 TO 1850

Painting from northern Europe is well covered, with Flemish, Dutch, German and English works by artists including Jan van Eyck, Vermeer, Hans Holbein and J M W Turner. The Spanish collection tends towards depictions of the tragic side of life, although several portraits by Goya are in a lighter vein.

The large collection of Italian paintings covers the period 1200 to 1800. Key figures of the Renaissance are here, including Giotto and Raphael. Several paintings by Leonardo da Vinci are as enchanting as his *Mona Lisa*.

The French collection ranges from the 14th century to 1848. There are superb works by Jean Fouquet, Georges de la Tour and Jean Watteau, as well as J H Fragonard, master of the Rococo.

MONA LISA: STORY OF AN ENIGMA

Acquired by King François I, this portrait of a mysterious woman, believed to be Italian noblewoman Lisa Gherardini, was one of the first paintings displayed in the Louvre when the museum opened. Its much-publicized theft in 1911 pushed it into the public eye, with reproductions appearing all over. Its masterful composition and the enigmatic expression of its sitter mean it remains one of the most valuable paintings in the world.

EUROPEAN SCULPTURE: 1100 TO 1850

←

Saint Mary Magdalene
by Gregor Erhart
(c 1515–20)

Early Flemish and German sculpture in the collection has many masterpieces, including an unusual life-size nude figure of the penitent Mary Magdalene by Gregor Erhart (early 16th century). The French section opens with early Romanesque works, such as a Figure of Christ by a 12th-century Burgundian sculptor and a Head of St Peter. With its eight black-hooded mourners, the Tomb of Philippe Pot is one of the more unusual pieces.

The works of Pierre Puget have been assembled inside the Cour Puget, while the Cour Marly houses the Marly Horses and other master-pieces of French sculpture.

The Italian sculpture collection includes pre-Renaissance works by Duccio and Donatello, and later masterpieces such as Michel-angelo's *Slaves* and Cellini's *Nymph of Fontainebleau*.

DECORATIVE ARTS

↑ Serpentine stone plate (1st century/ 9th century CE)

The Louvre has well over 8,000 "decorative art" objects, including jewellery, silver and glassware, bronzes, porcelain, snuffboxes and armour. Many of these precious objects are from the Abbey of St-Denis *(p305)*, where the kings of France were buried. The treasures include a serpentine stone plate from the 1st century CE with a 9th-century border of gold and precious stones, and the golden sceptre made for King Charles V in about 1380.

> **The French crown jewels include the coronation crowns of Louis XV and Napoleon, and the Regent, one of the purest diamonds in the world.**

The French crown jewels include the coronation crowns of Louis XV and Napoleon, and the Regent, one of the purest diamonds in the world.

The large collection of French furniture ranges from the 16th to the 19th centuries. On display are important pieces by prominent furniture-makers such as André-Charles Boulle, who was cabinet-maker to Louis XIV.

In 2012, the Islamic Art Department opened in the Cour Visconti, with around 18,000 objects on display covering 3,000 years of history from three continents. The museum also has decorative art galleries dedicated to objects from the reign of Louis XIV and the 18th century.

NEAR EASTERN, EGYPTIAN, GREEK, ETRUSCAN AND ROMAN ANTIQUITIES

The range of antiquities is impressive, with objects from the Neolithic period to the fall of the Roman Empire. Important works of Mesopotamian art include the seated figure of Ebih-il, from 2400 BCE, while the warlike Assyrians are represented by delicate carvings and a spectacular reconstruction of part of Sargon II's (722–705 BCE) palace. A fine example of Persian art is the enamelled brickwork depicting the king of Persia's personal guard of archers (5th century BCE).

Most Egyptian art was made for the dead to take to the afterlife. One exquisite example is the tiny carved funeral chapel built for a high official in about 2500 BCE. A special crypt dedicated to the god Osiris contains some colossal sarcophagi and mummified animals.

The department of Greek, Roman and Etruscan antiquities contains some exceptional pieces. The two most famous Greek statues in the Louvre, the *Winged Victory of Samothrace* and the *Venus de Milo*, belong to the Hellenistic period (late 3rd to 2nd century BCE), when more natural-looking human forms were first produced. The star of the Etruscan collection is the terracotta *Sarcophagus of the Cenestian Couple*, while the Roman section includes a bust of Agrippa and a splendid, powerful bronze head of Emperor Hadrian.

→

Winged Victory of Samothrace (c 190 BCE)

EXPERIENCE MORE

Palais-Royal

🅟H6 🏠Pl du Palais-Royal 75001 Ⓜ Palais-Royal
🆆 domaine-palais-royal.fr

This former royal palace, closed to the public, has had a turbulent history. Starting out in the early 17th century as Richelieu's Palais Cardinal, it passed to the Crown on his death and was the childhood home of Louis XIV. Under the control of the 18th-century royal dukes of Orléans, it was the scene of brilliant gatherings, as well as periods of debauchery and gambling. The cardinal's theatre, where Molière had performed, burned down in 1763, but was replaced by the Comédie-Française. After the Revolution, the palace became a gambling house. In 1815, it was reclaimed by the future King Louis-Philippe, one of whose librarians was Alexandre Dumas.

After being restored again between 1872 and 1876, the palace reverted to the state, and it now houses the Council of State, the supreme legal body for administrative matters, and the Constitutional Council. Another wing of the palace is occupied by the Ministry of Culture.

Jardin du Palais-Royal

🅟H5 🏠6 Rue de Montpensier, Pl du Palais-Royal 75001 Ⓜ Palais-Royal ⏱ Hours vary; check website 🆆 domaine-palais-royal.fr

The current garden is about one-third smaller than the original one, laid out by the royal gardener for Cardinal Richelieu in the 1630s. This is due to the construction, between 1781 and 1784, of 60 uniform houses bordering three sides of the square. Today, restaurants, art galleries and specialist shops line the square, which has numbered Jean Marais, Jean Cocteau and Colette among its famous former residents.

The courtyard contains the controversial black-and-white striped stone columns that form conceptual artist Daniel Buren's *Les Deux Plateaux*. The columns were installed in the pedestrianized Palais-Royal courtyard in 1986, despite vociferous opposition about their suitability for the space. Today, they are loved by children and adults alike.

Galerie Vivienne

🅟J5 🏠4 Rue des Petits Champs 75002 Ⓜ Bourse, Pyramides ⏱ Generally 8:30am–8:30pm daily 🆆 galerie-vivienne.com

The early 19th century saw the rise of fashionable covered *passages*, reminiscent of the souks explored during Napoleon's conquests in North Africa. At the height of their popularity there were over 100 of them; they were the shopping malls of their day, well before the department stores came of age. Galerie Vivienne, built in 1823, was a particularly sumptuous example of such a covered *passage*. Its lovely décor has been restored, including its atrium ceilings and mosaic floor with patterns reminiscent of

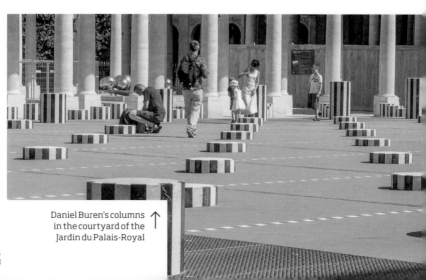

Daniel Buren's columns in the courtyard of the Jardin du Palais-Royal

decorations from Pompeii. It's the perfect all-weather retreat for a glass of wine, a little bit of shopping in the elegant boutiques, or browsing in the Librairie Jousseaume second-hand bookshop.

Galerie Colbert

📍 J5 🏠 4 Rue Vivienne 75002 Ⓜ Bourse, Pyramides 🕐 Generally 9am–8pm daily

Unlike nearby Galerie Vivienne, the covered Galerie Colbert – which is just as exquisite as its neighbour and was also completed in 1823 – is no longer used for commercial purposes. The two *passages* have historically been in competition to be Paris's favourite. It was in Galerie Colbert that composer Hector Berlioz, famous for *La Symphonie Fantastique*,

sang with crowds at the onset of the July Revolution in 1830. Today, it houses various institutions and parts of the University of Paris, all dedicated to the arts and cultural preservation. The *passage* is usually open to the public and is worth seeing for its lovely glass rotunda, with a statue of Eurydice beneath it. The *passage* can also be viewed from the adjacent brasserie Le Grand Colbert.

Tour Jean Sans Peur

📍 K5 🏠 20 Rue Étienne-Marcel 75002 Ⓜ Étienne-Marcel, Sentier 🕐 1:30–6pm Wed–Sun 🌐 tourjeansans peursite.wordpress.com

The Duc de Bourgogne feared reprisals after the Duc d'Orléans was assassinated on his orders in 1407. To protect himself, he had this 27-m (88-ft) tower built onto his home, the Hôtel de Bourgogne, and moved his bedroom up to the fourth floor (reached by a flight of 140 steps). The fine vaulted ceiling is decorated with stone carvings of oak leaves, hawthorn and hops, symbols of the Burgundys.

↑ The lofty, light-filled interior of the elegant Galerie Vivienne

EAT

Le Grand Colbert

This old-world brasserie still charms, and the traditional French food still pleases.

📍 J5 🏠 2 Rue Vivienne 75002 🌐 legrandcolbert.fr

Au Pied de Cochon

Onion soup is a staple of this Les Halles institution, which is open all night.

📍 J6 🏠 6 Rue Coquillière 75001 🌐 pieddecochon.com

Champeaux

Alain Ducasse's casual-yet-chic eatery under the new canopy at Forum des Halles serves French classics done just right.

📍 K6 🏠 La Canopée, Forum des Halles 75001 🌐 restaurant-champeaux.com

EXPERIENCE Louvre and Les Halles

7

St-Eustache

📍J6 🏠2 Impasse St-Eustache, Pl du Jour 75001 Ⓜ Les Halles 🚇 Châtelet-Les-Halles 🕐9:30am-7pm Mon-Fri, 10am-7pm Sat, 9am-7pm Sun 🌐 saint-eustache.org

With its Gothic plan and Renaissance decoration, St-Eustache is one of the most beautiful churches in Paris. Its interior layout is modelled on Notre-Dame (p70), with five naves and side and radial chapels. The 105 years (1532–1637) it took to complete the church saw the flowering of the Renaissance style, which is evident in the arches, pillars and columns. The stained-glass windows in the chancel are created from cartoons by Philippe de Champaigne.

Molière was buried in this church; and the Marquise de Pompadour, official mistress of Louis XV, was baptized here, as was Cardinal Richelieu. Don't miss a chance to attend one of the regular organ recitals that take place here.

8

Westfield Forum des Halles

📍J5 🏠101 Porte Berger 75001 Ⓜ Les Halles, Châtelet 🚇 Châtelet-Les-Halles 🕐Complex: 10am-8:30pm Mon-Sat, 11am-7pm Sun; restaurants & cinemas: 9am-11:30pm daily 🌐 forumdeshalles.com

Known simply as Les Halles and built amid controversy on the site of a famous produce market, this vast complex, much of it underground, is covered by an undulating glass-and-steel roof known as "La Canopée".

→

The manicured grounds of the Jardin des Tuileries

Shops and restaurants abound, and there are two multiscreen cinemas, a gym and swimming pool, and a cinema resource centre, the **Forum des Images**. Here, you can choose from thousands of cinema, television and amateur films, many featuring footage of the city of Paris. Above ground are peaceful gardens, pergolas and mini-pavilions.

Forum des Images

🏠2 Rue du Cinéma 🕐Tue-Sun; check website for details 🌐 forumdesimages.fr

---

9

St-Merry

📍K7 🏠76 Rue de la Verrerie 75004 Ⓜ Hôtel de Ville 🕐8am-8pm Mon-Sat, 9am-1pm & 3:30-6pm Sun 🌐 saintmerry.org

The site of this church dates back to the 7th century. St Médéric, the abbot of St-Martin d'Autun, was buried here at the beginning of the 8th century; he died while on pilgrimage in Paris. Construction of the church – in the Flamboyant Gothic style – took place in 1500–1550. The west front is especially

rich in decoration, and the northwest turret contains the oldest bell in Paris, dating from 1331. St-Merry was the wealthy parish church of the Lombard moneylenders, who gave their name to the nearby Rue des Lombards. Concerts, usually choral or piano, are held every Sunday afternoon.

10

Tour St-Jacques

📍K7 🏠Square de la Tour St-Jacques 75004 Ⓜ Châtelet, Hôtel de Ville 🕐Gardens: year-round; tower: by tour only, Jun-Nov: Fri-Sun 🌐 toursaint jacques.fr

This late-Gothic tower, dating from 1523, is all that remains of a church that was a rendezvous for pilgrims setting out on long journeys. The church was destroyed after the Revolution. Earlier, Blaise Pascal, the 17th-century mathematician, physicist, philosopher and writer, used the tower for experiments. Queen Victoria passed by on her state visit in 1854, giving her name to the nearby Avenue Victoria. The tower can be visited in the summer; book ahead online.

Statues set into the façade of the Gothic church of St-Merry ↑

⓫ Fontaine des Innocents

 K6   ⌂ Pl Joachim-du-Bellay 75001   Ⓜ Les Halles   Ⓡ Châtelet-Les-Halles

This carefully restored Renaissance fountain is a popular meeting place and a Les Halles landmark. It stands in the Place Joachim-du-Bellay, the area's main crossroads. Erected in 1549 on the Rue St-Denis, it was moved to its present location in the 18th century, when the square was constructed on the site of a former graveyard.

Originally set into a wall, the fountain had only three sides so a fourth had to be constructed. It is decorated with mythological figures.

⓬ Jardin des Tuileries

G6   ⌂ Pl de la Concorde 75001   Ⓜ Tuileries, Concorde   ⌚ Apr–Sep: 7am-9pm (to 11pm Jun-Aug); Oct-Mar: 7:30am-7:30pm

Once belonging to the old Palais des Tuileries, these gardens form part of the landscaped area between the Louvre and the Champs-Élysées. They were laid out in the 17th century by royal gardener André Le Nôtre, and later filled with striking sculptures. A staggering 125,000 plants are replanted annually.

STAY

Hotel Regina Louvre
Next to the Louvre, this hotel welcomes those seeking old-world charm and high-end service, with some rooms boasting views of the Eiffel Tower.

 H6   ⌂ 2 Place des Pyramides 75001   Ⓦ regina-hotel.com

€€€

Hôtel Thérèse
A chic boutique-hotel alternative to the big-name hotels in the area, with individually decorated rooms.

 H5   ⌂ 5 Rue Thérèse 75001   Ⓦ hoteltherese.fr

€€€

Grand Hôtel du Palais Royal
Tucked behind the Palais-Royal and overlooking its garden, this luxury property is central but has a secluded feel.

 H6   ⌂ 4 Rue de Valois 75001   Ⓦ grandhoteldupalais royal.com

€€€

Stained glass at
St-Germain l'Auxerrois →

JEU DE PAUME

Nobles used to play a version of handball, *jeu de paume*, in the former royal court that today houses the Galerie Nationale du Jeu de Paume. French players would yell "*tenez*" or "take it" to their opponents. As the game evolved, the word did, too, and the English began to call it tennis, or real tennis, and used rackets instead of their hands. Later, the Jeu de Paume became a storehouse during World War II, where the Nazis stashed stolen art. Those works deemed offensive, for example many Picasso and Dalí paintings, were burned in front of it in 1942.

13

Musée de l'Orangerie

📍 F6 🏛 Jardin des Tuileries, Pl de la Concorde 75001 Ⓜ Concorde ⏰ 9am–6pm Wed–Mon, advance booking recommended 🚫 1 May, 14 Jul am & 25 Dec 🌐 musee-orangerie.fr

Claude Monet's crowning work, the water lily series, or *Nymphéas*, can be found here. The series was painted in his garden at Giverny, near Paris, and presented to the public in 1927. These superb large-scale canvases are complemented well by the outstanding Walter-Guillaume collection of artists of the École de Paris, from the late-Impressionist era to the inter-War period. This is a remarkable concentration of masterpieces, including a room of dramatic works by Soutine and some 14 works by Cézanne – still lifes, portraits (*Madame Cézanne*) and landscapes, such as *Dans*

le Parc de Château Noir. Pierre-Auguste Renoir is represented by 27 canvases, including *Jeunes Filles au Piano (Young Girls at the Piano)*. There are early Picassos, works by Henri Rousseau – notably *La Carriole du Père Junier (Old Junier's Cart)* – and Matisse, and a portrait of Paul Guillaume by Modigliani. All are bathed in the natural light that flows through the windows. Temporary exhibitions are shown on the lower ground floor.

14

Galerie Nationale du Jeu de Paume

📍 F5 🏛 Jardin des Tuileries, 1 Pl de la Concorde 75008 Ⓜ Concorde ⏰ 11am–9pm Tue, 11am–7pm Wed–Sun 🚫 1 Jan, 1 May, 14 Jul & 25 Dec and in between exhibitions 🌐 jeude paume.org

The Jeu de Paume – or real tennis court – was built by Napoleon III in 1851. When real (royal) tennis was replaced in popularity by lawn tennis, the court was used to exhibit art. Eventually, an Impressionist museum was founded here. In 1986, the collection moved to the Musée d'Orsay (*p238*). Renovated in 2020–21, the Jeu de Paume now shows exhibitions of contemporary photography and film and video installations from both established and emerging artists.

15

Arc de Triomphe du Carrousel

📍 H6 🏛 Pl du Carrousel 75001 Ⓜ Palais-Royal

Built by Napoleon in 1806–8 as an entrance to the former Palais des Tuileries, this vast pink marble arch, inspired by ancient Roman triumphal arches, was once topped by the so-called Horses of St Mark's, which Napoleon had looted from Venice's St Mark's Cathedral. The original sculptures were returned to Venice in 1815 after Napoleon's defeat at the Battle of Waterloo and replaced by copies.

16

St-Germain l'Auxerrois

📍 J6 🏛 2 Pl du Louvre 75001 Ⓜ Louvre, Pont-Neuf ⏰ 9am–7pm daily 🌐 saintgermainauxerrois.fr

This church has been built in a combination of Renaissance and Gothic

Did You Know?

The façade of St-Germain l'Auxerrois is mirrored by the adjacent town hall.

styles. The first church on the site was constructed in the 12th century, of which only the foundations of the bell tower remain. The splendid rose stained-glass windows date from the Renaissance period.

After the Valois Court decamped to the Louvre in the 14th century, this became the favoured church of kings.

The church's many historical associations include the horrific St Bartholomew's Day Massacre on 24 August 1572, the eve of the royal wedding of Henri of Navarre and Marguerite de Valois. Thousands of Huguenots who had been lured to Paris for the wedding were murdered as the church bell tolled. Later, after the Revolution, the church was used as a barn and as a police station. Despite many restorations it remains a jewel of Gothic architecture. Check the website for details of the regular guided tours.

17

Place Vendôme

G5 **75001** **M** Tuileries

Perhaps the best example of 18th-century elegance in the city, the architect Jules Hardouin-Mansart's stately square was begun in 1698. The original plan was to house academies and embassies behind the arcaded façades. However, bankers moved in and created opulent homes. Miraculously, the square has remained virtually intact, and is home to jewellers and bankers. Among the famous, Frédéric Chopin died here in 1848 at No 12, and César Ritz established his luxury hotel at the turn of the 20th century at No 15.

 18

Ô Château

J5 **68 Rue Jean-Jacques Rousseau 75001** **M** Louvre-Rivoli, Étienne Marcel **4pm–midnight Mon-Sat** **W** o-chateau.com

With 50 wines served by the glass, this wine-tasting bar in the heart of Les Halles is one of the best places to learn about your soon-to-be favourite vintages (p53). You can stop in for a few drinks, or take a class or even a trip. They can organize outings to Champagne for tastings or prepare a multi-course meal served in one of their vaulted dining rooms. A sommelier pairs each dish with wine, explaining the particularities of French viticulture. English-speakers are catered for, so there's no chance of losing anything in translation.

←

The Galerie Nationale du Jeu de Paume

A SHORT WALK
TUILERIES QUARTER

Distance 2 km (1.25 miles) **Nearest Metro** Pyramides
Time 20 minutes

Elegant squares, formal gardens, street arcades and courtyards give this part of Paris its special character. Monuments to monarchy and the arts coexist with contemporary luxury: sumptuous hotels, world-famous restaurants, fashion emporiums and jewellers of international renown. Combine a walk around the area with a visit to the world-famous Louvre, and end the day with a well-deserved sit-down in the Jardin des Tuileries.

Metro
Pyramides

START

St-Roch is a remarkably long 17th-century church, unusually set on a north-south axis, and a treasure house of religious art.

The Normandy is an elegant hotel in the belle époque style, a form of graceful living that prevailed in Paris at the turn of the 20th century.

In Place des Pyramides is Frémiet's gilded statue of Joan of Arc, a focus of pilgrimage for royalists.

A highlight of the Musée des Arts Décoratifs' displays of art and design is the Art Nouveau collection.

The formal Jardin des Tuileries was designed by royal gardener André Le Nôtre in the 17th century.

RUE ST-HONORE

RUE DES PYRAMIDES

RUE DE L'ECHELLE

RUE DE

AVE DU GL LEMONNIER

FINISH

| 0 metres | | 100 | **N** |
| 0 yards | | 100 | ↑ |

←

Taking a break in the sunshine at the verdant Jardin des Tuileries

The elegant interior of the renowned restaurant Le Grand Véfour

The 18th-century décor makes Le Grand Véfour one of the most beautiful restaurants in Paris. Napoleon and Victor Hugo were two of the many famous people who dined here.

Locator Map
For more detail see p182

Tuileries Quarter

LOUVRE AND LES HALLES

With a fountain pool and benches, the Jardin du Palais-Royal is a city haven, bordered by arcades housing restaurants, art galleries and shops (p188).

France's national theatre, the Comédie-Française is the setting for the works of great dramatists, such as Molière.

In the 18th century, the Palais-Royal was a setting for brilliant gatherings, debauchery and gambling. Today, modern sculptures grace its square (p188).

Metro Palais-Royal, Musée du Louvre

Home to French kings for almost four centuries, the Musée du Louvre is now host to one of the world's greatest art collections (p184).

RUE STE ANNE

AVE DE L'OPERA

RUE DE RICHELIEU

RUE DE MONTPENSIER

RUE DE VALOIS

PL ANDRA MALRAUX

RUE DE ROHAN

RIVOLI

PL DU PALAIS-ROYAL

The iconic Eiffel Tower, illuminated at night

EIFFEL TOWER AND INVALIDES

On the Left Bank of the Seine, this quarter in the 7th arrondissement is monumental in scale. The construction of the Hôtel des Invalides in the late 17th century brought with it the urbanization of the surrounding area, and the neighbourhood quickly became popular with the city's nobles, who wanted more space for their palaces. Many wealthy residents of the Marais moved here in the early 18th century, building the aristocratic town houses that line the Rue de Varenne and Rue de Grenelle. Some of these were destroyed during the Revolution, while others were subsequently converted into national institutions, such as the Assemblée Nationale Palais-Bourbon, or embassies.

The quarter has long had a strong military connection as the home of the École Militaire. In 1889, the school's former parade ground, the Champ-de-Mars, was chosen as the site of an Exposition Universelle to commemorate the 100th anniversary of the Revolution. The centrepiece of that exhibition, the Eiffel Tower, is today the main draw for most visitors to the area.

B | **C** | **D**

Alma-Marceau Ⓜ

PLACE DE L'ALMA

Port de la Conférence 🚢

Trocadéro Ⓜ

CHAMPS-ÉLYSÉES AND CHAILLOT
p212

Pont de l'Alma

Berges de Seine ❽

Palais de Chaillot

Passerelle Debilly

Pont de l'Alma RER

❼ **Musée des Égouts**

QUAI D'ORSAY

Jardins du Trocadéro

Seine

QUAI BRANLY

PLACE DE LA RESISTANCE

RUE COGNACQ JAY

PLACE DE VARSOVIE

PORT DE LA BOURDONNAIS

Musée du Quai Branly-Jacques Chirac ❷

RUE DE L'UNIVERSITÉ

AVE FRANCO RUSSE

CITÉ DE L'ALMA

AVENUE

RAPP

RUE DE

PASSAGE LANDRIEU

RUE PIERRE VILLEY

RUE MALAR

ST-

Port de la Bourdonnais 🚢

AVENUE

AVE DE SAXE

RUE DE MONTESSUY

RUE VALENTIN

RUE DUPONT DES LOGES

ST-DOMINIQUE

Pont d'Iéna

La Branly

QUAI BRANLY

Port de Suffren 🚢

RUE DU GEN CAMOU

RUE DU MAL DU HARISPE

RUE SCHUTZ

RUE DE L'EXPOSITION

RUE BOSQUET

RUE CLER

Eiffel Tower ❶

AVE ELISÉE RECLUS

RUE AUGEREAU

Rue Cler ❻

AVE GUSTAVE EIFFEL

PLACE DU GENERAL GOURAUD

LA BOURDONNAIS

RUE DE

AVENUE

RUE VALADON

AVE OCTAVE GREARD

AVENUE

RUE DE CHAMP

DE MARS

❼ Le P'tit Trouquet

RUE DU CHAMP

RUE BOSQUET

Champ de Mars - Tour Eiffel RER

Parc du Champ-de-Mars

AVENUE

AVE EMILE

RUE DE BELGRADE

PASS DE LA VIERGE

ADRIENNE

DESCHANEL

École Militaire Ⓜ

PLACE JACQUES RUEFF

❶❶ **Champ-de-Mars**

ANATOLE

AVE CHARLES RISLER

AVE ELPLAY

PLACE DE L'ÉCOLE MILITAIRE

AVENUE I

THOMY

PIERRE

FRANCE

AVE DE LA MOTTE PICQUET

ALLÉE

LOTI

PLACE JOFFRE

BOUVARD

AVE DU GEN DERIE

THIERRY

École Militaire ❹

EIFFEL TOWER AND INVALIDES

AVE E ACOLLAS

RUE DUPLEIX

PLACE

AVENUE DE

Must Sees
❶ Eiffel Tower
❷ Musée du Quai Branly-Jacques Chirac
❸ Les Invalides

AVENUE DE LA MOTTE PICQUET

RUE DU LAOS

UNESCO

AVENUE DE SUFFREN

Experience More
❹ École Militaire
❺ Musée Rodin
❻ Rue Cler
❼ Musée des Egouts
❽ Berges de Seine
❾ Assemblée Nationale Palais-Bourbon
❿ Ste-Clotilde
❶❶ Champ-de-Mars

BLVD. DE GRENELLE

La Motte Picquet Grenelle Ⓜ

Square Cambronne

PLACE CAMBRONNE

RUE DU COMMERCE

RUE FREMICOURT

Cambronne Ⓜ

BOULEVARD

RUE MARIO NIKIS

RUE CAMBRONNE

Eat
① Le P'tit Trouquet
② David Toutain
③ Arpège

RUE DE LA CROIX NIVERT

RUE NIVERT

RUE MIOLLIS

RUE FRANÇOIS BONVIN

Stay
④ Hôtel de Varenne
⑤ Hôtel 7 Eiffel

RUE DE L'AMIRAL ROUSSIN

RUE

MADEMOISELLE

Square St-Lambert

RUE LECOURBE

RUE BLOMET

B | **C** | **D**

7 | 8 | 9 | 10

**LOUVRE AND
LES HALLES**
p180

Port des
Champs-Élysées

Pont de la
Concorde

QUAI D'ORSAY

Pont des
Invalides

Pont
Alexandre III

La Seine

PLACE DE
FINLANDE

QUAI ANATOLE FRANCE

Pont
Solférino

Invalides RER

BLVD

AVE R
SCHUMAN

AVE SULLY
PRUDHOMME

RUE DESGENETTES

RUE SURCOUF

RUE FABERT

AVE. DU MARÉCHAL GALLIÉNI

RUE R ESNAULT
PELTERIE

Assemblée
Nationale
Palais-Bourbon ❾

RUE A BRIAND

RUE DE COURTY

ST-GERMAIN

**Assemblée
Nationale**

Musée
d'Orsay
RER

L'UNIVERSITÉ

RUE JEAN NICOT

RUE

DE

L'UNIVERSITÉ

Ⓜ **Invalides**

PLACE DU
PRÉSIDENT
E HERRIOT

PLACE DU
PALAIS
BOURBON

RUE DE
SOLFÉRINO

RUE DE BELLECHASSE

RUE DE
L'UNIVERSITÉ

DOMINIQUE

RUE AMÉLIE

RUE DE LA COMÈTE

② **INVALIDES**

BLVD DE LA TOUR MAUBOURG

RUE FABERT

RUE DE CONSTANTINE

Esplanade des
Invalides

Institut
Géographique
National

RUE ST-DOMINIQUE

RUE DE BOURGOGNE

❿
Ste-
Clotilde

LAS

RUE DE
BELLECHASSE

Solférino
Ⓜ

PLACE J
BAINVILLE

RUE DE
L'UNIVERSITÉ

GRENELLE

⑤

PLACE DES
INVALIDES

RUE MARTIGNAC

RUE C PÉTRIER

CASES

**La Tour-
Maubourg** Ⓜ

RUE DUVIVIER

RUE CLER

AVENUE DE LA MOTTE PICQUET

RUE CHEVERT

RUE L CODET

Square
Santiago
du Chili

BLVD DE LA TOUR MAUBOURG

Square
d'Ajaccio

INVALIDES

④

RUE DE GRENELLE

③

Rue du Bac Ⓜ

BLVD RASPAIL

❸ Les
Invalides

Ⓜ **Varenne**

RUE

DE

VARENNE

RUE DE BELLECHASSE

**ST-GERMAIN-
DES-PRÉS**
p234

RUE J
GRANIER

DES

❺ Musée
Rodin

RUE BARBET DE JOUY

CITÉ VANEAU

RUE VANEAU

RUE DU BAC

AVENUE

DE

TOURVILLE

BOULEVARD

PLACE
VAUBAN

AVE DE VILLARS

Esplanade
du Souvenir
Français

RUE DE
CHANALEILLES

AVENUE DUQUESNE

AVENUE
DE LOWENDAL

RUE BIXIO

AVENUE

SÉGUR

DUQUESNE

RUE DE BABYLONE

RUE DE BABYLONE

LOWENDAL

RUE D'ESTRÉES

PLACE ANDRÉ
TARDIEU

Ⓜ **St-François
Xavier**

RUE MONSIEUR

Jardin
Catherine
Labouré

**Le Bon
Marché**

RUE DE SÈVRES

PLACE DE
FONTENOY

AVENUE
DE SAXE

DE

AVENUE

PLACE EL
SALVADOR

BOULEVARD DES INVALIDES

PLACE DU
PRÉSIDENT
MITHOUARD

RUE OUDINOT

RUE PIERRE LEROUX

RUE VANEAU

Vaneau
Ⓜ

RUE DE SÈVRES

RUE DE L'ABBÉ GRÉGOIRE

Ségur
Ⓜ

RUE L
VAUDOYER

RUE PÉRIGNON

AVENUE

VILLA DE SAXE

AVENUE DE BRETEUIL

RUE MASSERAN

AVENUE
COQUELIN

DUROC

RUE M DE LA
SIZERANNE

AVENUE
D'LESUEUR

RUE ROUSSELET

RUE DE SÈVRES

RUE ST ROMAIN

RUE DU CHERCHE MIDI

AVE. DE SUFFREN

RUE BOUCHUT

RUE R BONHEUR

RUE
BARTHELEMY

EBLE

RUE DU GÉNÉRAL BERTRAND

PLACE DE
BRETEUIL

DE

SAXE

Duroc
Ⓜ

PLACE L P
FARGUE

RUE MAYET

GARIBALDI

**Sèvres
Lecourbe** Ⓜ

PLACE
HENRI
QUEUILLE

RUE DE SÈVRES

**MONTPARNASSE AND
JARDIN DU LUXEMBOURG**
p278

BOULEVARD

PASTEUR

RUE LECOURBE

Falguière Ⓜ

EIFFEL TOWER
AND INVALIDES

RUE DE
VOLONTAIRES

RUE

DE

VAUGIRARD

Ⓜ
Pasteur

| 0 metres | 250 |
| 0 yards | 250 |

N
↑

Volontaires Ⓜ

ⓘ 🏷 🍴 🛍

EIFFEL TOWER

📍B7 🚇Quai Branly and Champ-de-Mars Ⓜ Bir Hakeim 🚌30, 42, 69, 82 to Champ-de-Mars 🚉Champ-de-Mars-Tour Eiffel 🕐Sep-Jun: 9:30am–11:45pm daily (6:30pm for stairs); Jul-Aug: 9am–12:45am 📅14 Jul 🌐toureiffel.paris

An impressive feat of engineering and the most distinctive symbol of Paris, the Eiffel Tower stands 324 m (1,063 ft) tall and offers unrivalled views over the city.

Originally built to impress visitors to the 1889 Exposition Universelle, the Eiffel Tower (Tour Eiffel) was meant to be a temporary addition to the Paris skyline. Built by the engineer Gustave Eiffel, it was fiercely decried by 19th-century aesthetes – the author Guy de Maupassant frequently ate lunch at the tower as it was the only place he could avoid seeing it. The world's tallest structure until 1931, when New York's Empire State Building was completed, the tower is now an icon of Paris and attracts almost 7 million visitors a year. The glass-floored first level houses a modern visitors' centre and an interactive museum chronicling the history of the tower.

THE TOWER IN FIGURES

276 m (905 ft): the height of the viewing gallery on the third level

1,665: the number of steps to the third level

2.5 million: the number of rivets holding the tower together

7 cm (2.5 in): the maximum amount that the tower ever sways

10,100 tonnes: the tower's total weight

60 tonnes: the amount of paint needed to decorate the ironwork

18 cm (7 in): how far the top can move in a curve under the effect of heat

↑ The view from the tower, ranging up to 72 km (45 miles)

← The Eiffel Tower under construction in April 1888, less than halfway complete

Did You Know?

Franz Reichelt died in 1912 after attempting to fly from the parapet using a modified cape as wings.

↑ A view of the Eiffel Tower from the Jardins du Trocadéro *(p220)*

② 🖊️ 🎵 🍴 🖥️ 🏛️

MUSÉE DU QUAI BRANLY-JACQUES CHIRAC

📍C6 🏠37 Quai Branly 🅜Alma-Marceau, Bir-Hakeim, Iéna
🚌42, 63, 72, 80, 82, 92 🚈Pont de l'Alma ⏰10:30am–7pm Tue–
Sun (to 10pm Thu) ⊘Mon (except during all school hols besides
summer hols), 1 May, 25 Dec 🌐quaibranly.fr

**This rich collection of artifacts from Africa, Asia, Oceania
and the Americas resides in a striking building that uses
surrounding greenery as a natural backdrop to the art.**

Widely regarded as former President Jacques Chirac's legacy to Paris's cultural scene, Quai Branly has proved a major tourist pull since it opened in 2006. The stylish Jean Nouvel building displays 3,500 exhibits from the French state's vast non-Western art collection, one of the world's most prolific. Items include an array of African instruments, Gabonese masks, Aztec statues and painted animal hides from North America. Outside, the grounds offer visitors breathing space, and in summer the museum's 500-seat auditorium opens onto an outdoor theatre for music and dance. The rooftop restaurant boasts breathtaking views.

GALLERY GUIDE

Tickets are bought outside the main building. Inside, a ramp around a large glass tower displaying musical instruments leads to the main collection level, where a suggested route passes through four colour-coded zones of Oceania, Asia, Africa and the Americas. Three mezzanine galleries house temporary exhibitions.

The museum's eye-catching exterior, with a glass wall and thickets of trees in the surrounding gardens

HIDDEN GEM
Key Object

The Africa collection houses a striking 1.91 m (6 ft 3 in) androgynous wooden statue from Mali, which combines a regal male head with the breasts of a woman.

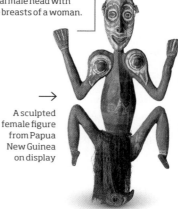

→ A sculpted female figure from Papua New Guinea on display

↑ Jean Nouvel's elegant building, an exhibit in itself from the inside and out *(inset)*

3

LES INVALIDES

📍 E7 🚪 6 Blvd des Invalides, Esplanade des Invalides Ⓜ La Tour-Maubourg, Varenne
🚌 28, 63, 69, 80, 82, 83, 87, 92, 93 to Les Invalides 🚇 Invalides 🚊 Tour Eiffel

This sizeable ensemble of monumental buildings is one of the most impressive sights in Paris. The complex takes its name from the imposing Hôtel des Invalides, built for wounded soldiers of the late 17th century, and is today home to a fascinating assortment of military museums. At its heart is the Dôme des Invalides, the final resting place of arguably the greatest French soldier of all, Napoleon Bonaparte.

① Hôtel des Invalides

🕐 10am–6pm daily (to 9pm Tue for temporary exhibitions) 🚫 1 Jan, 1 May, 25 Dec 🌐 musee-armee.fr

Founded by Louis XIV, the Hôtel des Invalides was France's first military hospital. Designed by Libéral Bruand and completed in 1675, it became home to French war veterans and disabled soldiers who, prior to its inauguration, had been reduced to begging on the streets.

Today, the classical façade is one of the most impressive sights in Paris, with its four storeys, the bank of cannon in the forecourt, garden and tree-lined esplanade that stretches to the Seine.

Part of the building is still home to veterans. The south side leads to St-Louis-des-Invalides, the soldiers' church, which backs on to the magnificent Dôme des Invalides of Jules Hardouin-Mansart (p206). The dome was regilded in 1989.

The splendid Hôtel des Invalides seen from Pont Alexandre III

② Musée de l'Armée

🚪 129 Rue de Grenelle (wheelchair access at 6 Blvd des Invalides) 🕐 10am–6pm daily (to 9pm Tue for temporary exhibitions) 🚫 1 Jan, 1 May, 25 Dec 🌐 musee-armee.fr

This is one of the world's most comprehensive museums of military history, with exhibits ranging from the Stone Age to the final days of World War II.

Situated in the northeast refectory, the Ancient Armoury department is worth visiting for the collection on display, one of the largest in the world, as much as for the 17th-century murals by Joseph Parrocel adorning the walls. These celebrate Louis XIV's military conquests.

The life of Charles de Gaulle and his role in World War II are

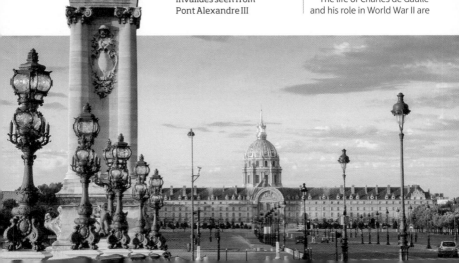

Metro La Tour-
Maubourg

PL DES INVALIDES

AVE DE LA MOTTE PICQUET

RUE DE GRENELLE

Metro
Varenne

BLVD DES INVALIDES

The Invalides
gardens were
designed by de
Cotte in 1704 and
are lined by bronze
cannons from the
17th and 18th
centuries.

The Cour d'Honneur is
still used for military
parades. Seurre's
statue of Napoleon,
known as the Little
Corporal, stands
above the south side.

AVE DE TOURVILLE

AVE DE SÉGOR

AVE DE VILLARS

↑ Map of the
Invalides complex

documented in the *Historial de Gaulle*, a film and interactive multimedia attraction (closed Mon). The Département Moderne is in two parts: the first (1648–1792) covers the reign of Louis XIV, while the second (1792–1871) displays a collection of Napoleon's mementos. Items include his campaign bed and his stuffed dog.

and was bestowed on those who made an outstanding contribution to the final victory in World War II. Among the recipients of the honour are French civilians and members of the armed forces, plus a number of overseas leaders such as King George VI, Winston Churchill and Dwight Eisenhower.

plot artillery positions. Out of a total of 260, around 100 of these three-dimensional maps are on display in the museum. The oldest model is that of Perpignan, dating from 1686. It shows the fortifications drawn up by the 17th-century military architect Vauban, who built the defences for several French towns, including Briançon.

Musée de l'Ordre de la Libération

🕑 10am–6pm daily (to 9pm Tue for temporary exhibitions; to 5pm Nov–Mar)
🚫 1 Jan, 1 May, 25 Dec
🌐 ordredelaliberation.fr

This museum is devoted to the wartime Free French and their leader, General Charles de Gaulle, as well as to the Resistance movement within France and the Resistance fighters who were deported.

The Order of Liberation was created by De Gaulle in 1940. It is France's highest honour

Musée des Plans-Reliefs

🕑 10am–6pm daily (Oct–Mar: to 5pm) 🚫 1st Mon of month (except Jul, Aug, Sep), 1 Jan, 1 May, 25 Dec
🌐 museedesplansreliefs.culture.fr

The detailed models of French forts and fortified towns, some dating back to Louis XIV's reign, were considered top secret until the 1950s, when they were put on public display. They were created between the reigns of Louis XIV and Napoléon III in order to plan town defences and

St-Louis-des-Invalides

🕑 10am–6pm daily (Nov–Mar: to 5pm) 🚫 1 Jan, 1 May, 25 Dec 🌐 musee-armee.fr

The "soldiers' church" was built in 1679–1708 by Jules Hardouin-Mansart from original designs by Libéral Bruand. The imposing but stark interior is decorated with banners seized in battle.

The first performance of Berlioz's *Requiem* was given on the fine 17th-century organ in 1837, with an orchestra accompanied by a battery of outside artillery.

⑥ ✎ Ⓜ 🖥 🛍

DÔME DES INVALIDES

🕐 10am–6pm daily (to 9pm Tue for temporary exhibitions)
🚫 1 Jan, 1 May, 25 Dec 🅦 musee-armee.fr

Built in the French Classical style on the orders of Louis XIV, this ornate church houses the tombs of Napoleon Bonaparte and a host of other great French military men. Its magnificent dome is a landmark on the city skyline and glistens as much now as it did when the Sun King had it first gilded in 1715.

The Dôme des Invalides was designed in 1676 by Jules Hardouin-Mansart for the exclusive use of Louis XIV and for the location of royal tombs. Slotted among the existing buildings of the Invalides military complex, the resulting masterpiece complements the surrounding structures and is one of the greatest examples of 17th-century French architecture. After Louis XIV's death, plans to bury the royal family in the church were abandoned, and it became a monument to Bourbon glory. In 1840, Louis-Philippe decided to install Napoleon's remains in the crypt, and the addition of the tombs of Vauban, Marshal Foch and other figures of military prominence have since turned this church into a French military memorial.

←

Charles de la Fosse's circular painting (1692) on the ceiling of the dome, showing the *Glory of Paradise*, with Saint Louis presenting his sword to Christ

NAPOLEON'S RETURN

King Louis-Philippe decided to bring the Emperor Napoleon's body back from St Helena as a gesture of reconciliation to the Republican and Bonapartist parties contesting his regime. The Dôme des Invalides, with its historical and military associations, was an obvious choice for Napoleon's final resting place. His body was encased in six coffins and finally placed in the crypt in 1861, at the culmination of a grand ceremony which was attended by Napoleon III.

Did You Know?

The dome stands 107 m (351 ft) high and was first gilded in 1706.

↑ The church with its glittering dome, which required 12 kg (26 lb) of gold to re-gild it in 1989

EXPERIENCE MORE

4

École Militaire

📍D8 🏠21 Pl Joffre 75007
📞01 80 50 14 00 Ⓜ École
Militaire

Founded in 1751 to educate
500 sons of impoverished
officers, the Royal Military
Academy was designed
by architect Jacques-Ange
Gabriel. The central pavilion,
a magnificent example of
the French classical style, is
graced with eight Corinthian
pillars and a quadrangular
dome. The ornate interior is
decorated in Louis XVI style;
of main interest are the chapel
and a Gabriel-designed
wrought-iron banister on
the main staircase.

One of the academy's
early cadets was Napoleon
Bonaparte, whose
passing-out report
stated that "he
could go far if the
circumstances are
right". Today, the
academy is used as a
cavalry training ground
and isn't generally open
to the public.

5

Musée Rodin

📍E7 🏠79 Rue de Varenne
75007 Ⓜ Varenne 🕐10am-
6:30pm Tue-Sun, advance
booking recommended
📅1 Jan, 1 May, 25 Dec
🌐musee-rodin.fr

Auguste Rodin, widely
regarded as one of the
greatest French sculptors
of the 19th century, lived
and worked in the elegant
18th-century Hôtel Biron
from 1908 until his death
in 1917. In return for a
state-owned flat

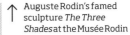

↑ Auguste Rodin's famed
sculpture *The Three
Shades* at the Musée Rodin

and studio, Rodin agreed
to leave his work to the
nation. Some 300 works
from Rodin's collection
can now be seen in the
museum. The attractive
grounds consist of a rose
garden, an ornamental garden and a relaxation area
with benches, and contain
some of Rodin's most
celebrated sculptures:
The Thinker, *The Burghers
of Calais*, *The Gates of Hell*
and *Balzac*. Spread across
18 rooms, the museum
combines a chronology of

The grandiose
classical façade of
the École Militaire ↓

The market street Rue Cler, with its many fine food shops ↑

Rodin's creative development with a thematic exploration of his workshop. It has even re-created a space exactly as it was when Rodin lived and worked here. The outdoor café makes a lovely spot for a drink in warmer weather.

Rue Cler

⬤D7 🏠75007 Ⓜ École Militaire, La Tour-Maubourg

This is a typically charming Parisian market street, albeit one chic enough for the 7th arrondissement, the richest in Paris. The bulk of senior civil servants, wealthy expatriates,

Did You Know?

If laid end to end, the city's 2,100 km (1,300 miles) of sewers would stretch from Paris to Istanbul.

business leaders and many diplomats live in this residential neighbourhood. Most of the food and drink stores – selling not just fresh produce but also cheese, chocolates, ice creams, patisseries and charcuterie – are gathered along the cobblestoned stretch south of Rue de Grenelle.

Musée des Égouts

⬤D6 🏠Pl Habib Bourguiba, opposite 93 Quai d'Orsay 75007 Ⓜ Alma-Marceau 🚆Pont de l'Alma 🕙10am-5pm Tue-Sun 🚫Jan, 1 May, 25 Dec 🌐musee-egouts.paris.fr

One of Baron Haussmann's finest achievements, the majority of Paris's sewers (égouts) date from the Second Empire (1852–70). In the 20th century, surprisingly the sewers became a popular attraction. The Musée des Égouts allows visitors to tour a small area around the Quai d'Orsay entrance. Display boards explain the history of Paris's water supply and waste management. It is a good idea to book guided tours in advance.

EAT

Le P'tit Trouquet
This cosy little restaurant offers classic French dishes.

⬤D7 🏠28 Rue de l'Exposition 75007 🚫Sat, Sun 🌐leptittrouquet.fr

David Toutain
Creative, two-star Michelin dining in a relaxed setting.

⬤E6 🏠29 Rue Surcouf 75007 🚫Sat, Sun 🌐davidtoutain.com

Arpège
Alain Passard's three-star restaurant is a worthwhile treat.

⬤F7 🏠84 Rue de Varenne 75007 🚫Sat, Sun 🌐alain-passard.com

STAY

Hôtel de Varenne
A hotel with refined décor in the chic 7th arrondissement.

⬤F7 🏠44 Rue de Bourgogne 75007 🌐hoteldevarenne.com

Hôtel 7 Eiffel
A modern option near the Eiffel Tower.

⬤D7 🏠17 bis Rue Amélie 75007 🌐hotel-7eiffel-paris.com

8

Berges de Seine

📍 D6 🏛 Quai d'Orsay 75007
Ⓜ Assemblée Nationale, Invalides

In 2013, this former busy roadway along the river bank was revamped for pedestrians, turning it into one of Paris's loveliest promenades. As well as offering spectacular views of the Louvre, Jardin des Tuileries and other monuments along the way, the 2.3-km (1½-mile) walkway is studded with activities for children, like mini playgrounds, climbing walls and floating gardens. The promenade also has *pétanque* courts, an athletics track, a fitness course and Vélib' bikes *(p313)*. Cyclists and joggers zigzag between pedestrians taking advantage of a traffic-free stroll. There are cafés and restaurants (some with board games to borrow) both on land and aboard boats, especially around Pont Alexandre III. Picnickers and evening revellers gather on the banks during the summer, making the Berges de Seine one of the liveliest places for evening tipples on the Left Bank.

Did You Know?
—
The Pont de la Concorde in front of the Assemblée Nationale was built using stones from the Bastille.

9

Assemblée Nationale Palais-Bourbon

📍 F6 🏛 126 Rue de l'Université 75007
Ⓜ Assemblée Nationale
🚉 Invalides 🌐 assemblee-nationale.fr

Built in 1722 for the Duchesse de Bourbon, daughter of Louis XIV, the Palais-Bourbon was confiscated during the Revolution. It has been home to the lower house of the French Parliament since 1830. During World War II, the palace became the Nazi administration's seat of government. The grand Neo-Classical façade with its fine columns was added in 1806, partly to mirror the façade of La Madeleine church facing it across the Seine *(p174)*. The adjacent Hôtel de Lassay is the residence of the president of the National Assembly. Group tours can be organized for a maximum of 50 people on the invitation of a member of parliament, with several months' prior notice.

10

Ste-Clotilde

📍 F7 🏛 23B Rue Las Cases 75007 Ⓜ Solférino, Varenne, Invalides ⏰ 9am–7:30pm Mon–Fri, 10am–8pm Sat & Sun. Times vary for Jul & Aug; check website 🔒 Non-religious public hols 🌐 sainte-clotilde.com

Designed by the German architect François-Christian

→
The Assemblée Nationale on the Left Bank of the Seine

The pretty Champ-de-Mars gardens at the foot of the Eiffel Tower

> **Picnickers and evening revellers gather on the banks during the summer, making the Berges de Seine one of the liveliest places for evening tipples on the Left Bank.**

Gau and the first of its kind to be built in Paris, this church, in Neo-Gothic style, was inspired by the mid-19th-century enthusiasm for the Middle Ages, made fashion-able by such writers as Victor Hugo. The church is noted for its imposing twin towers, visible from across the Seine, and there are sculptures of the Stations of the Cross inside. The composer César Franck was the organist here.

Champ-de-Mars

📍 C7 📮 75007 Ⓜ École Militaire 🚉 Champ de Mars-Tour Eiffel

The gardens stretching from the Eiffel Tower to the École Militaire were originally a parade ground for the officer cadets of the École Militaire *(p208)*. The area has since been used for horse-racing, hot-air balloon ascents and the mass celebrations for 14 July, the anniversary of the Revolution. The first Bastille Day ceremony was held in 1790 in the presence of a glum, captive Louis XVI. Vast exhibitions were held here in the late 19th century, including the 1889 World Fair for which the Eiffel Tower was erected. *Le Mur de la Paix*, Clara Halter and Jean-Michel Wilmotte's symbolic monument to world peace, stands at one end.

The park is popular with Parisian families and tour-ists, who come here to relax, walk their dogs (it is one of the few parks in Paris where dogs are allowed) and participate in the numerous activities for children, which include playgrounds, pony rides, puppet shows and a carousel. There is also an outdoor café.

CHAMPS-ÉLYSÉES AND CHAILLOT

This area radiates wealth and power, but it was once little more than open fields lying on the outskirts of Paris. In 1616, Marie de Medici, wife of Henri IV, commissioned a tree-lined approach road through here to the Tuileries Palace, which was expanded in the late 17th century by Louis XIV's landscape designer, André Le Nôtre. The avenue was christened Champs-Élysées in the 18th century, and became a fashionable location for the nobility to build grand town houses.

The nearby Chaillot quarter, however, remained just a village before becoming absorbed into the city of Paris in the 19th century. Subsequently bestowed with similarly wide avenues and grand mansions, it became one of the city's most elegant neighbourhoods. The districts' allure has not faded, and today they are home to numerous embassies and *haute couture* fashion houses, as well as five-star hotels and fine restaurants.

CHAMPS-ÉLYSÉES AND CHAILLOT

A
AVENUE DES TERNES
RUE D'ARMAILLE
AVENUE MAC-MAHON
AVENUE CARNOT

B
BLVD DE COURCELLES
RUE DARU
RUE DU FAUBOURG ST-HONORE
HOCHE
Courcelles Ⓜ
Ternes Ⓜ
AVE DE WAGRAM

C
AVE DE LA GRANDE ARMÉE
AVENUE FOCH

Place Charles de Gaulle (L'Étoile) ⑨
Arc de Triomphe ①
Ⓜ Charles de Gaulle-Étoile Ⓡ
RER
RUE LORD BYRON
RUE BALZAC
PLACE G GUILLAUMIN
AVENUE DE FRIEDLAND
RUE BEAUJON
②

Avenue des Champs-Élysées ⑧

4
AVENUE VICTOR HUGO
Kléber Ⓜ
RUE PAUL VALERY
RUE LAURISTON
AVENUE KLÉBER
RUE DE PRESBOURG
RUE VERNET
AVENUE DES
George V Ⓜ
CHAMPS-
⑥
RUE GALILEE
RUE DE BASSANO
AVENUE GEORGE V
RUE BAYARD
RUE WASHINGTON

Victor Hugo Ⓜ
PLACE VICTOR HUGO
RUE COPERNIC
RUE DE BELLOY
RUE JEAN GIRAUDOUX
RUE C COLOMB
RUE QUENTIN
④
⑪
③
RUE LINCOLN
RUE PIERRE CHARRON
RUE MARBEUF

AVE VICTOR HUGO
RUE ST DIDIER
RUE LAURISTON
RUE CIMAROSA
RUE GALILEE
RUE HAMELIN
PLACE DES ETATS UNIS
PLACE AMIRAL DE GRASSE
RUE DE BASSANO
RUE DE CHAILLOT
RUE PIERRE 1er DE SERBIE
RUE FRANCOIS

5
RUE LEO DELIBES
Boissière Ⓜ
RUE BOISSIERE
Galerie-Musée Baccarat
RUE DE LUBECK
Cathédrale Américaine

RUE ST-DIDIER
AVENUE KLÉBER
Musée National des Arts Asiatiques Guimet ①
RUE DE LONGCHAMP
PLACE D'IENA
Musée Galliera
AVENUE DU PRÉSIDENT WILSON
RUE FREYCINET
RUE GOETHE
Théâtre des Champs-Élysées
PLACE DE LA REINE ASTRID

6
CHAILLOT
AVENUE
Trocadéro Ⓜ
③ Cité de l'Architecture et du Patrimoine ⑦
Aquarium de Paris ⑦
DU
Ⓜ Iéna
Palais de Tokyo ㉑
RUE DE LA MANUTENTION
Alma-Marceau Ⓜ
PLACE DE L'ALMA
Pont de l'Alma

Cimetière de Passy ⑲
PLACE DU TROCADÉRO ET DU 11 NOVEMBRE
Palais de Chaillot
Musée National de la Marine ⑤
Musée de l'Homme ④
Jardins du Trocadéro ⑥
AVE D NATIONS UNIES
AVE ALBERT DE MUN
RUE FRESNEL
㉒ Musée d'Art Moderne de la Ville de Paris ㉑
Pont de l'Alma Ⓡ
RER
QUAI
PLACE DE LA RESISTANCE

AVE GEORGES MANDEL
AVE PAUL DOUMER
AVE D'EYLAU
PLACE DE VARSOVIE
Passerelle Debilly
AVENUE DE NEW YORK
Pont de l'Alma

EIFFEL TOWER AND INVALIDES *p196*

RUE B FRANKLIN
RUE LE TASSE
AVE DES NATIONS UNIES
Pont d'Iéna
Port de la Bourdonnais
Musée du Quai Branly-Jacques Chirac
AVENUE RAPP
AVENUE BOSQUET

7
PLACE DE COSTA RICA
RUE BEETHOVEN
SQUARE L'ALBONI
RUE L'ALBONI
AVE DU PRÉSIDENT KENNEDY
Passy Ⓜ
QUAI BRANLY
Champ de Mars-Tour Eiffel Ⓡ
Port de Suffren
Eiffel Tower
Parc du Champ-de-Mars
AVENUE DE LA BOURDONNAIS

AVE RENE BOYLESVE
Port de Passy
La Seine
Pont de Bir Hakeim
Pont de Passy
AVENUE DE SUFFREN

8
Bir Hakeim Ⓜ
QUAI DE GRENELLE

0 metres 300
0 yards 300

N ↑

A   **B**   **C**

CHAMPS-ÉLYSÉES AND CHAILLOT

Must Sees

1. Arc de Triomphe
2. Palais de Chaillot

Experience More

3. Cité de l'Architecture et du Patrimoine
4. Musée de l'Homme
5. Musée National de la Marine
6. Jardins du Trocadéro
7. Aquarium de Paris
8. Avenue des Champs-Élysées
9. Place Charles de Gaulle (L'Étoile)
10. Place de la Concorde
11. Grand Palais
12. Petit Palais
13. Pont Alexandre III
14. Palais de la Découverte
15. Avenue Montaigne
16. Parc Monceau
17. Musée Jacquemart-André
18. Palais de l'Élysée
19. Cimetière de Passy
20. Musée d'Art Moderne de la Ville de Paris
21. Palais de Tokyo

Eat

1. Astrance
2. Pierre Gagnaire
3. Relais de l'Entrecôte

Drink

4. Le Bar at the Four Seasons Hotel George V
5. Le Bar de l'Hôtel Belmont
6. Bar Kléber at the Peninsula
7. Le Bar Botaniste at the Shangri-La
8. Le Bar du Bristol

Stay

9. Hôtel Garden Élysées
10. Le Pavillon des Lettres
11. Hotel de Sers

30

shields just below the
Arc's roof each bear the
name of a victorious
Napoleonic battle.

The golden tones ↑
of the arch's stonework,
highlighted by the sunset

ARC DE TRIOMPHE

C4 **Pl Charles de Gaulle** **M / Charles de Gaulle-Étoile** **22, 30, 31, 52, 73, 92 to Pl Charles de Gaulle** **10am–10:30pm daily (to 11pm Apr–Sep)** **am only 8 May, 14 Jul, 11 Nov; all day 1 Jan, 1 May, 25 Dec** **paris-arc-de-triomphe.fr**

Situated at the heart of Place Charles de Gaulle, overlooking the Champs-Élysées, the Arc de Triomphe was commissioned by Napoleon to celebrate France's military might. The exterior is adorned with sculptures depicting various battles, while the viewing platform at the top affords one of the best views in Paris.

After his greatest victory, the Battle of Austerlitz in 1805, Napoleon promised his men, "You shall go home beneath triumphal arches." The first stone of what was to become the world's most famous triumphal arch was laid the following year, but disruptions to architect Jean Chalgrin's plans and the demise of Napoleonic power delayed the completion of this monumental building until 1836. Standing 50 m (164 ft) high, the Arc is now the customary starting point for victory celebrations and parades.

← The twelve avenues radiating from Place Charles de Gaulle

→ The symbolic torch at the Tomb of the Unknown Soldier

NUPTIAL PARADE

Napoleon divorced Josephine in 1809 because she was unable to bear him children. A diplomatic marriage was arranged in 1810 with Marie-Louise, daughter of the Austrian emperor. Napoleon was determined to impress his bride by passing through the Arc on their way to the wedding, but work had barely started, so Chalgrin built a full-scale mock-up of the arch on the site for the couple to go through.

Timeline

1806
▼ Napoleon commissions Chalgrin to build the triumphal Arc following the Battle of Austerlitz in the previous year

1815
Napoleon abdicates after defeat at the Battle of Waterloo, causing work on the Arc to cease

1919
Victory parade of Allied armies through the Arc to celebrate the end of World War I

1836
King Louis-Philippe completes the Arc during the Bourbon Restoration

1944
▲ De Gaulle leads the crowd from the Arc following the liberation of Paris

2 🖥 🛍

PALAIS DE CHAILLOT

📍 B6 🏠 Pl du Trocadéro 75016 Ⓜ Trocadéro

The Palais, with its huge, curved colonnaded wings each culminating in an immense pavilion, was designed in Neo-Classical style for the 1937 World Fair (Exposition Universelle) by Léon Azéma, Louis-Hippolyte Boileau and Jacques Carlu. Today it houses three major museums: the Cité de l'Architecture et du Patrimoine, the Musée de l'Homme and the Musée National de la Marine.

The present Palais replaced the Trocadéro palace built for the World Fair of 1878. It is adorned with sculptures and bas-reliefs, and on the walls of the pavilions are gold inscriptions by the poet and essayist Paul Valéry. The *parvis*, or square, situated between the two pavilions is decorated with large bronze sculptures and ornamental pools. On the terrace in front of the *parvis* stand two bronzes, *Apollo* by Henri Bouchard and *Hercules* by Albert Pommier. Stairways lead from the terrace to the Théâtre National de Chaillot, which, since World War II, has enjoyed huge fame for its avant-garde productions.

↑ One of the galleries in the Cité de l'Architecture et du Patrimoine *(p220)*

THÉÂTRE NATIONAL DE CHAILLOT

In addition to being a prestigious performance venue, the Théâtre National de Chaillot has also played an important role in world history. It was here that the Universal Declaration of Human Rights was signed in 1948.

← View of the Palais de Chaillot from the Eiffel Tower

Exhibits from the anthropology and ethnology collection of the Musée de l'Homme *(p220)* ↑

PICTURE PERFECT
Eiffel Tower

The palace's terrace boasts magnificent views of the Eiffel Tower. Head here to get a panoramic shot of the Iron Lady.

← The bronze *Hercules* statue on the terrace

EXPERIENCE MORE

3

Cité de l'Architecture et du Patrimoine

📍 B6 🏛 Palais de Chaillot, Pl du Trocadéro 75016 Ⓜ Trocadéro ⏰ 11am–7pm Wed–Mon (to 9pm Thu) 🔒 1 Jan, 1 May, 14 Jul, 25 Dec 🌐 citedelarchitecture.fr

In the east wing of the Palais de Chaillot, this museum charts the development of French architecture through the ages. Among the unmissable displays is the Galerie des Moulages, which covers the period from the Middle Ages to the Renaissance. Here, you will find three-dimensional models of great French cathedrals, such as Chartres. Also worth a look is the Galerie d'Architecture Moderne et Contemporaine, with a reconstruction of an apartment designed by Le Corbusier.

4

Musée de l'Homme

📍 A6 🏛 Palais de Chaillot, Pl du Trocadéro 75016 Ⓜ Trocadéro ⏰ 11am–7pm Wed–Mon 🔒 1 Jan, 1 May, 14 Jul, 25 Dec 🌐 musee delhomme.fr

Situated in the west wing of the Chaillot palace, this museum traces the process of human evolution, from prehistoric times to the present, through anthropological exhibits from around the world. It houses one of the world's most comprehensive prehistoric collections. Displays show how humans have adapted to the environment, and there is also a focus on the development of language and culture.

5

Musée National de la Marine

📍 B6 🏛 Palais de Chaillot, Pl du Trocadéro 75016 Ⓜ Trocadéro 🔒 For renovation until Oct 2023 🌐 musee-marine.fr

This museum recounts French maritime history from the days of the royal wooden warships to today's aircraft carriers and nuclear submarines through wonderfully exact scale models (most of them two centuries old), mementos of naval heroes, paintings and navigational instruments. The museum was set up by Charles X in 1827, and was moved to the Chaillot palace in 1943. Extensive renovations are currently underway to modernize the museum and create new spaces to explore historical and contemporary maritime themes.

↑ Henri Bouchard's *Apollo* statue outside the Musée de l'Homme

6

Jardins du Trocadéro

📍 B6 🏛 75016 Ⓜ Trocadéro

These charming gardens were created for the Exposition Universelle in 1937, at the same time as the Palais de Chaillot *(p218)*. Their centre-piece is a long rectangular ornamental pool, bordered by stone and bronze-gilt statues, which look spectacular at night when the fountains are illuminated. The statues include *Man* by Pierre Traverse and *Woman* by Daniel Bacqué, *Bull* by Paul Jouve and *Horse* by Georges Guyot. On either side of the pool, the slopes of the Chaillot hill lead down to the Seine and the Pont d'Iéna. The 10-ha (25-acre) park is laid out with flowering trees, small streams and bridges,

WORLD FAIR

In 1889, the World Fair (or Exposition Universelle) saw the construction of the Eiffel Tower *(p200)*. The 1937 edition initiated the building of the Palais de Chaillot *(p218)*, which replaced the Palais du Trocadéro, itself erected for the 1878 World Fair. Numerous other temporary structures dotted the area around the Champs de Mars, but today, only the Iron Lady remains. If it weren't for the fact that the Eiffel Tower proved useful as a radio tower, it, too, would have been dismantled.

and is a romantic place for a stroll. There is an aquarium in the northeast corner of the gardens, and in winter an outdoor ice-skating rink is open to visitors.

Aquarium de Paris

B6 5 Ave Albert de Mun 75016 Trocadéro, Iéna 10am–6pm daily (to 8pm Sat), advance booking required 14 Jul aquariumdeparis.com

Originally built in 1878 for the Exposition Universelle, this is now a state-of-the-art aquarium which is home to over 500 species of sea creatures from around the world, including seahorses, clown-fish and some spectacular sharks and rays, plus the Médusarium, with more than 50 species of jellyfish..

The building is located in a former quarry and has been designed to blend in entirely with the Chaillot hillside. Cinema screens showing cartoons and animal documentaries are interspersed with the aquariums, and there are art exhibitions and shows for children in the theatre.

→

The Eiffel Tower seen from the Jardins du Trocadéro

One of the ornamental fountains in the huge Place de la Concorde ↑

 8

Avenue des Champs-Élysées

Q D4 **⌂** 75008
M Franklin D. Roosevelt, George V

Paris's most famous and popular thoroughfare had its beginnings in about 1667, when the royal landscape garden designer André Le Nôtre extended the royal view from the Tuileries by creating a tree-lined avenue which eventually became known as the Champs-Élysées (Elysian Fields). It has been France's national "triumphal way" ever since the homecoming of Napoleon's body from St Helena in 1840. With the addition of cafés and restaurants in the second half of the 19th century, the Champs-Élysées became the place in which to see and be seen. The Rond-Point des Champs-Élysées is the prettiest part, with chestnut trees and flower beds. A number of major brands, such as Zara and Lancôme, have their flagship stores here, while fast-food cafés jostle for space with more upmarket establishments such as Fouquet's brasserie. In July, the avenue is the setting for the exhilarating sprint finish of the annual Tour de France cycle race.

> One of Europe's most magnificent and historic squares, Place de la Concorde covers more than 8 ha (20 acres) in the middle of Paris.

9

Place Charles de Gaulle (l'Étoile)

Q C4 **⌂** 75008 **M** Charles de Gaulle-Étoile

Known as the Place de l'Étoile until the death of Charles de Gaulle in 1969, the area is still referred to simply as l'Étoile, "the star". The present *place* was laid out in accordance with Baron Haussmann's plans of 1854 (p55). For motorists, it is the ultimate challenge.

10

Place de la Concorde

Q F5 **⌂** 75008
M Concorde

One of Europe's most magnificent and historic squares, Place de la Concorde covers more than 8 ha (20 acres) in the middle of Paris. Starting out as Place Louis XV, displaying a statue of the eponymous king, it was built in the mid-18th century by architect Jacques-Ange Gabriel, who chose to make it an open octagon with only the north side containing mansions. In the square's next incarnation, as the Place de la Révolution, the statue was replaced by the guillotine. The death toll in the square in two and a half years was 1,119, and victims included Louis XVI, Marie-Antoinette (who died in view of the secret apartment she kept at No 2 Rue Royale) and the Revolutionary leaders Danton and Robespierre.

In the spirit of reconciliation, the square was then renamed Concorde (originally by chastened Revolutionaries). Its grandeur was enhanced in the 19th century by the arrival of the 3,200-year-old Luxor obelisk – a gift from Egypt, 23-m (75-ft) tall and covered in hieroglyphics – as well as two fountains and eight statues personifying French cities. It has become the culminating point of triumphal parades down the Champs-Élysées each 14 July, most notably on the memorable Bastille Day of 1989 when the Revolution's bicentenary was celebrated by a million people, including many world leaders.

11 Grand Palais

📍 E5 🚪 Porte A, Ave du Général Eisenhower 75008 Ⓜ Champs-Élysées-Clemenceau 🕐 Until 2024 🌐 grandpalais.fr

Built at the same time as the Petit Palais and the Pont Alexandre III, the exterior of this massive palace combines an imposing classical stone façade with a riot of Art Nouveau ironwork. The enormous glass roof (15,000 sq m/160,000 sq ft) has Récipon's colossal bronze statues of flying horses and chariots at its four corners. The metal structure supporting the glass weighs 8,500 tonnes, some 500 tonnes more than the Eiffel Tower's. Today, the restored Grand Palais hosts art exhibitions and other events. In winter, the nave turns into the world's biggest indoor ice rink. Major touring and temporary exhibitions are held at the Galeries Nationales in the same building; these are often very popular and it's worth booking ahead.

The Grand Palais will remain closed to the public until the 2024 Olympics.

12 Petit Palais

📍 E5 🚪 Ave Winston Churchill 75008 Ⓜ Champs-Élysées-Clemenceau 🕐 10am–6pm Tue–Sun (to 7pm Fri for temporary exhibitions) 🔒 Public hols 🌐 petitpalais.paris.fr

Built for the Exposition Universelle in 1900, this jewel of a building now houses the Musée des Beaux-Arts de la Ville de Paris. Arranged around a pretty courtyard, the palace is similar in style to the Grand Palais, and is graced with Ionic columns, a grand porch and a dome. The wing nearest the river is used for temporary exhibitions, while the Champs-Élysées side of the palace houses the permanent collections: Greek and Roman artifacts; medieval and Renaissance ivories and sculptures; Renaissance clocks and jewellery; and 17th-, 18th-, and 19th-century art and furniture. There are also many works by Impressionist artists.

↓ The Neo-Classical entrance to the Petit Palais

EAT

Astrance
Go for broke at this three-Michelin-star restaurant with epic tasting menus.

📍 B5 🚪 32 Rue de Longchamp 75016 🌐 astranceparis.fr

€€€

Pierre Gagnaire
One of Paris's best chefs wows diners with a contemporary dining experience.

📍 C4 🚪 6 Rue Balzac 75008 🌐 pierre-gagnaire.com

€€€

Relais de l'Entrecôte
Steak, chips and nothing else. It's a family favourite; just go early to queue up - it doesn't take long to get a table.

📍 D5 🚪 15 Rue Marbeuf 75008 🌐 relaisentrecote.fr

€€€

↑ A ceiling painting by Maurice Denis inside the Petit Palais

The Avenue des Champs-Élysées, looking towards the Arc de Triomphe and La Défense

⑬
Pont Alexandre III

◉ E5 🏠 75008
Ⓜ Champs-Élysées-Clemenceau

This is Paris's prettiest bridge with its exuberant Art Nouveau decoration of lamps, cherubs, nymphs and winged horses at either end. It was built between 1896 and 1900, in time for the Exposition Universelle, and it was named after Tsar Alexander III of Russia, whose son Nicholas II laid the foundation stone in October 1896.

The style of the bridge reflects that of the Grand Palais, to which it leads on the Right Bank. The construction of the bridge is a marvel of 19th-century engineering, consisting of a 6-m- (18-ft-) high single-span steel arch that stretches across the Seine. The design was subject to strict controls that prevented the bridge from obscuring the view of the Champs-Élysées (p222) or the Dôme des Invalides (p206) so, today, you can still enjoy magnificent views from here.

⑭
Palais de la Découverte

◉ E5 🏠 Ave Franklin D Roosevelt 75008
Ⓜ Franklin D. Roosevelt
🕑 Until 2025 Ⓦ palais-decouverte.fr

Opened in a wing of the Grand Palais (p223) for the World Fair of 1937, this science museum is a Paris institution. Demonstrations and displays, including a planetarium, cover many subjects and explain such phenomena as electromagnetism. The Palais de la Découverte will remain closed to the public until 2025.

⑮
Avenue Montaigne

◉ D5 🏠 75008
Ⓜ Franklin D. Roosevelt

In the 1800s, this avenue was famous for its dance halls and its Winter Garden, where Parisians went to hear Adolphe Sax play his newly invented saxophone. Today, it is still a fashionable street, bustling with restaurants, hotels and designer boutiques. At one end lies the Art Deco Théâtre de Champs-Élysées, built in 1913.

⑯
Parc Monceau

◉ D3 🏠 35 Blvd de Courcelles 75017
Ⓜ Monceau, Courcelles
🕑 7am–8pm daily (to 10pm summer)

This green haven dates back to 1778 when the Duc de Chartres (later Duc d'Orléans) commissioned the painter-writer and amateur landscape designer Louis Carmontelle to create a magnificent garden. Also a theatre designer, Carmontelle created a "garden of dreams", an exotic landscape full of architectural follies in imitation of English and German fashions of the time. In 1783, the Scottish landscape gardener Thomas Blaikie laid out an area of the garden in English style. The park was the scene of the first recorded parachute landing,

The ornamental pond in the charming Parc Monceau ↑

made by André-Jacques Garnerin on 22 October 1797. Over the years, the park changed hands and in 1852 it was acquired by the state and half the land sold off for property development. The remaining land was made into public gardens. These were restored and new buildings erected by Adolphe Alphand, architect of the Bois de Boulogne *(p292)* and the Bois de Vincennes *(p294)*.

The park, one of the most chic in Paris, has lost many of its early features. A *naumachia* basin – an ornamental version of a Roman pool used for simulating naval battles – remains, flanked by Corinthian columns. Other remaining features include a Renaissance arcade, pyramids, statues, a river and the Pavillon de Chartres, a charming rotunda designed by Nicolas Ledoux which was once used as a tollhouse. Just south of here is a huge red Chinese pagoda, which now houses a gallery devoted to Asian art.

17

Musée Jacquemart-André

🔲 **E3** 🏠 **158 Blvd Haussmann 75008** Ⓜ **Miromesnil, St-Philippe-du-Roule** 🕐 **10am–6pm daily (to 8:30pm Mon)** 🌐 **musee-jacquemart-andre.com**

This museum is known for its collection of Italian Renaissance and French 18th-century works of art, as well as its beautiful frescoes by Tiepolo. Highlights include works by Mantegna, Uccello's master-piece *St George Defeating the Dragon* (c 1435), paintings by Boucher and Fragonard and 18th-century tapestries.

←

Pont Alexandre III, with its flamboyant Art Nouveau decoration

18 Palais de l'Élysée

◉ E4 ⬛ 55 Rue du Faubourg-St-Honoré 75008 Ⓜ St-Philippe-du-Roule 🕐 To the public

Built for the Comte d'Evreux in 1718, the Élysée Palace has been the official residence of the President of the Republic since 1873. From 1805 to 1808, it was occupied by Napoleon's sister, Caroline, and her husband, Joachim Murat. Two rooms have been preserved from this period: the Salon Murat and the Salon d'Argent. General de Gaulle gave press conferences in the Hall of Mirrors. The president's modernized apartments are on the first floor in the east wing, opposite the Rue de l'Élysée. The palace is open to the public only during the Journées du Patrimoine in September.

↑ The imposing Art Deco Palais de Tokyo, housing two galleries of modern art

← Edouard Manet's gravestone in the Cimetière de Passy

19 Cimetière de Passy

◉ A6 ⬛ 2 Rue du Commandant-Shloesing 75016 Ⓜ Trocadéro 🕐 8am–5:30pm Mon–Fri, 8:30am–5:30pm Sat, 9am–5:30pm Sun (to 6pm 16 Mar–5 Nov) 🌐 cimetiere-de-passy.com

This small cemetery, opened in 1820, is packed with the graves of eminent Parisians. Figures buried here include the composers Claude Debussy, Gabriel Fauré and Jacques Ibert, and renowned painter Edouard Manet, as well as many politicians and aristocrats, such as Ghislaine Dommanget, Princess of Monaco and Leila Pahlavi, daughter of the Shah of Iran.

20   Musée d'Art Moderne de la Ville de Paris

◉ C6 ⬛ 11 Ave du Président-Wilson 75116 Ⓜ Iéna, Alma Marceau 🕐 10am–6pm Tue–Sun (to 9:30 Thu) 🕐 Public hols 🌐 mam.paris.fr

This large lively museum houses the city of Paris's own renowned collection of modern art. It has about 10,000 works representing major 20th- and 21st-century artistic movements and artists. Established in 1961, the museum is one of two within the vast Palais de Tokyo, which was built for the 1937 World Fair.

One of the museum's highlights is Raoul Dufy's gigantic mural *The Spirit of Electricity*, which traces the history of electricity through the ages. It was designed for the Electricity Pavilion at the 1937 fair. One of the largest paintings in the world, measuring 600 sq metres (6,500 sq ft), this curved mural takes up a whole room of the museum. Also notable are the Cubists, Amedeo Modigliani, George Rouault, Duchamp, Klein and the Fauves. This group of avant-garde artists, including Dufy and Derain, was dominated by Matisse, whose celebrated mural *La Danse* is on display here; you can see both the incomplete early version and the finished version. Entry to the permanent exhibition is free, while the frequent temporary exhibitions require a ticket.

Did You Know?

During World War II, the Nazis stored hundreds of pillaged pianos in the Palais de Tokyo.

Palais de Tokyo

📍C5 📌13 Ave du Président-Wilson 75116 Ⓜ Iéna, Alma Marceau ⏰Noon–midnight Wed-Mon 🚫1 Jan, 1 May, 25 Dec 🌐palaisdetokyo.com

This enormous modern art gallery is adjacent to the Musée d'Art Moderne de la Ville de Paris within the imposing 1937 Palais de Tokyo. It presents an innovative, changing programme of contemporary art exhibitions, fashion shows and avant-garde performances. Installations by artists such as Pierre Joseph, Wang Du and Frank Scurti have earned the Palais de Tokyo a reputation as one of the most cutting-edge art houses in Europe. It also has a good bookshop and two restaurants, while club nights regularly take place in its basement space, Le Yoyo.

DRINK

Here are five of the best hotel bars for enjoying a decadent sundowner around Champs-Élysées.

Le Bar at the Four Seasons Hotel George V
📍C5 📌31 Ave George V 75008 🌐fourseasons.com

Bar de l'Hôtel Belmont
📍C5 📌30 Rue de Bassano, 75116 🌐belmont-paris-hotel.com

Le Bar Kléber at the Peninsula
📍B4 📌19 Ave Kléber 75116 🌐peninsula.com

Le Bar Botaniste at the Shangri-La
📍B6 📌10 Ave d'Iéna 75116 🌐shangri-la.com

Le Bar du Bristol
📍E4 📌112 Rue du Faubourg-St-Honoré 75008 🌐oetkercollection.com

A SHORT WALK
CHAMPS-ÉLYSÉES

Distance 2 km (1.25 miles) **Nearest Metro** Invalides
Time 20 minutes

The formal gardens that line the Champs-Élysées from the Place de la Concorde to the Rond-Point have changed little since they were laid out by the architect Jacques Hittorff in 1838. The Grand Palais and Petit Palais, which were created as showpieces of the Third Republic for the Exposition Universelle of 1900, sit on either side of an impressive vista that stretches from Place Clémenceau across the elegant curve of the Pont Alexandre III to the Invalides.

There are plaques on the back door of the Théâtre du Rond-Point representing Napoleon's campaigns.

Metro Franklin D. Roosevelt

AVE DES CHAMPS

AVE G. EISENHOWER

Christian Dior and other haute couture houses are based on chic Avenue Montaigne.

RUE JEAN GOUJON

AVE FRANKLIN D ROOSEVELT

Designed by Charles Girault, the 19th-century Grand Palais is being refurbished for the 2024 Olympic Games (p223).

Restaurant Lasserre is decorated in the style of a luxurious ocean liner from the 1930s.

RUE FRANÇOIS PREMIER

Outside the Palais de la Découverte is a pair of equestrian statues (p226).

PL DU CANADA

COURS LA

PONT DES INVALIDES

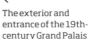

← The exterior and entrance of the 19th-century Grand Palais

Avenue des Champs-Élysées was the setting for the victory parades following the two World Wars, and for the bicentennial parade in 1989 (p222).

Metro Champs-Élysées-Clemenceau

AVE GABRIEL

ELYSÉES

AVE DE MARIGNY

M

PL CLÉMENCEAU

AVE DES CHAMPS ELYSÉES

FINISH

AVE WINSTON CHURCHILL

REINE

PONT ALEXANDRE III

START

CHAMPS-ÉLYSÉES AND CHAILLOT

Champs-Élysées

Locator Map
For more detail see p214

The Jardins des Champs-Élysées, with their fountains, flower beds, paths and pleasure pavilions, became very popular towards the end of the 19th century. Fashionable Parisians, including Marcel Proust, often came here.

↑ Strolling through the tree-lined Jardins des Champs-Élysées

Lit by natural light, the Petit Palais is as much a work of art as the wide-ranging collections it contains, from antiquity to the belle époque (p223).

Pont Alexandre III's four columns help to anchor the piers that absorb the immense forces generated by such a large single-span structure (p226).

0 metres		100	N
0 yards		100	↑

A LONG WALK
PARC MONCEAU

Distance 3 km (2 miles) **Walking time** 45 minutes **Nearest Metro** Monceau

This leisurely walk passes through the exquisite late-18th-century Parc Monceau *(p226)*, the centrepiece of a smart Second Empire district. The park is the most fashionable green space in Paris, full of well-heeled residents from the opulent mansions nearby. A stroll through the surrounding streets offers a fascinating glimpse of Paris at its most grand.

Take the second path on the left past the **monument to Guy de Maupassant** *(1897), one of six French writers and musicians memorialized in the park.*

The walk starts at the **Monceau Metro station** *on the Boulevard de Courcelles.*

PLACE DU
GENERAL
CATROUX

RUE FORTUNY

RUE DE PHALSBOURG

RUE G. BERGER

RUE MEDERIC

RUE DE PRONY

RUE DE CHAZELLES

Enter the park where Nicolas Ledoux's 18th-century **tollhouse** *stands. On either side are sumptuously gilded wrought-iron gates.*

START
Monceau Ⓜ
Tollhouse

Guy de Maupassant Monument

Parc Monceau

Ambroise Thomas Monument

DE COURCELLES

BLVD Ⓜ **Courcelles**

Emile Menier Mansion

PLACE GEN BROCARD

RUE MURILLO

RUE DE MONCEAU

No 5 Avenue Van Dyck *is an impressive Neo-Baroque mansion built by chocolate manufacturer Émile-Justin Menier.*

AVENUE HOCHE

Pagoda Paris

RUE DE COURCELLES

Immediately behind the **monument to the musician Ambroise Thomas** *(1902) is a lovely artificial mountain with cascade.*

At the corner of the Rue Rembrandt and the Rue de Courcelles is a striking red **Chinese pagoda**.

The most important remaining folly in the park is a moss-covered **Corinthian colonnade**, *running around the edge of a tiny lake with an island in the centre.*

The Corinthian colonnade at the edge of the small lake in Parc Monceau

Locator Map
For more detail see p214

Parc
Monceau

CHAMPS-ÉLYSÉES
AND CHAILLOT

→
The impressive
interior of the
Église St-Augustin

AVE DE VILLIERS

Ⓜ Villiers

BLVD DE COURCELLES

Musée
Cernuschi

RUE DE

RUE DE MONCEAU

RUE DE NAPLES

RUE DE VÉZELAY

RUE DU GÉNÉRAL FOY

RUE DE MADRID

RUE DE TEHERAN

RUE DE LISBONNE

BOULEVARD MALESHERBES

MIROMESNIL

RUE DE LA
BIENFAISANCE

PLACE DE
NARVIK

AVE DE MESSINE

BOULEVARD   HAUSSMANN

RUE DU ROCHER

On the left, approaching the Boulevard
Haussmann, looms the great **Église
St-Augustin**, built in the 19th century
by Victor-Louis Baltard.

Église
St-Augustin

Square
M Pagnol

At the end of the walk, in
Place St-Augustin, is a
bronze statue of Joan of Arc.

● Joan of
Arc Statue

PLACE ST-
AUGUSTIN

RUE DE LA PEPINIERE

Ⓜ St-Augustin
FINISH

RUE LA BOETIE

Square
Louis XVI

RUE ROQUEPINE

The long **Boulevard
Malesherbes**,
with its dignified six-storey
apartment buildings, is typical
of the great avenues
cut through Paris by Baron
Haussmann.

| 0 metres | | 300 |
| 0 yards | | 300 |

N
↑

ST-GERMAIN-DES-PRÉS

Named after a Benedictine abbey that was founded here in the 6th century, St-Germain-des-Prés came to prominence in the 1950s as the nucleus of the city's intellectual life. Largely working class, the neighbourhood attracted numerous writers and philosophers with its nonconformist atmosphere and profusion of bookshops and publishing houses. Leading figures such as Jean-Paul Sartre and Simone de Beauvoir held court at the district's celebrated cafés, most notably Café de Flore, Les Deux Magots and Le Procope. They and their disciples may have left, but this area is still renowned for its youthful student atmosphere and literary traditions. Since the 1970s, the neighbourhood has become progressively more upmarket, with the emergence of numerous fashionable boutiques. Rue de Seine is lined with charming restaurants and contains many high-end galleries where the smart set purchase their art.

E   F   G

PLACE DE LA CONCORDE

Galerie Nationale du Jeu de Paume

RUE DE RIVOLI

Tuileries Ⓜ

PLACE DES PYRAMIDES

Musée de l'Orangerie

Jardin des Tuileries

QUAI DES TUILERIES

6

Palais Bourbon Assemblée Nationale

PLACE DU PRESIDENT E HERRIOT

QUAI ANATOLE FRANCE

Ⓜ Assemblée Nationale

Pont Solférino

PLACE H DE MONTHERLANT

LOUVRE AND LES HALLES *p180*

La

INVALIDES

Musée de la Légion d'Honneur ❷

RER Musée d'Orsay

Quai de Solférino

🚈

Quai du Louvre

RUE ST-DOMINIQUE

RUE DE SOLFERINO

RUE DE BELLECHASSE

RUE DE LILLE

❶ Musée d'Orsay

Pont Royal

Seine

QUAI VOLTAIRE

Institut Géographique National

RUE DE POITIERS

Ⓜ Solférino

RUE DE VILLERSEXEL

RUE

RUE DU BAC

RUE DE BEAUNE

RUE

DE

LILLE

VERNEUIL

PLACE J BAINVILLE

DE

L'UNIVERSITE

RUE DE BOURGOGNE

EIFFEL TOWER AND INVALIDES *p196* ◄

BOULEVARD

RUE DE BELLECHASSE

RUE DE SAINT SIMON

RUE P.L. COURIER

Deyrolle ⓰

RUE DU BAC

RUE MONTALEM-BERT

PLACE ST THOMAS D'AQUIN

RUE DE LUYNES

RUE DES SAINTS-PERES

RUE DU PRE AUX CLERCS

RUE PERRONET

7

Ⓜ Varenne

RUE DE VARENNE

RUE DE GRENELLE

⓽

Ⓜ Rue du Bac

ST-

GERMAIN

Musée Rodin

RUE DE VARENNE

Hôtel Matignon

⓯ Musée Maillol

BOULEVARD RASPAIL

RUE DE GRENELLE

RUE ST-GUILLAUME

RUE DES SAINTS-PERES

RUE DU DRAGON

RUE B PALISSY

RUE DU SABOT

RUE DE BABYLONE

RUE VANEAU

RUE BARBET DE JOUY

RUE DU BAC

RUE DE COMMAILLE

RUE DE LA CHAISE

CARREFOUR DE LA CROIX ROUGE

RUE

RUE DE BABYLONE

RUE CHOMEL

Sèvres-Babylone Ⓜ

RUE DE SEVRES

RUE D. VIEUX COLOMBIER

8

RUE MONSIEUR

RUE OUDINOT

RUE VANEAU

Jardin Catherine Labouré

RUE VELPEAU

Le Bon Marché ⓬

Square Boucicaut

RUE DE SEVRES

PLACE LE CORBUSIER

PLACE DEVILLE

RUE DU CHERCHE MIDI

RUE COETLOGON

St-Sulpice Ⓜ

RENNES

RUE DE MEZIERES

⓾

RUE DUPIN

RUE SAINT-PLACIDE

RUE DU CHERCHE MIDI

RUE DU REGARD

BOULEVARD

RUE DE RENNES

RUE D'ASSAS

RUE CASSETTE

RUE MADAME

Vaneau Ⓜ

Rennes Ⓜ

RASPAIL

RUE DE L'ABBE GREGORE

RUE SAINT-PLACIDE

9

0 metres   250

0 yards   250

N ↑

St-Placide Ⓜ

E   F   G

ST-GERMAIN-DES-PRÉS

ST-GERMAIN-DES-PRÉS

Must See

1 Musée d'Orsay

Experience More

2 Musée de la Légion d'Honneur
3 Académie Française
4 École Nationale Supérieure des Beaux Arts
5 Musée Eugène Delacroix
6 St-Germain-des-Prés
7 Monnaie de Paris
8 Rue St-André-des-Arts
9 Cour du Commerce St-André
10 Le Procope
11 St-Sulpice
12 Le Bon Marché
13 Café de Flore
14 Les Deux Magots
15 Musée Maillol

16 Deyrolle
17 Pont des Arts

Eat

① Semilla
② Le Comptoir du Relais
③ Ze Kitchen Galerie

Stay

④ Hôtel de Saint Germain
⑤ Relais Christine
⑥ Hôtel Récamier

Shop

⑦ Rue Lobineau
⑧ Rue Bonaparte
⑨ Rue du Bac
⑩ Rue de Sèvres
⑪ Rue de Buci

❶ MUSÉE D'ORSAY

📍 G6 📮 1 Rue de la Légion d'Honneur Ⓜ Solférino 🚌 68, 69, 87 to Quai A
France; 73 to Rue Solférino; 63, 83, 84, 94 to Blvd St-Germain Ⓡ Musée d'Orsay
🕐 9:30am–6pm Tue–Sun (to 9:45pm Thu) 🚫 1 May, 25 Dec 🌐 musee-orsay.fr

**The Musée d'Orsay picks up where the Louvre ends, showing a variety of
art forms from 1848 to 1914. Its star attraction is a superb collection of
Impressionist art, which includes famous works by Monet, Renoir, Manet
and Degas, as well as pieces by Georges Seurat, Gaugin and Van Gogh.**

In 1986, 47 years after it had closed as a
mainline railway station, Victor Laloux's superb
late-19th-century building was reopened as
the Musée d'Orsay. Originally commissioned
by the Orléans railway company to be its Paris
terminus, the structure avoided demolition in
the 1970s after being classified as a historical
monument. During the conversion into a
museum, much of the original architecture was
retained. The collection was set up to present
each of the arts of the period from 1848 to
1914 in the context of contemporary society
and other forms of creative activity happening
at the time. The displays are constantly evolving,
and American collectors made large donations
of works in 2016 and 2019.

↑ The light and spacious entrance hall,
with curved glass ceiling

GREAT VIEW
City Panorama

Make your way to the rear escalator, ride it all the way up, and head to the small rooftop terrace for a great bird's-eye view of the city.

① The clock face on the fifth floor provides views over the Seine to the Jardin des Tuileries.

② *Le Déjeuner sur l'herbe* (1863) by Manet caused a scandal when it was first exhibited.

③ Monet's *Le Déjeuner sur l'herbe* (1865–6) was a tribute to the work of the same name by Manet.

GALLERY GUIDE

The collection occupies three levels and a linked decorative arts pavilion. The ground floor, with sculptures down the central aisle, houses Academic, Realist and Symbolist works. Temporary exhibits appear on the middle level, along with displays on Art Nouveau and Naturalism. The upper level has an outstanding array of Impressionist and Post-Impressionist art.

←

The former railway station, designed by Victor Laloux for the Exposition Universelle of 1900

EXPERIENCE MORE

2

Musée de la Légion d'Honneur

📍 G6 **🏠** 2 Rue de la Légion d'Honneur (Parvis du Musée d'Orsay) 75007 **Ⓜ** Solférino **ⓇⒺⓇ** Musée d'Orsay **🕐** 1–6pm Wed–Sun **🕐** 1 Jan, 1 May, 15 Aug, 1 Nov, 24 & 25 Dec **🌐** legiondhonneur.fr

Next to the Musée d'Orsay is the truly massive Hôtel de Salm. It was one of the last great mansions to be built in the area (1782). The first owner was a German count, Prince de Salm-Kyrbourg, who was guillotined in 1794.

Today, the building contains a museum where you can learn all about the Legion of Honour, a decoration launched by Napoleon I. Those awarded the honour wear a small red rosette in their buttonhole. The impressive displays of medals and insignia are complemented by paintings. In one of the rooms, Napoleon's Legion of Honour is on display with his sword and breastplate.

The museum also contains examples of decorations from most parts of the world, among them the British Victoria Cross and the American Purple Heart.

3

Académie Française

📍 H7 **🏠** 23 Quai de Conti 75006 **Ⓜ** Pont Neuf, St-Germain-des-Prés **🌐** academie-francaise.fr

This striking Baroque edifice was built as a school for young noblemen in 1688 and given over to the Institut de France in 1805. Its cupola was designed by architect Louis Le Vau to harmonize with the Palais du Louvre.

The Académie Française is the oldest of the five academies of the institute. Founded in 1635 by Cardinal Richelieu, it is charged with regulating the French language by deciding acceptable grammar and vocabulary, and with the compilation of an official

 INSIDER TIP
Mega Macaron

Sample the city's most innovative macarons, such as jasmine and wild strawberry, at Pierre Hermé's flagship, on Rue Bonaparte, near St-Germain-des-Prés.

dictionary of the French language. From the beginning, membership has been limited to 40 scholars, who are entrusted with a lifelong commitment to working on the dictionary. The building is only open to the public during the Journées du Patrimoine (Heritage Days) on the third weekend of September.

École Nationale Supérieure des Beaux-Arts

H7 13 Quai Malaquais & 14 Rue Bonaparte 75006 St-Germain-des-Prés beauxartsparis.com

The main French school of fine arts occupies an enviable position at the corner of Rue Bonaparte and the riverside Quai Malaquais. The school is housed in several buildings, the most imposing being the

19th-century Palais des Études. A host of budding French and foreign painters and architects have crossed the large courtyard to study in the ateliers of the school. Young American architects, in particular, have frequented the halls since the late 19th century. Works from its collections can be viewed in regular exhibitions; see website.

Musée Eugène Delacroix

H7 6 Rue de Fürstemberg 75006 St-Germain-des-Prés, Mabillon 9:30am-5:30pm Wed-Mon, advance booking recommended 1 Jan, 1 May, 25 Dec musee-delacroix.fr

The leading nonconformist Romantic painter Eugène Delacroix, known for his passionate and highly coloured canvases, lived and worked here from 1857 to his death in 1863. Here, he painted *The Entombment of Christ* and *The Way to Calvary* (which now hang in the museum). He also created superb murals for the Chapel of the Holy Angels in the nearby St-Sulpice church *(p243)*, which is part of the reason why he moved to this area. The first-floor apartment and garden studio now form a national museum, where regular exhibitions of Delacroix's work are held. The apartment has portraits, studies for future works and artistic memorabilia.

The charm of Delacroix's garden is reflected in the tiny Fürstemberg square. With its purple-flowering Paulownia trees and old-fashioned street lamps, the square is one of Paris's most romantic corners.

The Académie Française, ultimate arbiter of French language and grammar

St-Germain-des-Prés

H7 3 Pl St-Germain-des-Prés 75006 St-Germain-des-Prés 9:30am-8pm Sun & Mon, 8:30am-8pm Tue-Sat eglise-saintgermain despres.fr

This is the oldest church in Paris, originating in 543 when King Childebert built a basilica to house holy relics. It became a powerful Benedictine abbey, which was suppressed during the French Revolution, when most of the buildings were destroyed by a fire. The present church dates from about the 11th century and was restored in the 19th century. The interior is a mix of architectural styles, with a number of 6th-century marble columns, Gothic vaulting and Romanesque arches. Famous tombs include that of René Descartes.

TOP 5 SHOPPING STREETS

Rue Lobineau
H8
Home of the St-Germain food market.

Rue Bonaparte
H8
Full of swanky shops, including the Pierre Hermé flagship.

Rue du Bac
G7
Plenty of pastry shops and other confections.

Rue de Sèvres
G8
The location of Le Bon Marché *(p243)*, Paris's first department store.

Rue de Buci
H8
A former market street that today houses cafés and appealing shops.

7

Monnaie de Paris

⊙H7 ♨11 Quai de Conti 75006 Ⓜ Pont Neuf, Odéon ⊙11am–6pm Tue-Sun (to 9pm Wed) ♦1 Jan, 1 May, 25 Dec Ⓦmonnaiedeparis.fr

In the late 18th century, when Louis XV decided to rehouse the Mint, he launched a design competition for the new building. The Hôtel des Monnaies is the result. It was completed in 1775, and the architect, Jacques Antoine, lived here until his death.

Coins were minted in the mansion until 1973, when the process was moved to Pessac in the Gironde. The whole complex can now be visited, including its interior court-yards, garden and museum, the Musée du 11 Conti.

Centred around a tranquil public space and surrounded by artists' workshops, the permanent gallery focuses on the history of coins and minting. Regular exhibitions of contemporary art are also staged here, as well as work-shops for both families and adults, such as making coins out of chocolate. There are also shops selling work by resident artisans, a gastro-nomic restaurant run by chef Guy Savoy and a more casual café.

Did You Know?

Remnants of the old Paris wall can be found in the chocolate shop on Cour du Commerce St-André.

8

Rue St-André-des-Arts

⊙J8 ♨75006 Ⓜ St-Michel, Odéon

Extending from Place St-André-des-Arts, where the square's namesake church once stood, this little street boasts numerous historical monuments. Dating back to 1179, it once led to the gate of the city in the former Philippe Auguste wall. The mansion at No 27 was owned by Louis XIII's geographer in the 1600s, while grammarian and encyclopaedist Pierre Larousse lived at No 49 in the 19th century. Peeling south off Rue St-André-des-Arts is the cobbled Cour du Commerce.

9

Cour du Commerce St-André

⊙J8 ♨75006 Ⓜ Odéon

No 9 in this historic passage has a particularly grisly past, because it was here that Dr Guillotin is supposed to have perfected his "philanthropic decapitating machine". In fact, although the idea was Guillotin's, it was Dr Antoine Louis, a Parisian surgeon, who was responsible for putting

← A coin press at the Musée du 11 Conti

The picturesque Cour du Commerce St-André enchants at twilight ↑

the "humane" plan into action. When the guillotine was first used for execution in 1792, it was known as a *Louisette*.

10

Le Procope

⊙J8 ♨13 Rue de l'Ancienne-Comédie 75006 Ⓜ Odéon ⊙Noon- midnight daily (to 1am Thu-Sat) Ⓦprocope.com

Founded in 1686 by the Sicilian Francesco Procopio dei Coltelli, this claims to be the world's first coffee house. It quickly became popular with the city's political and cultural elite.

Its illustrious patrons have included the philosopher Voltaire – who supposedly drank 40 cups of his favourite mixture of coffee and choco-late every day – and the young Napoleon, who would leave his hat as security while he went searching for the money to pay the bill. Le Procope is now an 18th-century-style restaurant serving *coq au vin* and other brasserie classics.

Café de Flore

H7 172 Blvd St-Germain 75006 St-Germain-des-Prés 7:30am-1:30am daily cafedeflore.fr

The classic Art Deco interior of this café has changed little since World War II. Like its neighbouring rival Les Deux Magots (p244), Café de Flore has hosted most of the French intellectuals during the post-War years.

EAT

Semilla
Sharing plates and fresh, innovative cooking with local ingredients are on the menu here.

H7 54 Rue de Seine 75006 semillaparis.com

€€€

Le Comptoir du Relais
This bistro is a staple of the area for inventive French cooking at lunch and dinner.

H8 9 Carrefour de l'Odéon 75006 hotel-paris-relais-saint-germain.com

€€€

Ze Kitchen Galerie
French cooking is infused with international inspirations at this relaxed one-Michelin star restaurant.

J7 4 Rue des Grands Augustins 75006 Sat, Sun zekitchengalerie.fr

€€€

11

St-Sulpice

H8 2 Rue Palatine, Pl St-Sulpice 75006 St-Sulpice 8am-7:45pm daily paroisse saintsulpice.paris

It took over a century, from 1646, for this imposing church to be built. The result is a simple two-storey west front with two tiers of elegant columns. The overall harmony of the building is marred only by the towers, one at each end, which do not match.

Large arched windows fill the interior with light. By the front door are two huge shells given to François I by the Venetian Republic – they rest on bases sculpted by Jean-Baptiste Pigalle.

In the side chapel to the right of the main door are three magnificent murals by Eugène Delacroix: *Jacob Wrestling with the Angel*, *Heliodorus Driven from the Temple* and *St Michael Killing the Dragon*. If you are lucky, you can catch an organ recital. There are regular guided tours of the church and chapel; see the website for details.

12

Le Bon Marché

G8 24 Rue de Sèvres 75007 Sèvres-Babylone 10am-7:45pm Mon-Sat, 11am-8pm Sun lebon marche.com

Welcoming as many as 15,000 customers per day, "The Good Market" (or "The Good Deal") is the swankiest department store in Paris, selling luxury goods as well as gourmet foods in its annexe La Grande Épicerie at No 38 Rue de Sèvres. The designer clothing section is well sourced, the high-end accessories are excellent, and the own-brand linen has a good quality-to-price ratio.

Le Bon Marché is also the world's oldest department store, founded in 1852 by Aristide Boucicaut and his wife. The Boucicauts used their keen sense of commerce to introduce innovative practices – fixed prices, sales, home delivery, advertising and guarantees – that became the standard for other *grands magasins*. Designed by Louis-Charles Boileau and Gustave Eiffel, it is an architectural landmark.

14

Les Deux Magots

 H7 🏠 6 Pl St-Germain-des-Prés 75006 Ⓜ St-Germain-des-Prés ⏱ 7:30am–1am daily 🗓 One week in Jan 🌐 lesdeuxmagots.com

Established in 1914, this café still trades on its reputation as the meeting place of the city's literary and intellectual elite. This derives from the patronage of Surrealist artists and writers, including Ernest Hemingway, in the 1920s and 1930s, and existentialist philosophers and writers in the 1950s.

The present clientele is more likely to consist of tourists or people-watchers than the new Hemingway. The café's name comes from the two wooden statues of Chinese commercial agents *(magots)* that adorn one of the pillars. This is a good place for enjoying an old-fashioned hot chocolate or a classic French omelette and watching the world go by from a seat on the wraparound terrace.

15

Musée Maillol

 G7 🏠 59/61 Rue de Grenelle 75007 Ⓜ Sèvres-Babylone, Rue du Bac ⏱ 10:30am–6:30pm daily (to 10pm Wed) 🗓 1 Jan, 25 Dec 🌐 museemaillol.com

Once the home of novelist Alfred de Musset, this museum was created by Dina Vierny, former model of Aristide Maillol, in an 18th-century building that used to be a convent. All aspects of the artist's work are here: drawings, engravings, paintings, sculpture and decorative objects. Also

---

STAY

Hôtel de Saint Germain

It's all about the location at this simple, no-frills, yet well-designed hotel.

 G8 🏠 50 Rue du Four 75006 🌐 hotel-de-saint-germain.fr

Relais Christine

This luxury property includes a spa for guests who are after a bit of pampering.

 J7 🏠 3 Rue Christine 75006 🌐 relais-christine.com

Hôtel Récamier

Elegance and comfort are on order at this tiny property tucked behind St-Sulpice.

 H8 🏠 3B Place St-Sulpice 75006 🌐 hotelrecamier.com

> At night, illuminated every so often by the Bateaux Mouches cruising underneath, the Pont des Arts is an especially romantic place to walk or picnic in warmer months.

The Pont des Arts with its prime view of the Institut de France

displayed is Vierny's private collection, including works by Matisse, Picasso and Rodin. The museum stages regular temporary art exhibitions, which are usually on themes and artists associated with Maillol.

Large allegorical figures of the city of Paris, the River Seine and the four seasons decorate Edme Bouchardon's fountain, *La Fontaine des Quatre Saisons*, built in 1739–45, in front of the house.

Deyrolle

G7 📍**46 Rue du Bac 75005** Ⓜ**Rue du Bac**
🕐 **10am–7pm Mon–Sat**
🌐 **deyrolle.com**

A Parisian institution since 1831 and beloved by artists like Salvador Dali, Deyrolle is a cabinet of curiosities that continues to delight all who enter its doors. Originally a taxidermy shop, it has evolved over the years, and now part of its mission is to raise awareness about wildlife conservation. The casual visitor, however, can simply enjoy the collection of taxidermied animals, from giant elephants and rhinos to the most delicate birds and crustaceans. There is a wide range of insects housed in drawers. Iridescent beetles and colourful butterflies sit alongside terrifying tarantulas and scorpions. Everything is for sale, mostly at decent prices considering the quality.

Pont des Arts

H7 📍**75006**
Ⓜ**Louvre-Rivoli**

Sometimes referred to as the Passerelle des Arts, this picturesque iron bridge, part of the UNESCO-listed Parisian riverfront, has more often been called the "Love Lock Bridge" in recent years. The nickname refers to the now-forbidden practice of couples fixing padlocks to the bridge to signify their love; the practice had to be stopped because the locks exerted too much weight on the structure and started to destroy it. Now revived and restored – following the removal of almost a million locks weighing 45 tonnes – this pedestrian bridge, built under Napoleon from 1801 to 1804, has been returned to its 19th-century splendour. The first iron bridge in Paris, it links the Institut de France with the Louvre, offering resplendent views of the Île de la Cité from above the river. At night, illuminated every so often by the Bateaux Mouches cruising gently underneath, the Pont des Arts is an especially romantic place to walk or picnic in warmer months.

THE CELEBRATED CAFÉS OF PARIS

One of the most enduring images of Paris is the café scene. For the visitor, it is the romantic vision of great artists, writers or eminent intellectuals consorting in one of the Left Bank's celebrated cafés. For the Parisian, the café is one of life's constants, an everyday experience, providing people with a place to tryst, drink and meet friends, to conclude business deals, or to simply watch the world go by.

The most famous cafés are on the Left Bank, in St-Germain and Montparnasse. Sartre and his intellectual peers, among them the writers Simone de Beauvoir and Albert Camus, gathered to work and discuss their ideas in Les Deux Magots and Café de Flore.

↑ Les Deux Magots, where the literary and intellectual elite used to gather

A SHORT WALK
ST-GERMAIN-DES-PRÉS

Distance 1.5 km (1 mile) **Nearest Metro** St-Germain-des-Prés
Time 15 minutes

A walk around this area is to follow in the footsteps of some of Paris's most iconic inhabitants. After World War II, St-Germain-des-Prés became synonymous with intellectual life centred on bars and cafés. Philosophers, writers, actors and musicians mingled in the cellar nightspots and brasseries, where existentialist philosophy co-existed with American jazz. The area is now smarter than in the heyday of Jean-Paul Sartre and Simone de Beauvoir, but the writers are still around, enjoying the pleasures of café life.

Descartes and Casimir, King of Poland, are among the notables buried in Paris's oldest church, St-Germain-des-Prés (p241).

In the 1950s, French intellectuals wrestled with new philosophical ideas in the Art Deco interior of the Café de Flore (p243).

Les Deux Magots is famous for its celebrity patrons such as Ernest Hemingway (p244).

Colourful ceramics decorate the famous Brasserie Lipp, once frequented by politicians.

START

BLVD ST-GERMAIN

RUE DU DRAGON

RUE DU SABOT

RUE DE RENNES

RUE BONAPARTE

RUE

0 metres 100
0 yards 100
N ↑

RUE DU FOUR

Café terraces, boutiques, cinemas, restaurants and bookshops characterize the central section of the Left Bank's Boulevard St-Germain.

Les Deux Magots, on the pleasant Boulevard St-Germain

↑ Admiring the works of the Romantic painter at the Musée Eugène Delacroix

Locator Map
For more detail see p236

Picasso's sculpture Homage to Apollinaire is a tribute to the artist's friend, the poet Guillaume Apollinaire. It was erected in 1959, near the Café de Flore.

The tiny square of Rue de Fürstemberg, with its old-fashioned street lamps, is often used as a film set.

The Musée Eugène Delacroix is dedicated to the life and works of the Romantic painter (p241).

Rue de Buci was once the site of some real tennis courts. It now holds a lively daily market.

Le Palais Abbatial was the residence of abbots from 1586 till the 1789 Revolution.

Danton's statue (1889), by Auguste Paris, is a tribute to the Revolutionary leader.

Ⓜ Metro Odéon

Marché St-Germain is an old covered food market which opened in 1818, taking over the site of a former fairground.

Metro Mabillon

LATIN QUARTER

Located on the Left Bank, the Latin Quarter spreads over the 5th and 6th arrondissements. One of the oldest and best-known areas of Paris (the Rue St-Jacques is probably the oldest street in the city), this lively neighbourhood exudes a bohemian charm. It emerged in the Middle Ages as a student quarter, with the celebrated Sorbonne University attracting scholars from all over Europe. Much of the area's character was established at this time, as it grew up into a maze of tiny cobblestoned streets leading to gardens and churches. The Latin Quarter was at the centre of the riots that erupted out of the student protests and workers' strike in May 1968, but since then the Boulevard St-Michel, the area's spine, has turned increasingly to commerce, not demonstrations. Today there are cheap shops and fast-food outlets, and the cobbled streets are now pedestrianized and filled with small cafés, global boutiques and second-hand bookshops.

LATIN QUARTER

Must See

1 Panthéon

Experience More

2 Musée de Cluny
3 Musée de la Préfecture de Police
4 Collège de France
5 La Sorbonne
6 St-Séverin
7 Place St-Michel
8 Gibert Jeune Bookshops
9 St-Julien-le-Pauvre
10 Marché Maubert
11 St-Étienne-du-Mont
12 Grand Action Cinéma
13 Bibliothèque Ste-Geneviève
14 Shakespeare and Company
15 Square René Viviani

Eat

1 Shakespeare and Co Café
2 Chez Gladines
3 La Tour d'Argent

Drink

4 Monk Le Taverne de Cluny
5 Le Piano Vache
6 Le Bombardier

Stay

7 Hôtel Design Sorbonne
8 Hôtel des Grands Hommes
9 Les Degrés de Notre-Dame

❶ ⓒ ⓜ

PANTHÉON

⬤ J9 **⌂ Pl du Panthéon** **Ⓜ Cardinal Lemoine, Maubert-Mutualité**
🚌 84 to Panthéon; 21, 27, 38, 82, 85, 89 to Gare du Luxembourg
🚆 Luxembourg **🕐 10am–6:30pm daily (Oct-Mar: to 6pm); Dome:
Apr-Oct** **🚫 1 Jan, 1 May, 1 & 11 Nov, 25 Dec** **🌐 paris-pantheon.fr**

Inspired by the Pantheon in Rome, Paris's Panthéon was originally
built as a church. Today a public building, it provides a fitting final
resting place for the nation's great figures.

When Louis XV recovered from desperate
illness in 1744, he was so grateful to be alive
that he conceived a magnificent church to
honour Sainte Geneviève. The design was
entrusted to the French architect Jacques-
Germain Soufflot, who planned the church
in Neo-Classical style. Work began in 1757
and was completed in 1790, ten years after
Soufflot's death, under the supervision of
Guillaume Rondelet. But with the Revolution
under way, the church was soon turned into
a pantheon – a location for the tombs of
France's great and good. Napoleon returned
it to the Church in 1806, but it was secularized
and then desecularized once more before
finally being made a civic building in 1885.

←

The colonnade
encircling the dome,
both decorative and
part of an ingenious
supporting system

Pediment relief

Entrance

THE PANTHÉON'S ENSHRINED

The first of France's great men to be
entombed here (though later removed
on the orders of Robespierre) was
the popular orator Honoré Mirabeau.
Voltaire followed, as did other literary
notables, including Jean-Jacques
Rousseau, Victor Hugo and Émile
Zola. In the 1970s, the remains of the
wartime Resistance leader Jean Moulin
were reburied here. Pierre and Marie
Curie's remains were transferred here
in 1995, followed by Alexandre Dumas
in 2002. In 2015, four more Resistance
fighters - two of them women - took
their places in the Panthéon.

↑ The elegant arches linking the four
pillars that support the dome

↑ Alphonse Terroir's statue (1925)
to the political writer Denis Diderot

Did You Know?

The dome was inspired
by St Paul's in London
and the Dôme des
Invalides *(p206)*.

Dome lantern

Dome galleries

Colonnade

Crypt

Dome arches

↑ The church, designed
in the shape of a
Greek cross

A collection of exquisitely decorated medieval armour and shields at the Musée de Cluny

EXPERIENCE MORE

Curiosities on show include arrest warrants for figures such as the famous Revolutionary Danton, and a rather sobering display of weapons and tools used by famous criminals. There is also a section on the part that the police played in the Resistance and subsequent liberation of Paris.

② Musée de Cluny

🔲 J8 🏠 28 Rue du Sommerard 75005
Ⓜ Cluny-La Sorbonne, Odéon, St-Michel
🕐 9:30am–6:15pm Tue–Sun 🌐 musee-moyenage.fr

The National Museum of the Middle Ages is housed in the former town house of the abbots of Cluny, the Hôtel de Cluny. Surrounded by imaginatively recreated medieval gardens, it is a unique combination of Gallo-Roman ruins incorporated

into a medieval mansion, with striking modern architectural touches, and contains one of the world's finest collections of medieval art. Highlights include the *Lady with the Unicorn*, an outstanding series of six tapestries, and the Gallery of the Kings, which contains 22 of the 27 stone heads of the Kings of Judah (carved around 1220 and removed from Notre-Dame in the 18th century).

③ Musée de la Préfecture de Police

🔲 K8 🏠 4 Rue de la Montagne Ste-Geneviève 75005 📞 01 44 41 52 50
Ⓜ Maubert-Mutualité
🕐 9:30am–5pm Mon–Fri, 10:30am–5pm 3rd Sat of month 🔒 Sun & public hols

A darker side to Paris's history is exposed in this small, rather old-fashioned museum. Created in 1909, the collection traces the development of the police in Paris from the Middle Ages to the 20th century.

A statue of Guillaume Budé, Collège de France

④ Collège de France

🔲 J9 🏠 11 Pl Marcelin-Berthelot 75005
Ⓜ Maubert-Mutualité
🕐 Sep–Jun: 9am–6pm Mon–Fri 🔒 School hols
🌐 college-de-france.fr

One of Paris's great institutes of research and learning, the college was established in 1530 by François I. Guided by the great humanist Guillaume Budé, the king aimed to counteract the rigidity and traditionalism of the Sorbonne. A statue of Budé stands in the west courtyard, and the unbiased approach to learning is reflected in the inscription on the old college entrance: *docet omnia* (all are taught here). Lectures are free and open to the public – see the website for details.

🔍 HIDDEN GEM
Thermes de Cluny

These Roman baths were built at the end of the 1st century AD. In the 14th century the Cluny monks built their abbey over the ruins and today they can be seen as part of a visit to the Musée de Cluny.

5
La Sorbonne

☷ J9 **⌂** 1 Rue Victor Cousin 75005 **Ⓜ** Cluny-La Sorbonne, Odéon **Ⓦ** sorbonne-universite.fr

The Sorbonne, seat of the University of Paris, was established in 1253 by Robert de Sorbon, confessor to Louis IX, for 16 poor students to study theology. The college soon became the centre of scholastic theology. In 1469, the rector had three printing machines brought over from Mainz, thereby founding the first printing house in France. The college's opposition to liberal 18th-century philosophy led to its suppression during the Revolution. It was re-established by Napoleon in 1806. The buildings built by Richelieu in the early 17th century were replaced by the ones seen today, with

→

The chapel of La Sorbonne, with its elegant dome

the exception of the chapel. You can book onto a guided tour by emailing ahead.

6
St-Séverin

☷ J8 **⌂** 3 Rue des Prêtres-St-Séverin 75005 **Ⓜ** St-Michel **Ⓞ** 9:30am-1pm & 2-7:30pm Mon-Sat, 9am-1pm & 3-8pm Sun **Ⓦ** saint-severin.com

One of the most beautiful churches in Paris and a popular venue for concerts, St-Séverin, named after a 6th-century hermit who lived in the area, is a perfect example of the Flamboyant Gothic style. Construction finished during the early 16th century and included a double ambulatory circling the chancel. In 1684, the Grande Mademoiselle, cousin to Louis XIV, adopted St-Séverin after breaking with St-Sulpice and had the church's chancel modernized.

EAT

Shakespeare and Co Café
Sip coffee and nibble cakes outside the iconic bookshop (p258).

☷ K8 **⌂** 37 Rue de la Bûcherie 75005 **Ⓦ** shakespeareand company.com

€€€

Chez Gladines
Hearty and affordable no-frills French meals.

☷ K8 **⌂** 44 Blvd St-Germain 75005 **Ⓦ** chezgladinesparis.fr

€€€

La Tour d'Argent
Try the legendary duck at this historic restaurant that was much loved by Henri IV.

☷ L8 **⌂** 15 Quai de la Tournelle 75005 **Ⓒ** Sun, Mon **Ⓦ** tourargent.com

€€€

➐ Place St-Michel

📍 J8 📮 75005
Ⓜ St-Michel

This square at a busy intersection is a popular meeting place for Parisians and tour groups. Created in 1855, it's defined by the statue of Saint Michael the archangel slaying Satan, part of the monumental fountain built into the side of an adjacent building. The mix of colours and motifs earned it some criticism initially, and it was the last monumental wall fountain to be built in the city, ending the Renaissance-era trend brought to Paris by Catherine de Medici. Originally the fountain was meant to honour Napoleon Bonaparte, but the city council thought better of it and opted not to ruffle the feathers of anti-Bonaparte reactionaries. Nowadays, the fountain is a memorable welcome to the Latin Quarter for visitors entering the district from Île St-Louis. It is surrounded by cafés and bookshops which are popular with local university students.

➑ Gibert Jeune Bookshops

📍 J8 📮 Multiple locations, Quai St-Michel 75005
Ⓜ St-Michel ⏰ 10am–7pm Mon-Sat 🌐 gibert jeune.fr

A former professor, Joseph Gibert opened his first shop in 1886. He started by selling books on the Quai St-Michel along with the other *bouquinistes* (used-book sellers who ply their wares out of green boxes along the Seine). Gibert's sons continued the family business, opening separate outposts under the name in the fifth arrondissement, selling a mix of new and secondhand books. Sadly with sales down due to the pandemic, the iconic French bookstore's flagship shop on Place St-Michel has now closed, but book lovers can still visit the two stores that remain open on Quai St-Michel. Look out, too, for the Gibert Joseph shops on Boulevard St-Michel.

300,000

books are held in the green boxes of the *bouquinistes* along the river.

➒ St-Julien-le-Pauvre

📍 K8 📮 79 Rue Galande 75005 📞 01 43 54 52 16 Ⓜ St-Michel 🚇 St-Michel-Notre-Dame
⏰ 2–6:30pm daily

At least three saints can claim to be patron of this church, but the most likely is St Julian the Hospitaller. The church, together with St-Germain-des-Prés, is one of the oldest in Paris, dating from between 1165 and 1220. The university

→ The monumental fountain in Place St-Michel

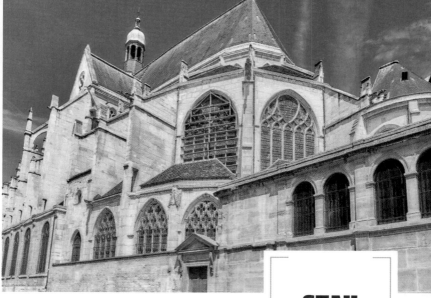
↑ The Gothic-Renaissance church of St-Étienne-du-Mont

held its official meetings in the church until 1524, when a student protest created so much damage that meetings were barred from the church by parliament. Since 1889, it has belonged to the Melchite sect of the Greek Orthodox Church, and it is now the setting for chamber and religious music concerts.

10 Marché Maubert

K8 ☖ Place Maubert 75005 🕒 7am–2:30pm Tue & Thu, 7am–3pm Sat Ⓜ Maubert-Mutualité

Popular with locals, this is one of the city's oldest outdoor markets, dating back to 1547. In earlier times the square was a place where carriage drivers emptied their waste, creating a truly gut-wrenching stench that drove out many inhabitants. Eventually the city cleaned up the mess and repurposed the square as a place for public executions, installing breaking wheels and gibbets here in the 16th

century. By the 19th century the square had returned to commercial use, and included a unique market where beggars would sell unused tobacco that they collected from the streets. Today the market is entirely wholesome, and you can browse stalls selling organic strawberries, cheese and dried hams.

11 St-Étienne-du-Mont

K9 ☖ Pl Ste-Geneviève 75005 Ⓜ Cardinal Lemoine 🕒 Opening hours vary; check website for details 🌐 saintetiennedumont.fr

This remarkable church houses the shrine of Sainte Geneviève, patron saint of Paris, as well as the remains of the great literary figures Racine and Pascal. Some parts are in the Gothic style and others date from the Renaissance, including a magnificent rood screen that crosses the nave like a bridge. The stained-glass windows are also of note.

STAY

Hôtel Design Sorbonne

Stylish and central, this boutique hotel is in an excellent location.

📍 J9 ☖ 6 Rue Victor Cousin 75005
 ⓦ hotelsorbonne.com

€€€

Hôtel des Grands Hommes

Sleep in 19th-century grandeur at this tasteful property.

📍 J9 ☖ 17 Place du Panthéon 75005
ⓦ hoteldesgrands hommes.com

€€€

Les Degrés de Notre-Dame

Stylish simplicity in central Paris, right across from Notre-Dame.

📍 K8 ☖ 10 Rue des Grands Degrés 75005
📞 01 55 42 88 88

€€€

12

Grand Action Cinéma

📍K9 🏠5 Rue des Écoles 75005 Ⓜ Cardinal Lemoine, Jussieu 🌐legrandaction.com

Located in the heart of the Latin Quarter, this tiny independent operation is one of the most exciting cinematic experiences in Paris. The site has been a handball court, a Revolutionaries' meeting place and a dance hall over the years. Today it welcomes all sorts of films and retrospectives, ranging from niche independent films to Oscar-nominated pictures. The director and local student clubs regularly host industry professionals for talks to the public on themes such as science-fiction movies or Russian films. There are just two theatres with rows of red-cushioned seats, but the Grand Action perseveres even as multiplexes have risen in popularity.

13

Bibliothèque Ste-Geneviève

📍J9 🏠10 Place du Panthéon 75005 Ⓜ Maubert-Mutualité 🕐10am–10pm Mon–Sat 🌐bsg.univ-paris3.fr

This massive, sober-looking library houses some two million documents salvaged from the nearby abbey of Ste-Geneviève. Visitors to the neighbourhood may completely overlook it, as the enormous dome of the Panthéon tends to command more attention. It was, however, the first French library that was built without any connection to a palace or school building. It opened to the public in 1851, and architect Henri Labrouste incorporated a soaring glass-and-iron ceiling into the main reading room. There is usually a queue to enter the library, and visitors may be required to register at the front desk, but it is worth it to work in such a grand setting.

14

Shakespeare and Company

📍K8 🏠37 Rue de la Bûcherie 75005 🕐10am–8pm Mon–Sat, noon–7pm Sun Ⓜ St-Michel 🌐shakespeareandcompany.com

George Whitman opened this now-iconic shop in 1951. Originally called Le Mistral, it was renamed Shakespeare

> ## Did You Know?
> —
> This district was the scene of violent clashes between angry students and police in the riots of May 1968.

↑ The legendary American-run English-language bookshop Shakespeare and Company

Square René Viviani, a perfect retreat from the bustle of the city ↑

and Company in 1964 after the renowned bookshop run by Sylvia Beach on nearby Rue de l'Odéon, which closed in 1941 during the Occupation. Whitman sought to emulate the spirit of Beach's shop, attracting expat writers like Henry Miller and Anaïs Nin. Over the years, the owner allowed young writers to sleep in the shop for free, asking them only to read, help at the shop and write a page-long autobiography. The shop continues Whitman's traditions under his daughter Sylvia, named after Beach. There are always literary events taking place, some featuring big names like David Sedaris. The shop is tiny, but well stocked with contemporary literature, Paris-themed books and English travel books. Next door is a coffee shop *(p255)*, where you can sit with a book at one of the outdoor tables facing Notre-Dame.

15

Square René Viviani

K8 **25 Quai de Montebello 75005** **St-Michel, Maubert-Mutualité** **8am-5pm Mon-Fri, 9am-5pm Sat-Sun (to 8:30pm in summer)**

One of many little green oases in Paris, Square René Viviani has views of Notre-Dame that beat all others. The park was once a graveyard belonging to the 6th-century basilica that formerly stood here. Now, the church St-Julien-le-Pauvre *(p256)*, begun in the 12th century, sits adjacent to the park. Its most notable feature is a black locust tree *(Robinia pseudoacacia)*, allegedly planted in 1601. Held up by a couple of concrete stilts, it is generally accepted to be the oldest tree in Paris, having survived shell damage during World War I. The square owes its name to France's first Labour Minister, René Viviani, who once spoke out in support of women's suffrage – albeit, in a limited fashion.

DRINK

Monk La Taverne de Cluny
Craft beer has infiltrated the Parisian scene, and this is the place for it on the Left Bank.

J8 **51 Rue de la Harpe 75005** **01 43 54 28 88**

Le Piano Vache
Students and locals hit the bar at this rowdy watering hole.

K9 **8 Rue Laplace 75005** **01 46 33 75 03** **Sun**

Le Bombardier
Paris has a few pubs worthy of the name, but this one has earned its stripes.

K9 **2 Place du Panthéon 75005** **bombardierpub.fr**

> **Shakespeare and Company allowed young writers to sleep in the shop for free, asking them only to read, help at the shop and write a page-long autobiography.**

A SHORT WALK
LATIN QUARTER

Distance 2 km (1.25 miles) **Nearest Metro** Cluny - La Sorbonne
Time 20 minutes

This riverside quarter, dating back to Roman times, acquired its name from early Latin-speaking students. The area is generally associated with artists, intellectuals and the bohemian way of life, but it also has a history of political unrest. In 1871, Place St-Michel became the centre of the Paris Commune, and in May 1968, it was the site of the student uprisings. Though now sufficiently chic to contain the homes of some of the establishment, the quarter is still full of bookshops and cafés, perfect for an afternoon of browsing.

Place St-Michel contains a fountain by Davioud. The bronze statue by Duret shows St Michael fighting the devil.

Metro St-Michel

No 22 Rue St-Séverin is the narrowest house in Paris and used to be the residence of Abbé Prévost, author of Manon Lescaut.

The northern end of the Boulevard St-Michel is a lively mélange of cafés, bars, bookshops and clothes stores.

Begun in the 13th century, the beautiful St-Séverin took three centuries to build and is a fine example of the Flamboyant Gothic style (p255).

Metro Cluny – La Sorbonne

QUAI ST-

BLVD ST-MICHEL

RUE DE LA HARPE

RUE DU

RUE ST-JACQUES

RUE DES ÉCOLES

RUE THENARD

START

One of the finest collections of medieval art in the world is kept at the superb Musée de Cluny (p254).

↑ Davioud's decorative fountain, found in Place St-Michel

↑ The iconic Shakespeare and Company bookshop and accompanying café

Locator Map
For more detail see p250

Rue du Chat qui Pêche translates as "street of the fishing cat".

Little Athens is a lively place in the evenings, especially at the weekend, when the Greek restaurants situated in the touristy streets around St-Séverin are at their busiest.

Shakespeare and Company at No 37 Rue de la Bûcherie is a delightful, if chaotic, bookshop. Any books purchased here are stamped with Shakespeare & Co Kilomètre Zéro Paris (p258).

Did You Know?

Rue du Chat qui Pêche is the narrowest street in Paris at just 1.8 m (6 ft) wide.

One of the oldest churches in Paris, St-Julien-le-Pauvre has 13th-century Romanesque architecture. The vault was added in the 17th century (p256).

Rue du Fouarre used to host lectures in the Middle Ages. The students sat on straw (fouarre) in the street.

Metro – Maubert Mutualité

Rue Galande was home to the rich and the chic in the 17th century, but subsequently became notorious for its taverns.

| 0 metres | | 100 |
| 0 yards | | 100 |

N ↑

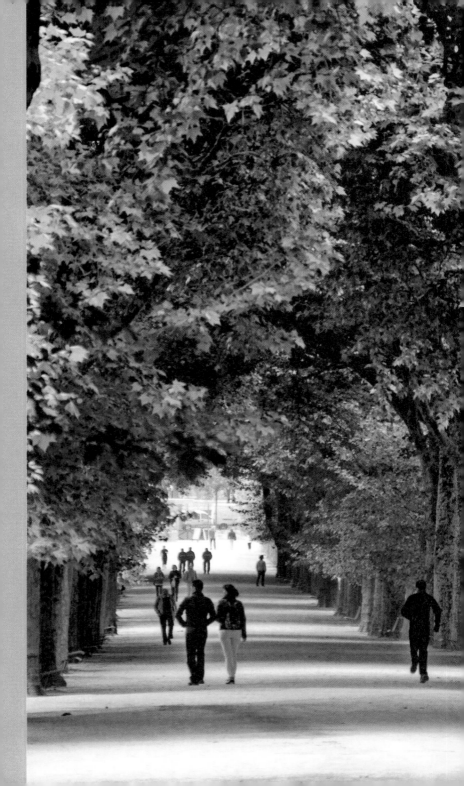

JARDIN DES PLANTES AND PLACE D'ITALIE

This is one of the oldest areas in Paris, with a history dating back to ancient times. Part of the Roman settlement of Lutetia, it housed the large Arènes de Lutèce amphitheatre. The Rue Mouffetard was also established during the Roman era, and remained an important market street throughout the ensuing centuries. In 1626, Louis XIII founded the Jardin des Plantes as the royal medicinal plant gardens, and it soon became a scientific laboratory and botanical research centre – in the 18th century it was the stomping ground of naturalists Georges Louis Leclerc, Comte de Buffon and Jean-Baptiste Lamarck, whose research eventually influenced Charles Darwin and his *On the Origin of Species*. In more recent years, the area has become home to a sizable Muslim community, focused on the Grande Mosquée de Paris and the Institut du Monde Arabe cultural centre.

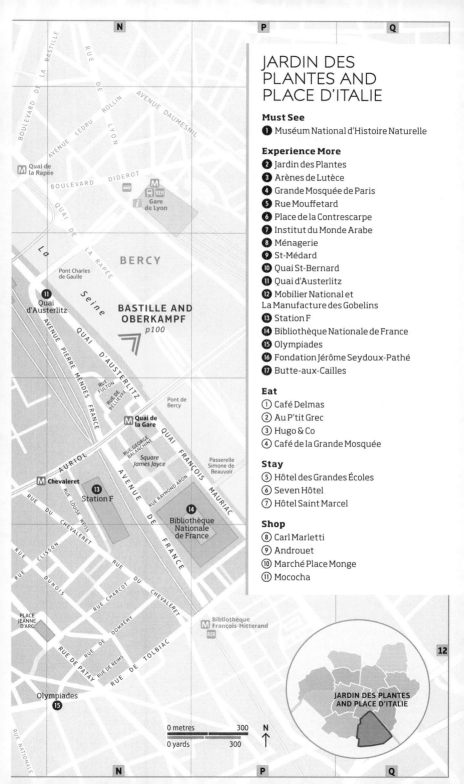

JARDIN DES PLANTES AND PLACE D'ITALIE

Must See

1 Muséum National d'Histoire Naturelle

Experience More

2 Jardin des Plantes
3 Arènes de Lutèce
4 Grande Mosquée de Paris
5 Rue Mouffetard
6 Place de la Contrescarpe
7 Institut du Monde Arabe
8 Ménagerie
9 St-Médard
10 Quai St-Bernard
11 Quai d'Austerlitz
12 Mobilier National et
La Manufacture des Gobelins
13 Station F
14 Bibliothèque Nationale de France
15 Olympiades
16 Fondation Jérôme Seydoux-Pathé
17 Butte-aux-Cailles

Eat

① Café Delmas
② Au P'tit Grec
③ Hugo & Co
④ Café de la Grande Mosquée

Stay

⑤ Hôtel des Grandes Écoles
⑥ Seven Hôtel
⑦ Hôtel Saint Marcel

Shop

⑧ Carl Marletti
⑨ Androuet
⑩ Marché Place Monge
⑪ Mococha

The spectacular
Grande Galerie
de l'Évolution ↑

1 🗺️ 💻 🏛️

MUSÉUM NATIONAL D'HISTOIRE NATURELLE

📍**L10** 🏛️**Grande Galerie de l'Évolution and Galerie de Géologie et de Minéralogie: 36 Rue Geoffroy St-Hilaire 75005; Galerie de Paléontologie et d'Anatomie: 2 Rue Buffon 75005**
Ⓜ**Jussieu, Gare d'Austerlitz** 🕐**10am–6pm Wed–Mon** 🚫**1 Jan, 1 May, 25 Dec** 🌐**mnhn.fr**

This collection of galleries in the Jardin des Plantes houses an impressive display of natural history specimens tracing the evolution of life on Earth.

A botany research centre in the 17th century, this museum was founded in 1793 to include zoology. It has three galleries in the Jardin des Plantes: the Galerie de Géologie et de Minéralogie, with crystals, gems and meteorites; the Galerie de Paléontologie et d'Anatomie Comparée, housing dinosaur skeletons and fossils; and the Grande Galerie de l'Évolution, featuring stuffed tigers and elephants. The 67 million specimens here form the world's third-largest research collection. The Galerie des Enfants, in the Grande Galerie de l'Évolution, is an environment-focused exhibition for children.

The museum also encompasses several other sites in the Jardin des Plantes, including the greenhouses and the zoo *(p270)*.

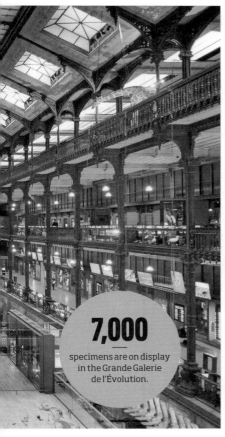

LA GALERIE DE PALÉONTOLOGIE ET D'ANATOMIE COMPARÉE

Built in 1898 for the Exposition Universelle of 1900, the Galerie de Paléontologie et d'Anatomie Comparée mesmerizes young visitors with its collection of dinosaur skeletons, including a Triceratops and a Tyrannosaurus rex. Beginning in the Paleozoic Era, the exhibition takes visitors on a 540-million-year journey through each stage in the development of animal life. Keep a special eye out for the skeleton of Louis XV's rhino; one of the museum's longest-held specimens, it once lived at Versailles.

TYRANNOSAURUS REX SKULL

[1] A wide range of flora is on show in the greenhouses.

[2] The museum sits amid the glorious Jardin des Plantes.

[3] The Galerie de Géologie et de Minéralogie is home to giant crystals and Martian meteorites.

EXPERIENCE MORE

②

Jardin des Plantes

⑨ L9 **⌂** 57 Rue Cuvier 75005 **Ⓜ** Jussieu, Gare d'Austerlitz **◷** 7:30am-8pm daily (8am-5:30pm winter) **ⓦ** jardin desplantesdeparis.fr

A treasure to locals in the 5th arrondissement, the Jardin des Plantes comprises a museum, a zoo, botanical gardens, a science lab and a university research centre. Previously known as the Jardin du Roi, it started life as a medicinal herb garden created by Guy de la Brosse and Jean Hérouard, King Louis XIII's physicians, in 1626. After opening to the public in 1640 and offering a free school of botany, chemistry and anatomy, it quickly attracted renowned scientists, such as the Comte de Buffon, whose studies were to shape Darwin's views on evolution.

Today, this popular botanical garden is home to three galleries of the Muséum National d'Histoire Naturelle (p266). It includes a small zoo (p270), a rose garden and a labyrinth that kids adore. As well as beautiful vistas and walkways flanked by ancient trees and punctuated with statues, the park features a remarkable alpine garden with plants from the Alps, the Himalayas, Corsica and Morocco, and an unrivalled display of herbaceous and wild plants. It also has the first cedar of Lebanon planted in France, originally from Britain's Kew Gardens.

---

③

Arènes de Lutèce

⑨ K9 **⌂** 49-59 Rue Monge/4 Rue des Arènes 75005 **☎** 01 45 35 02 56 **Ⓜ** Jussieu, Cardinal Lemoine **◷** 8/9am-6/7:30/8:30pm, depending on the time of year

The remains of this vast Roman arena (Lutetia was the Roman name for Paris) date from the late 1st century AD. Its destruction began towards the end of the 3rd century at the hands of the Barbarians, and later, parts of it were used to build the walls of the Île de la Cité. The arena was then gradually buried and its exact location preserved only in old documents and the local name Clos des Arènes.

 HIDDEN GEM
Dodo Manège

This unique merry-go-round in the Jardin des Plantes allows you to ride on a host of strange and exotic animals, including a dodo, a triceratops, a horned turtle and even a sivatherium, a giraffe-like animal with antlers.

It was rediscovered in 1869 during the construction of Rue Monge and the allocation of building plots nearby. Action towards its restoration began with the campaigning of Victor Hugo (among others) in the 19th century, but work did not get underway until 1918.

With a seating capacity of 15,000, arranged in 35 tiers, the original arena was used both for theatrical performances and as an amphitheatre for gladiator fights. This type of combined use was peculiar to Gaul (France), and the arena is similar to the other ones in Nîmes and Arles.

---

④

Grande Mosquée de Paris

⑨ L10 **⌂** 2 bis Pl du Puits de l'Ermite 75005 (Turkish baths/tearoom: 39 Rue Geoffroy St-Hilaire) **Ⓜ** Jussieu, Place Monge **◷** 9am-6pm Sat-Thu; baths: 10am-9pm Wed-Mon **⌂** Muslim hols **ⓦ** mosqueedeparis.net

Built in the 1920s in the Hispano-Moorish style,

←

People enjoying a stroll on a spring day in the Jardin des Plantes this complex is the spiritual centre of Paris's Muslim community and the home of the Grand Imam. It comprises religious, educational and commercial sections; and at its heart is a mosque. Each of the mosque's domes is decorated in a different style, and the minaret stands nearly 33 m (100 ft) high. Inside is a grand patio with mosaics on the walls and tracery on the arches.

Once used only by scholars, the mosque's place in Parisian life has grown over the years. The complex now houses Turkish baths (strictly for women only), as well as a tearoom and restaurant set in a peaceful tree-shaded courtyard. It serves Moorish specialities and makes a lovely spot for a glass of mint tea and sticky cakes.

The tranquil, tiled gardens of the Grande Mosquée de Paris

⑤

Rue Mouffetard

🔲 K10 🏠 75005 Ⓜ Censier-Daubenton, Place Monge 🅱 Market Place Monge: 7am–2:30pm Wed, Fri, Sun (to 3pm Sun)

A major thoroughfare since Roman times, when it linked Lutetia (Paris) and Rome, this street is one of the oldest in the city. In the 17th and 18th centuries, it was known as the Grande Rue du Faubourg St-Marcel, and many of its buildings date from that time. Some of the small shops still have ancient painted signs, and some houses have mansard roofs.

> **Did You Know?**
>
> Ernest Hemingway lived in the area in the 1920s, at 74 Rue du Cardinal Lemoine.

No 125 has an attractive, restored Louis XIII façade, and the entire front of No 134 is beautifully decorated with wild beasts, flowers and plants. No 69 sports an old shop sign featuring a carved oak tree, while at No 60, the *Fontaine de Pot-de-Fer* is a small fountain dating from Roman times. In the 17th century, it was connected to an aqueduct used by Marie de Médici to take water to the Palais du Luxembourg and its gardens *(p286)*.

The area is known for its open-air markets, especially those in Place Monge (set around the Monge fountain) – a flurry of colours, flavours and delicious smells well worth a visit.

At night, the street bustles with people enjoying the Greek, Italian, Lebanese and other cuisines on offer at the many small restaurants.

6 Place de la Contrescarpe

⊙ K9 ⌂ 75005 Ⓜ Place Monge

At one time, this site lay outside the city walls. It gets its name from the backfilling of the moat that ran along Philippe Auguste's wall. The present square was laid out in 1852, but the fountain was added in 1994. At No 1, there is a memorial to the old "pine-cone club"; here, a group of writers known as *La Pléiade* used to meet in the 16th century. Four hundred years later, authors such as Ernest Hemingway, James Joyce and George Orwell also found the streets of this historically working-class neighbourhood a great source of inspiration.

The area has always been used for meetings and festivals. Today, it still embodies old Paris, with its narrow cobblestoned streets and charming cafés, and is very lively at weekends.

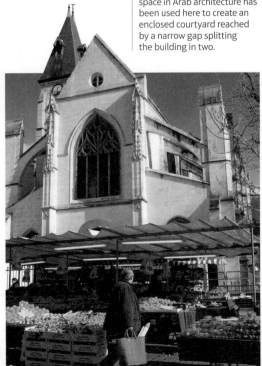

7 Institut du Monde Arabe

⊙ L9 ⌂ 1 Rue des Fossés St-Bernard, Pl Mohammed V 75005 Ⓜ Jussieu, Cardinal Lemoine Ⓞ Museum & temp exhibits: 10am–6pm Tue, Wed & Fri, 10am–7pm Thu, Sat & Sun Ⓦ imarabe.org

This cultural institute was founded in 1980 by France and 20 Arab countries with the intention of fostering cultural links between the Arab world and the West. It is housed in a magnificent building designed by Jean Nouvel (who was also responsible for the Musée du quai Branly and the Philharmonie), combining modern materials with the spirit of traditional Islamic architecture. The white marble book tower, which can be seen through the glass of the west wall, spirals upwards, bringing to mind the minaret of a mosque. The emphasis that is traditionally placed on interior space in Arab architecture has been used here to create an enclosed courtyard reached by a narrow gap splitting the building in two.

↑ Flamingos in the Ménagerie, France's oldest public zoo

From floors four to seven, there's a fascinating display of Islamic works of art from the 9th to the 19th centuries, including ceramics, sculpture, carpets and astrolabes. The centre also houses a library and media archive, and puts on a lively programme of lectures and concerts.

8 Ménagerie

⊙ L9 ⌂ 57 Rue Cuvier/Rue Buffon 75005 Ⓜ Jussieu, Gare d'Austerlitz Ⓞ 9am–6pm Mon–Sat, 9am–6:30pm Sun & public hols (winter: earlier closure), advance booking recommended Ⓦ zoodujardindesplantes.fr

Opened in 1794, France's oldest public zoo sits in the pleasant surroundings of the Jardin des Plantes (*p268*). The Ménagerie was set up during the Revolution to house the survivors from

← St-Médard and a Rue Mouffetard street market

the royal menagerie at Versailles – all four of them. The state then expanded the collection with animals rounded up from circuses and exotic creatures sent from abroad. Tragically, during the Prussian siege of Paris (1870–71), most of the animals were slaughtered in order to feed the hungry citizens.

The zoo specializes in small mammals, insects, birds, primates and reptiles. It is a great favourite with children as it allows them to get close to the animals, and feeding times are especially popular. The big cat house contains panthers from China, and other attractions include a large monkey house, a waterfowl aviary, and wild sheep and goats. The displays in the vivarium (enclosures of live animals in their natural habitat) are changed at regular intervals, and there is a permanent exhibition of micro-arthropods (also known as creepy-crawlies).

St-Médard

♥ K10 **⌂ 141 Rue Mouffetard 75005** **Ⓜ Censier-Daubenton** **⏱ 9am-7:30pm Tue-Sat, 9am-8pm Sun** **🌐 saintmedard.org**

The origins of this church go back to the 9th century. St Médard, counsellor to the Merovingian kings, was known for giving a wreath of white roses to young girls noted for their virtue. The churchyard became notorious in the 18th century as the centre of the cult of the Convulsionnaires, whose fits were brought on by the contemplation of miracle cures. The interior has many paintings, including the 17th-century *St Joseph Walking with the Christ Child* by Francisco de Zurbarán, and the organ loft is adorned with Renaissance statues.

STAY

Hôtel des Grandes Écoles

A garden terrace and old-world feel make this a perpetual favourite.

♥ K9 **⌂ 75 Rue du Cardinal Lemoine 75005** **🌐 hoteldesgrandes ecoles.com**

€€€

Seven Hôtel

Swanky décor sets this modern hotel apart from most in the area.

♥ J10 **⌂ 20 Rue Berthollet 75005** **🌐 sevenhotel paris.com**

€€€

Hôtel Saint Marcel

A great location and amenities such as a wine bar stocked with the family's own wine make this hotel a real treat.

♥ L11 **⌂ 43 Blvd St-Marcel 75013** **🌐 hotel-saint-marcel-paris.com**

€€€

⑩
Quai St-Bernard

📍 M9 🏛 75005
Ⓜ Gare d'Austerlitz

Running along the river from the Pont de Sully as far as the Pont d'Austerlitz is the peaceful Quai St-Bernard. Not always so sedate, Quai St-Bernard was famous during the 17th century as a spot for nude bathing, until scandalized public opinion made it illegal. The quay is studded with contemporary sculptures, but its main draw is the green space known as the Jardin Tino-Rossi, named for the Coriscan singer who recorded "Petit Papa Noël" in 1946, one of France's best-selling songs ever. The park is alive with music in the summer, from French folk to salsa and tango. Dancers of all levels meet here at night, turning the park into an outdoor dance hall.

Butting up to the left-hand corner of the Institut du Monde Arabe, the Pont de Sully links the Île St-Louis with both banks of the Seine. Opened in 1877 and built of cast iron, the Pont de Sully is not an especially beautiful structure. Despite this, it is well worth pausing for a moment on the bridge for a view of Notre-Dame rising dramatically behind the graceful Pont de la Tournelle.

⑪
Quai d'Austerlitz

📍 M10 🏛 75013
Ⓜ Gare d'Austerlitz
🌐 citemodedesign.fr

Stretching along the Left Bank from Gare d'Austerlitz towards the Bibliothèque, this riverfront promenade is closed to traffic and offers a pleasant stroll with views of the Seine. Several boats host cafés serving coffee and wine. The impressive contemporary cultural centre known as Les Docks, Cité de la Mode et du Design, perches over the Seine, with its green undulating façade looking northwards. Housed in a former industrial warehouse, it is home to an assortment of bars, cafés and restaurants, as well as a fashion institute, and hosts regular exhibitions. Further south, along Quai François Mauriac, is the Port de la Gare where, in the summer, outdoor restaurants and cafés line the riverfront. Le Bateau Phare, a floating bar, restaurant and concert space, and the Piscine Josephine Baker, a floating public pool, also moor here year-round.

> ### Did You Know?
>
> The Bateau Phare was a working Irish lightship from 1955 to 1975s.

⑫
Mobilier National et La Manufacture des Gobelins

📍 K11 🏛 42 Ave des Gobelins 75013 Ⓜ Les Gobelins 🕐 11am–6pm Tue–Sun (temporary exhibitions) 🚫 1 Jan, 1 May, 25 Dec 🌐 mobiliernational. culture. gouv.fr

Originally a dyeing workshop set up in about 1440 by the

→
The striking façade of Les Docks, Cité de la Mode et du Design

Gobelin brothers, the building became a tapestry factory early in the 17th century. Louis XIV took it over in 1662 and gathered together the greatest craftsmen of the day – carpet-weavers, cabinet-makers and silversmiths – to furnish his new palace at Versailles (p296). Working under the direction of court painter Charles Le Brun, 250 Flemish weavers laid the foundations for the factory's international reputation. Today, weavers continue to work in the traditional way but with modern designs, including those of Picasso and Matisse. Guided tours on Wednesday afternoons can be booked via the website.

Station F

N11 ⌂ **5 Parvis Alan Turing 75013** Ⓜ **Chevaleret** ⓦ **stationf.co**

This converted train station, which opened in 2017, houses Paris's burgeoning innovation scene. The world's largest "start-up campus", Station F is as long as the Eiffel Tower is high. The venue hosts a variety of events about business and technology, with registration available on its website. Visitors can take a tour of the new ventures or cosy up with entrepreneurs at the public café. Locals flock here for the various Italian food options served at La Felicità, an enormous, trendy cafeteria-style eatery. Be prepared to queue and be quick to grab one of the many communal tables available.

SHOP

Carl Marletti

Daring confectionaries fill Marletti's celebrated patisserie, with ephemeral favourites like the *fraisier* popping up each year.

K10 ⌂ **51 Rue Censier 75005** ⓦ **carlmarletti.com**

Androuet

Expert artisan cheeses from here have pleased Parisians since 1909, including classics such as Camembert.

K10 ⌂ **134 Rue Mouffetard 75005** ⓦ **androuet.com**

Marché Place Monge

Vendors stock fresh produce that changes with the seasons at this outdoor market with a focus on quality over quantity.

K10 ⌂ **1 Place Monge 75005** ◷ **7am-2:30pm Wed, Fri (to 3pm Sun)**

Mococha

Surprising combinations deck the shelves of this boutique, run by a team of inspired chocolatiers.

K10 ⌂ **89 Rue Mouffetard 75005** ⓦ **chocolatsmococha.com**

Bibliothèque Nationale de France

N11 **Quai François Mauriac 75013**
M Bibliothèque François-Mitterrand **2–8pm Mon, 9am–8pm Tue–Sat, 1–7pm Sun** **Public hols** **bnf.fr**

The national library collection dates back to the 1300s, when King Charles V began a library at the Louvre. Royals added to the shelves, even involuntarily, as Revolutionaries confiscated thousands of volumes from aristocrats during the French Revolution. Nowadays, the symbol of the BNF is the ultra-modern building rising over the Quai François Mauriac. The structure looks like four giant glass books opening onto a courtyard, and is largely used by scholars. Commissioned by President Mitterrand and completed in 1996, it houses the world's largest selection of medieval manuscripts and boasts over 14 million books in total. Temporary exhibitions take place throughout the year, as well as in the other BNF sites located around the city.

Olympiades

N12 **75013**
M Olympiades

This modern corner of Paris, with several impressive street-art murals, is part of the city's larger vision of urban development. It is marked by the Olympiades towers, an innovative housing complex where each tower is named after a different Olympic host city. Today, the area is largely known as Paris's largest Chinatown, where the annual Chinese New Year parade takes place in February. Parisians head here for delicious Chinese and Vietnamese food, including some of the best *bo bun* in the entire city. Its affordable fare and grocery stores, such as Tang Frères, are huge draws for anyone interested in a break from *steak-frites* and cheese. The district is bordered on the south by the tramline that stretches around southern Paris.

Fondation Jérôme Seydoux-Pathé

L11 **73 Ave des Gobelins 75013** **M Place d'Italie, Les Gobelins** **Salle Charles Pathé & Exhibitions: 2–8:30pm Tue & Fri, 2–7pm Wed & Thu, 11:30am–7pm Sat; research centre: by appt only** **1 Jan, 25 Dec** **fondation-jerome seydoux-pathe.com**

The headquarters of the Fondation Jérôme Seydoux-Pathé sits on the site of a mid-19th-century theatre that was transformed into one of Paris's first cinemas in the early 1900s. Pathé, a major French film production and distribution company, is the second-oldest operating film company in the world. The foundation is dedicated to the preservation of its legacy and to promoting cinematography. The building has a

Dominique Perrault's modern Bibliothèque Nationale de France ↑

Did You Know?

The Bibliothèque Nationale de France is one of the oldest libraries in the world.

68-seat screening room for silent films, plus temporary and permanent collections of films, cameras, projectors, programmes and posters dating back to 1896. It is a treasure trove for film enthusiasts and researchers. Guided tours are held on Saturdays at noon.

Butte-aux-Cailles

K12 **75013**
M Place d'Italie, Corvisart

Named after landowner Pierre Caille who grew grapes here in the 1500s, this little hill was once an important area for tanneries and other industry. The La Bièvre river, which now runs underground, used to run right through

→ A water fountain in Chinatown

it. Limestone quarries underground made the land unsuitable for Haussmann's large construction projects, and as a result the area has more of a village feel than most parts of Paris – the Rue des Cinq-Diamants is a great example of this. Interestingly, it was in this area, in 1783, that the first official hot-air balloon trip landed successfully. Today the district is full of local character in its bars and cafés; they are relatively cheap, making the area especially popular among young university types. The area is also an excellent place to discover some great street art, with lots of examples of the work of the late tagger Miss.Tic.

↑ The dome of Ste-Anne-de-la-Buttes-aux-Cailles church in the picturesque Butte-aux-Cailles district

EAT

Café Delmas
Traditional French café overlooking a square.

📍K9 🏠2 Place de la Contrescarpe 75005
🌐cafedelmas.com

€€€

Au P'tit Grec
A popular spot serving huge take-away crêpes.

📍K10 🏠68 Rue Mouffetard 75005
🌐auptitgrec.com

€€€

Hugo & Co
Convivial restaurant serving chic dishes.

📍K9 🏠48 Rue Monge, 75005 📅Sat & Sun
🌐tomygousset.com/hugo-and-co

€€€

Café de la Grande Mosquée
A lovely tea room attached to the mosque.

📍L10 🏠39 Rue Geoffroy St-Hilaire 75005

€€€

A SHORT WALK

JARDIN DES PLANTES QUARTER

Metro Cardinal Lemoine

START ▶

Distance 2.5km (1.5 miles) **Nearest Metro** Cardinal Lemoine
Time 25 minutes

A well-to-do residential patchwork of 19th- and early-20th-century buildings, this area also has one or two surprises up its sleeve, including a Roman amphitheatre and a Hispano-Moorish mosque. The area began life in 1626 as a royal medicinal herb garden, the work of two physicians to Louis XIII, Jean Hérouard and Guy de la Brosse. The herb garden and gardens of various religious houses gave the region a rural character. In the 19th century, the population and thus the area expanded and it became more built up, transforming into the area you see today.

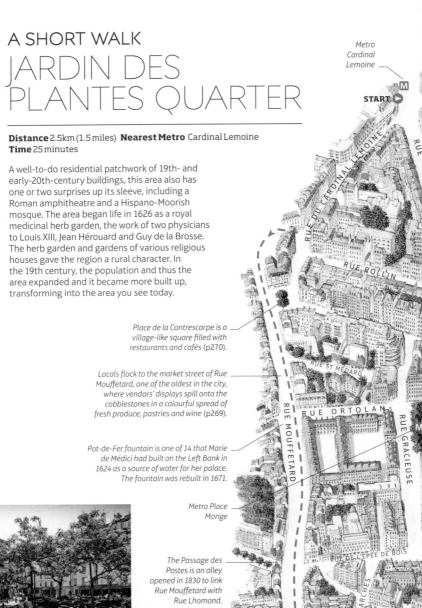

Place de la Contrescarpe is a village-like square filled with restaurants and cafés (p270).

Locals flock to the market street of Rue Mouffetard, one of the oldest in the city, where vendors' displays spill onto the cobblestones in a colourful spread of fresh produce, pastries and wine (p269).

Pot-de-Fer fountain is one of 14 that Marie de Médici had built on the Left Bank in 1624 as a source of water for her palace. The fountain was rebuilt in 1671.

Metro Place Monge

The Passage des Postes is an alley opened in 1830 to link Rue Mouffetard with Rue Lhomond.

The church of St-Médard dates to the mid-1400s. In 1784, the choir was revamped and the nave's windows replaced with contemporary stained glass (p271).

↑ Taking time out on the cobbled square of Place de la Contrescarpe

The Arènes de Lutèce, a Roman amphitheatre, was used for burials in the 4th century (p268).

Rue des Arènes is round the corner from the Arènes de Lutèce. No 5 is an interesting Gothic Revival house in which the writer Jean Paulhan lived from 1940.

Jardin des Plantes Qurarter

JARDIN DES PLANTES AND PLACE D'ITALIE

Locator Map
For more detail see p264

The Cuvier Fountain is a memorial to naturalist Georges Cuvier. It was erected in 1840 by P Vigouroux, with figures carved by Jean-Jacques Feuchère.

RUE DES COULANGERS

MONGE

RUE DES ARÈNES

FINISH

RUE LINNÉ

RUE DE NAVARRE

RUE   LACÉPÈDE

RUE QUATREFAGES

RUE GEOFFROY-ST-HILAIRE

RUE DE LA CLEF

RUE LARREY

RUE G. DESPIAS DU GRIL

RUE MONGE

RUE DAUBENTON

DE MIRBEL

↑ The Hispano-Moorish Grande Mosquée de Paris and its garden

Did You Know?

The Grande Mosquée honours Muslims who died on French battlefields during World War I.

Metro Censier-Daubenton

The Grande Mosquée de Paris, the centre of Paris's Muslim community, includes within its walls a Turkish bath, and a Moorish café and restaurant (p268).

0 metres   100   N
0 yards   100   ↑

MONTPARNASSE AND JARDIN DU LUXEMBOURG

Montparnasse takes its name from the Mount Parnassus of Ancient Greece, the home of Apollo, god of poetry and music. In the first three decades of the 20th century, Montparnasse was a thriving artistic literary centre. Many modern painters and sculptors, new novelists and poets were drawn to this bohemian area, where they would frequent cafés such as La Closerie des Lilas and La Coupole. The great epoch ended with World War II, and change continued with the destruction of many ateliers and the construction of the soaring Tour Montparnasse, Paris's tallest office tower, which heralded the more modern quarter.

The Jardin du Luxembourg was initiated by Marie de Médici in 1612, inspired by the Boboli Gardens of her native Florence. Baron Haussmann redeveloped the area around the park in the 19th century; his changes were deeply unpopular with the public for encroaching on the gardens and reducing their size. Nonetheless, the area has retained its own unique charm of winding streets, beautiful buildings, bookshops and art galleries.

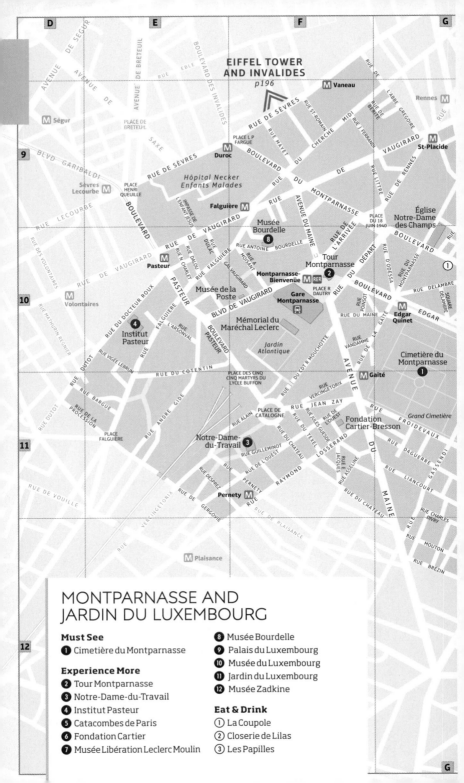

MONTPARNASSE AND JARDIN DU LUXEMBOURG

Must See
1. Cimetière du Montparnasse

Experience More
2. Tour Montparnasse
3. Notre-Dame-du-Travail
4. Institut Pasteur
5. Catacombes de Paris
6. Fondation Cartier
7. Musée Libération Leclerc Moulin

8. Musée Bourdelle
9. Palais du Luxembourg
10. Musée du Luxembourg
11. Jardin du Luxembourg
12. Musée Zadkine

Eat & Drink
1. La Coupole
2. Closerie de Lilas
3. Les Papilles

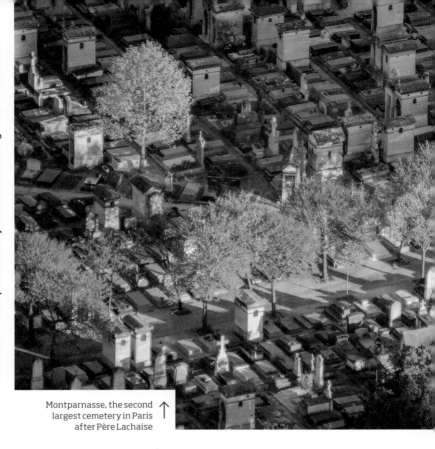

Montparnasse, the second largest cemetery in Paris after Père Lachaise ↑

❶ CIMETIÈRE DU MONTPARNASSE

📍 G10 🏠 3 Blvd Edgar Quinet 75014 Ⓜ Edgar Quinet 🚌 28, 58, 68, 82, 83, 88, 91 to Port Royal 🚈 Port Royal 🕐 Mid-Mar-mid-Nov: 8am-6pm Mon-Fri, 8:30am-6pm Sat, 9am-6pm Sun (mid-Nov-mid-Mar: to 5:30pm)

This cemetery is the resting place of many illustrious Parisians. Sculptures nestle among the funerary art, creating a peaceful haven in the tree-lined grounds.

The Montparnasse Cemetery was planned by Napoleon outside the city walls to replace the numerous, congested, small cemeteries within the old city, viewed as a health hazard at the turn of the 19th century. It was opened in 1824 and contains the graves of many notable, particularly Left Bank, personalities. Like all French cemeteries, it is divided into rigidly aligned paths. The Rue Émile Richard cuts it into two parts, the Grand Cimetière and the Petit Cimetière.

The Kiss by Brancusi, who is buried just off Rue Émile Richard ↑

Did You Know?

The cemetery's tower is the remains of a 17th-century windmill.

Jean-Paul Sartre and Simone de Beauvoir

△ The famous existentialist couple, undisputed leaders of the post-War literary scene, lie here close to their Left Bank haunts.

Jean Seberg

▶ The Hollywood actress, chosen by Jean-Luc Godard as the star of his film *À Bout de Souffle*, was the epitome of American blonde beauty, youth and candour.

Serge Gainsbourg

The French singer, composer and pop icon of the 1970s and 80s is best known for his wistful and irreverent songs. He was married to the actress Jane Birkin.

Samuel Beckett

◀ The great Irish playwright, renowned for *Waiting for Godot*, spent most of his life in Paris. He died in 1989.

Man Ray

The American photographer immortalized the Montparnasse artistic and café scene in the 1920s and 30s.

André Citroën

▶ The engineer and industrialist, who died in 1935, founded the famous French car firm.

CHARLES BAUDELAIRE

The cemetery contains the cenotaph of Charles Baudelaire, the great poet and critic. Baudelaire, who was born and died in Paris, shocked the world with his frank and decadent collection of poems *Les Fleurs du Mal*, published in 1857. His work has had a widespread literary influence, and has even inspired rock stars such as Mick Jagger.

EXPERIENCE MORE

②

Tour Montparnasse

📍F10 🏠33 Ave du Maine
75015 Ⓜ Montparnasse-
Bienvenüe ⏱9:30am-
10:30pm Sun-Thu (to 11pm
Fri & Sat) 🌐tourmont
parnasse56.com

This was Europe's largest office
block when it was built in 1973.
At 210 m (690 ft) high, it totally
dominates the area's skyline. A
lift takes you up to the obser-
vation floor with its panoramic
bar. For the best views you'll
need to climb up the last three
floors to the open-air observa-
tory. The views from here
are spectacular – up to 40 km
(25 miles) on a clear day. The
tower will be closed for major
renovations – current plans
include the installation of solar
panels and a green roof – in the
run-up to the Olympics from
some time in 2021 to 2024.

③

Notre-Dame-du-Travail

📍F11 🏠36 Rue
Guilleminot 75014
Ⓜ Pernety ⏱7:30am-
7:45pm Mon-Fri, 8:45am-
7:30pm Sat & Sun
🌐notredamedutravail.net

This church dates from 1901
and is made of an unusual
mix of materials: stone, rubble
and bricks over a riveted
steel-and-iron framework.
It was the creation of Father
Soulange-Bodin, a priest who
organized cooperatives and
sought to reconcile labour and
capitalism. Local parishioners
raised the money for its
construction, but lack of funds
meant that many features,
such as the bell towers, were
never built. On the façade
hangs the Sebastopol Bell,
a trophy from the Crimean
War given to the people
of the Plaisance district by
Napoleon III. The Art Nouveau
interior has been restored and
features paintings of saints.

---

④

Institut Pasteur

📍E10 🏠25-28 Rue du
Docteur Roux 75015
Ⓜ Pasteur 🌐pasteur.fr

The Institut Pasteur, France's
leading medical research
centre, was founded by the
scientist Louis Pasteur in
1888–9. He discovered the
process of milk pasteurization,
as well as vaccines against
rabies and anthrax. In 2020, the
institute set up a coronavirus
task force to launch and
coordinate COVID-19 research
projects. The centre houses
a museum that includes a
reconstruction of Pasteur's

Tour Montparnasse,
as seen from the
Eiffel Tower ↓

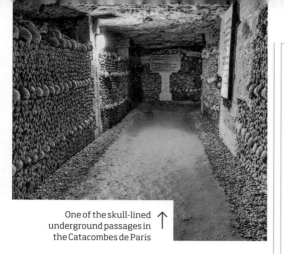

One of the skull-lined underground passages in the Catacombes de Paris

apartment and laboratory. Pasteur's tomb is in a basement crypt built in the style of a small Byzantine chapel. The museum is currently closed for renovation and will reopen in late 2024.

Catacombes de Paris

📍H11 🏠1 Ave du Colonel Henri Rol-Tanguy 75014 Ⓜ️Denfert-Rochereau ⏰9:45am–8:30pm Tue–Sun, advance booking recommended 🗓1 Jan, 1 May, 25 Dec 🌐catacombes. paris.fr

In 1786, a monumental project began here: the removal of the millions of skulls and bones from the unsanitary city cemetery in Les Halles to the quarries at the base of the three "mountains": Montparnasse, Montrouge and Montsouris. Initially the bones were placed haphazardly, but from the early 19th century they were used to adorn the walls in decorative patterns.

During World War II, the French Resistance set up its headquarters here. Above the door outside are the words "Stop! This is the empire of death." Visiting the catacombs has become very popular, so reserving your ticket well in advance is advised. Guided tours in French are at 1pm on Thursdays.

Fondation Cartier

📍H11 🏠261 Blvd Raspail 75014 Ⓜ️Raspail ⏰11am–8pm Tue–Sun (to 10pm Tue) 🗓1 Jan, 25 Dec 🌐fondationcartier.com

This foundation for art and architecture is in a building designed by Jean Nouvel. He has created an air of transparency and light, as well as incorporating a cedar of Lebanon, which was planted in 1823 by François-René de Chateaubriand. The structure complements the nature of the exhibitions of progressive art, which showcase personal, group or thematic displays.

Musée Libération Leclerc Moulin

📍H11 🏠4 Ave du Colonel Rol-Tanguy – Place Denfert Rochereau 75014 Ⓜ️Denfert-Rochereau ⏰10am–6pm Tue–Sun 🌐museeliberation-leclerc-moulin.paris.fr

Opened in 2019, on the 75th anniversary of Paris's liberation, the Museum of the Liberation of Paris joins the Musée du Général Leclerc and Musée de Jean Moulin in a new facility to celebrate the city's emancipation during World War II. The museum displays some 7,000 objects, with original newspapers, photos and audio displays allowing visitors to relive this pivotal time in French history.

If you head underground, you can see a reconstruction of the command centre during the Liberation, where Colonel Rol-Tanguy directed Parisian forces at the end of the German Occupation. Not only interesting and engaging, the entire collection is also free.

EAT & DRINK

La Coupole

An Art Nouveau brasserie serving up meaty classics.

📍G10 🏠102 Blvd du Montparnasse 75014 🌐lacoupole-paris.com

€€€

Closerie des Lilas

A classic brasserie, once frequented by Hemingway.

📍H10 🏠171 Blvd du Montparnasse 75006 🌐closeriedeslilas.fr

€€€

Les Papilles

Wine bottles line the walls of this friendly local.

📍J9 🏠30 Rue Gay-Lussac 75005 🗓Sun, Mon 🌐lespapillesparis.fr

€€€

8 Musée Bourdelle

📍 F10 🏛 18 Rue Antoine Bourdelle 75015
Ⓜ Montparnasse-Bienvenüe, Falguière
🕐 10am-6pm Tue-Sun
🚫 Public hols 🌐 bourdelle.paris.fr

The prolific sculptor Antoine Bourdelle lived and worked in the studio here from 1884 until his death in 1929. The house, studio and garden are now a museum. Among the 900 sculptures on display are the original plaster casts of his monumental works planned for wide public squares. They include the group of sculptures for the relief decoration of the Théâtre des Champs-Élysées. Frequent temporary exhibitions, for which there is an entry fee, complement the free permanent collection.

9 Palais du Luxembourg

📍 H9 🏛 15 Rue de Vaugirard 75006
Ⓜ Odéon 🚉 Luxembourg
🌐 senat.fr/visite

Now the home of the French Senate, this palace was designed by Salomon de Brosse in the style of Florence's Pitti Palace to remind Marie de Médici, widow of Henri IV, of her native town. By the time it was finished (1631), Marie had been banished, but it remained a royal palace until the Revolution. In World War II, it was the headquarters of the Luftwaffe. The building is currently accessible to individual visitors only during the European Heritage Days, which take place on the third weekend in September.

10 Musée du Luxembourg

📍 H9 🏛 19 Rue de Vaugirard 75006 Ⓜ St-Sulpice 🚉 Luxembourg
🕐 10:30am-7pm daily during exhibitions; check website 🚫 1 May & 25 Dec
🌐 museeduluxembourg.fr

Orginally housed in the east wing of the Palais du Luxembourg, France's first public gallery moved to this building, the palace's grand former orangery, in 1886. The collection contained works by renowned artists such as Leonardo da Vinci, Van Dyck and Rembrandt, many of which have since been moved to the Louvre. Following extensive renovations, today the museum hosts impressive temporary exhibitions on leading artists, including Rubens, Cézanne and Pissaro.

←

One of the many statues in the Musée Bourdelle

11 Jardin du Luxembourg

📍 H9 🏛 Blvd St-Michel/Rue Guynemer 75006 Ⓜ Odéon
🚉 Luxembourg 🕐 Dawn-dusk daily 🌐 senat.fr/visite/jardin

A green oasis covering 25 ha (60 acres) in the heart of the Left Bank, the Jardin du Luxembourg is one of the most popular parks in Paris. The beautifully landscaped gardens are centred around the Palais du Luxembourg and feature an octagonal basin that is often surrounded by children sailing wooden toy boats, which can be hired here.

The Jardin du Luxembourg was created at the request of Marie de Médici, who had it designed as a fitting reminder of the Boboli Gardens at the Pitti Palace, in her home town of Florence. The original garden measured 8 ha (20 acres); what remains of it today are the large pond, the Fontaine Médicis and

↑ The stately Palais du Luxembourg in the gorgeous Jardin du Luxembourg

A green oasis covering 25 ha (60 acres) in the heart of the Left Bank, the Jardin du Luxembourg is one of the most popular parks in Paris.

2,000 elm trees. Statues were placed throughout the park in 1848. They include those of the queens of France, famous French women – Sainte Geneviève is an impressive example – and, later, famous writers and artists, too, totalling 106 statues.

The garden is a great space for children, with activities such as a puppet theatre starring the famous character Guignol, a fenced-in play-ground, a carousel and tennis courts. Adults can play chess or bridge, wander through the open-air photography exhibitions or grab a chair and enjoy a free concert.

12

Musée Zadkine

🔲 H10 🏠 100 bis Rue d'Assas 75006 Ⓜ Notre-Dame-des-Champs 🕐 10am–6pm Tue–Sun 🚫 Public hols 🌐 zadkine. paris.fr

The Russian-born sculptor Ossip Zadkine lived here from 1928 until his death in 1967.

The small house, studio and garden contain his works. Here he produced his great commemorative sculpture *Ville Détruite*, commissioned by Rotterdam after World War II, and two monuments to Vincent van Gogh. The museum's works span the development of Zadkine's style, from his Cubist begin-nings to Expressionism and Abstractionism.

FONTAINE MÉDICIS

This Baroque fountain in the Jardin du Luxembourg, thought to have been designed by Salomon de Brosse, was built in 1624 in the style of an Italian grotto. It stands at the end of a long pond filled with goldfish. The mythological figures were added much later by Auguste Ottin (1866) and represent Polyphemus discovering the lovers Acis and Galatea.

A SHORT WALK
MONTPARNASSE

Distance 2.5 km (1.5 miles) **Nearest Metro** Gaîté
Time 25 minutes

Renowned for its mix of art and high living (Picasso, Hemingway, Matisse and Modigliani were frequent visitors to the area), Montparnasse offers a pleasant mixture of bars, cafés and art galleries. Take a detour on this walk by visiting the Cimetière du Montparnasse, where, along tree-lined avenues, you'll be able to pay your respects to many Parisian and international icons.

Did You Know?

Artists Giacometti and Modigliani were students at the Académie de la Grande-Chaumière.

The Tour Montparnasse, once Europe's tallest tower block, rests on 56 piles that extend 62 m (203 ft) below the surface (p284).

0 metres   100
0 yards   100   N ↑

↑ Sculpture at the Cimetière du Montparnasse

RUE DU DÉPART

RUE D' ODESSA

RUE DU MONTPARNASSE

BLVD DU

BLVD EDGAR

M

Metro Edgar Quinet

The Cimetière du Montparnasse is the final resting place of several Parisian icons (p282).

RUE DE LA GAÎTÉ

The Théâtre Montparnasse at No 31 has fully restored its original 1880s décor.

▶ **START**

↑ The Art Deco-style interior
of the iconic La Coupole

The statue of Balzac by Auguste
Rodin was erected in 1939, and
stands 3 m (10 ft) tall.

Rue Bréa has a variety of shops,
restaurants and hotels, all
within a 90-m (300-ft) stretch.

La Coupole, a traditional
brasserie-style café, with
its large enclosed terrace,
opened in 1927 and
became a famous
meeting place for artists
and writers (p285).

The celebrated Académie
de la Grande-Chaumière
art school was founded
at No 14 in 1904.

MONTPARNASSE

RUE BRÉA

RUE J. CHAPLAIN

RUE NOTRE DAME DES CHAMPS

RUE DE LA GDE CHAUMIÈRE

Metro
Vavin

SQ DELAMBRE

RUE HUYGHENS

BLVD RASPAIL

RUE LÉOPOLD ROBERT

QUINET

FINISH

Metro
Raspail

Must Sees

❶ Bois de Boulogne

❷ Château and Bois de Vincennes

❸ The Palace and Gardens of Versailles

❹ Disneyland® Paris

Experience More

❺ La Défense

❻ Musée Marmottan Monet

❼ Basilique-Cathédrale de St-Denis

❽ Potager du Roi

❾ Marché aux Puces de St-Ouen

❿ Marché aux Puces de la Porte de Vanves

BEYOND THE CENTRE

The area beyond the Périphérique (ring road) once served as a country retreat for the aristocracy, with the medieval Château de Vincennes as the royal residence. It was usurped in the 17th century by Louis XIV's spectacular palace at Versailles, where the excessive displays of opulence were brought to a violent end during the Revolution of 1789. An industrial boom in the 19th century was followed by a number of large-scale construction projects in the 20th century, including blocks of social housing and the Périphérique. Today, the varied neighbourhoods of the suburbs are home to the vast majority of Paris's citizens.

BOIS DE BOULOGNE

🏠 75016 Ⓜ Porte Maillot, Porte Dauphine, Porte d'Auteuil, Les Sablons 🕐 Wood: 24 hrs daily;
gardens: 8/9/9:30/10am–dusk daily (depending on season) ⓦ Jardin d'Acclimatation:
jardindacclimatation.fr; Théâtre de Verdure du Jardin Shakespeare: letheatredeverdure.
com; Fondation Louis Vuitton: fondationlouisvuitton.fr

Between the western edges of Paris and the Seine, this 865-ha (2,137-acre) park
offers greenery for strolling and a boating lake, plus opportunities for horse-riding,
picnicking or a day at the races. It is a favourite outdoor retreat with Parisians,
especially on summer weekends.

The remains of a royal hunting ground, the many beautiful areas around the Bois include the Hippodrome de Longchamp racecourse, the Jardin d'Acclimatation amusement park and Roland Garros, home to the French Tennis Open championships. Hidden within its borders is the Théâtre de Verdure, an open-air playhouse that puts on Shakespeare, dance and musical performances in summer. The charming Bagatelle Gardens feature architectural follies and an 18th-century orangery famous for its rose garden. Opened in 2014, Frank Gehry's stunning Fondation Louis Vuitton is a cultural centre dedicated to modern art.

Did You Know?

The orangery was built in 64 days as a bet between the Comte d'Artois and Marie-Antoinette.

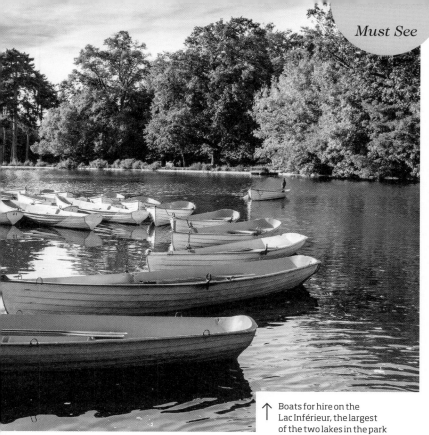

↑ Boats for hire on the Lac Inférieur, the largest of the two lakes in the park

EAT

Le Frank
A high-end restaurant within the Fondation Louis Vuitton.

🏠 8 Ave du Mahatma Gandhi, 75116 🕐 Noon-7pm daily, dinner Fri & Sat 🌐 restaurant lefrank.fr

€€€

① The "sails" of the Fondation Louis Vuitton are made of 3,600 glass panels.

② The Château de Bagatelle was built by Louis XVI's brother, the Comte d'Artois.

③ A statue of French tennis legend Henri Cochet stands outside Roland Garros.

2

CHÂTEAU ET BOIS DE VINCENNES

⬛ 1 Ave de Paris, 94300 Vincennes Ⓜ Château de Vincennes 🚆 Vincennes
🕐 Château: mid-May–mid-Sep: 10am–6pm daily (mid-Sep–mid-May: to 5pm daily); Bois de Vincennes: 24 hrs daily 🚫 Château: 1 Jan, 1 May & 25 Dec
🌐 chateau-de-vincennes.fr

Guarded by an imposing medieval keep, the sprawling Bois de Vincennes is a verdant wonderland. With boating lakes, formal gardens and numerous walking and cycling trails, it is the perfect playground in which to escape the city.

The Château de Vincennes was once a royal residence; it was here that Henry V of England died of dysentery in 1422. Abandoned when the Palace of Versailles was completed, the château was subsequently converted into an arsenal by Napoleon.

The 14th-century keep is the tallest in Europe and is a fine example of medieval military architecture. It houses the château's museum. The Gothic chapel features beautiful stone rose windows, while two 17th-century pavilions house a fascinating museum of army insignia.

Once a royal hunting ground, the Bois de Vincennes was given to the City of Paris by Napoleon III in 1860. Baron Haussmann's landscape architect added a number of ornamental lakes and cascades. Among the forest's main attractions is the oldest funfair in France (open from Palm Sunday to end of May) and the renovated Parc Zoologique de Paris.

> **Once a royal hunting ground, the Bois de Vincennes was given to the City of Paris by Napoleon III in 1860.**

The château, used as a prison from the 16th to the 19th centuries ↑

↑ Lake Daumesnil, one of four artificial lakes in the park

EAT

Le Château des Vignerons
French dishes with an international twist.

⬛ 17 Rue des Vignerons, 94300 Vincennes
🕐 Sun 🌐 chateau desvignerons.com

€€€

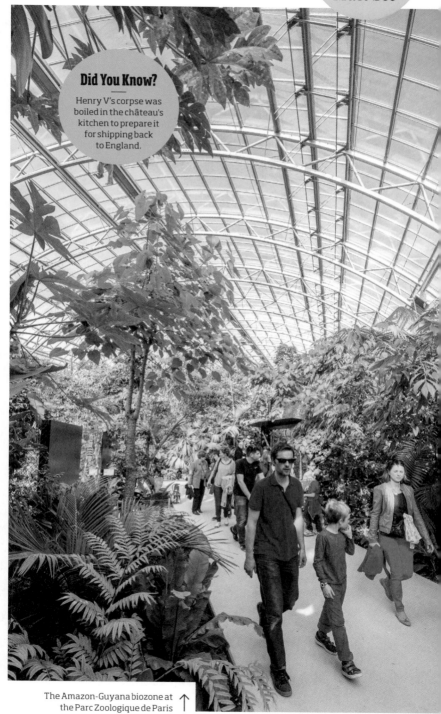

Did You Know?

Henry V's corpse was boiled in the château's kitchen to prepare it for shipping back to England.

The Amazon-Guyana biozone at the Parc Zoologique de Paris ↑

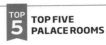

THE PALACE AND GARDENS OF VERSAILLES

🏛 Place d'Armes, 78000 Versailles 🚌 Versailles Express from Eiffel Tower 🚆 Versailles-Château-Rive Gauche, Versailles Chantiers ⏰ Palace: 9am–5pm Tue–Sun; gardens: 8am–6pm; booking required 🚫 Mon, 1 Jan, 25 Dec 🌐 chateauversailles.fr

This stunning royal residence is overwhelming in its scale and opulence. The spectacular, lavishly decorated palace and vast gardens, complete with fountains, landscaped topiary and even a model farm, make Versailles the top day trip from the centre of Paris.

The Palace

Starting around 1662 with his father's hunting lodge, Louis XIV built the largest palace in Europe, housing up to 20,000 people at a time. Architects Louis Le Vau and Jules Hardouin-Mansart designed the buildings, which grew as a series of "envelopes" around the lodge. The Opera House was added in 1770.

The sumptuous main apartments are on the first floor of the vast château complex. These were richly decorated by Charles Le Brun with coloured marbles, stone and wood carvings, murals, velvet, silver and gilded furniture. The climax is the Hall of Mirrors, where 357 great mirrors face 17 tall arched windows.

TOP FIVE PALACE ROOMS

Salon de Vénus
A statue of Louis XIV stands amid this room's rich marble décor.

Salon d'Apollon
Designed by Le Brun and dedicated to the god Apollo, this was Louis XIV's throne room.

Salon de la Guerre
The room's theme of war is dramatically reinforced by the stuccoed relief of Louis XIV riding to victory.

Hall of Mirrors
This glittering room stretches 73 m (240 ft) along the west façade.

Queen's Bedchamber
In this room, the queens of France gave birth to the royal children in full public view.

The palace and gardens of Versailles, the epitome of royal grandeur ↓

EXPERIENCE Beyond the Centre

1 The Marble Courtyard is decorated with marble paving, urns, busts and a gilded balcony.

2 Mansart's last great work, the two-storey Baroque Chapelle Royale was Louis XIV's final addition to Versailles.

3 The South Wing's original apartments for great nobles were replaced by Louis-Philippe's museum of French history.

The formal gardens, complete with geometric paths and shrubberies

The Gardens

The grounds of Versailles are no less impressive than the palace. Designed by the great landscaper André Le Nôtre, the formal gardens are a masterpiece: sculptural fountains and secluded groves sit amid geometric flower beds and hedges. The 1.7-km- (1-mile-) long Grand Canal leads from the gardens to the enormous park, which features wooded areas and agricultural fields delineated by a network of footpaths. The grounds also encompass the Grand Trianon and Petit Trianon palaces, built as private apartments for Louis XIV and Louis V, as well as the Queen's Hamlet – a life-size model village built for Marie-Antoinette that was also a functioning farm.

> The formal gardens are a masterpiece: sculptural fountains and secluded groves sit amid geometric flower beds and hedges.

The Grand Trianon, built by Louis XIV in 1687 to escape the rigours of court life

EAT

Ore
This Alain Ducasse dining experience in the Pavillon Dufour is as luxurious as the château it occupies.

🏠 Château de Versailles, 78000 Versailles
Ⓦ ducasse-chateauversailles.com

€€€

Angelina
The iconic tea house has two outposts in Versailles – one in the Pavillon d'Orléans and one at the Petit Trianon – both serving a selection of snacks and delectable pastries.

🏠 Château de Versailles, 78000 Versailles
Ⓦ angelina-paris.fr

€€€

Did You Know?

One-third of the estate's budget went to the fountains. Today they only go on during the summer months.

1 The cottages in the Queen's Hamlet were inspired by rural French architecture. Although rustic on the exterior, inside they were richly furnished.

2 During the Grands Eaux Nocturnes in the summer, the gardens of Versailles come alive with superb illuminations and installations.

3 Built in 1762 as a retreat for Louis XV, the Petit Trianon became a favourite of Marie-Antoinette.

❹ 🎟️ 🎭 🍽️ 🖥️ 🛍️

DISNEYLAND®
PARIS

🏠 **77777 Marne-la-Vallée** 🚌 **Disneyland® Paris Express
from Gare du Nord, Opéra, Châtelet and the Eiffel Tower**
🚆 **Marne-la-Vallée–Chessy** 🕐 **Disneyland® Park: 10am–
11pm in high season (closes earlier in low season); Walt
Disney Studios® Park: 10am–9pm in high season (closes
earlier in low season)** 🌐 **disneylandparis.com**

**Unbeatable for complete escapism, combined with
vibrant excitement and sheer energy, Disneyland®
Paris offers extreme rides, gentle experiences and
phenomenal visual effects.**

The resort is built on a huge scale – the 53-ha
(140-acre) site encompasses two theme parks; seven
hotels; a shopping, dining and entertainment village; an
ice-skating rink; a lake; two convention centres; and a golf
course. The theme parks are split into Disneyland® Park and
the Walt Disney Studios® Park. The former, with more than
50 rides and attractions, celebrates Hollywood folklore and
fantasies, while the latter highlights the ingenuity involved
in cinema, animation and television production with
interactive exhibits and live shows.

DISNEY VILLAGE

The fun does not
have to end when
the two parks close.
Disney Village offers
a host of evening
entertainment
options – including
a cinema, concerts
and Buffalo Bill's
Wild West Show –
as well as numerous
restaurants and
shops. Seasonal
events take place
all year, including
celebrations for
Easter, Halloween
and New Year.

Did You Know?

Sleeping Beauty's castle was designed to contrast with the grey Parisian skies.

↑ The view from Alice's Curious Labyrinth in Disneyland® Park

1 Crush's Coaster® is one of the many thrilling rides in Walt Disney Studios® Park.

2 Take a spin in the Mad Hatter's Tea Cups in Disneyland® Park's Fantasyland®.

3 The parade in Disneyland® Park features characters from films such as *Toy Story*.

DISNEYLAND® PARK

Disneyland® Park is comprised of five areas. Main Street represents a fantasy small-town America, its Victorian façades fronting interesting stores and food outlets. Frontierland®, a homage to America's Wild West, hosts some of the park's most popular attractions, while wild rides and Audio-Animatronics are the draw at Adventureland®. The buildings in Fantasyland® are modelled on those in animated movies, and contain many attractions for younger children. Science fiction and the future are the themes at Discoveryland®, home to the popular multi-loop ride Star Wars Hyperspace Mountain.

TOP 3 RIDES IN DISNEYLAND® PARK

Star Wars Hyperspace Mountain
Formerly known as Space Mountain®, this iconic rollercoaster draws crowds from the outset but at the end of the day you can often walk straight on.

Big Thunder Mountain
This wild rollercoaster ride on a speeding runaway mine train is a crowd favourite.

Pirates of the Caribbean
This boat ride takes you on a thrilling journey through underground prisons and past fighting galleons.

← The park, home to rides such as Indiana Jones™ and the Temple of Peril *(below)*

The entrance to Walt Disney Studios® Park, with the Earful Tower ↑

↑ The four-wheeled Cars Quatre Roues Rallye attraction

↑ The underwater animated world of Crush's Coaster®

WALT DISNEY STUDIOS® PARK

The five production zones at Walt Disney Studios® Park reveal the secrets of movie-making. Inside the giant studio gates on the Front Lot, Disney Studio 1 houses a film set boulevard, complete with stylized street façades and venues such as the 1930s-style Club Swankedero. Toon Studio® and Worlds of Pixar® contain rides and exhibits inspired by various iconic Disney and Pixar characters, and includes La Place de Rémy, home to the 4D experience Ratatouille: A Recipe for Adventure. The Production Courtyard® offers the chance to see behind the scenes on the Studio Tram Tour®, among other attractions; while rides at the Avengers Campus® enable you to save the world alongside Marvel heroes.

→ Mickey Mouse casting his magic over the Toon Studio® zone

EXPERIENCE MORE

La Défense

📍 1 Parvis de la Défense
Ⓜ/🚇 La Défense 🕐 La
Grande Arche: 10am–
7pm daily 🌐 parisla
defense.com

This skyscraper business district on the western edge of Paris is one of Europe's largest modern office developments and covers 80 ha (198 acres). It was launched in 1958 to create a new home for leading French and multinational companies. Since then, a major artistic scheme has transformed several of the squares into fascinating open-air museums.

In 1989, one of Paris's most striking landmarks, La Grande Arche, was added to the complex – an enormous hollow cube large enough to contain Notre-Dame cathedral. This was designed by Danish architect Johan Otto von Spreckelsen as part of major construction works,

or *Grands Travaux*, which were initiated by (and are now a memorial to) the late President François Mitterrand. You can take a lift to the top of the arch for some great views. There's also a restaurant and an exhibition space for photojournalism.

Musée Marmottan Monet

📍 2 Rue Louis-Boilly 75016
Ⓜ Muette 🕐 10am–6pm
Tue–Sun (to 9pm Thu)
🔒 1 Jan, 1 May, 25 Dec
🌐 marmottan.fr

In 1932, art historian Paul Marmottan bequeathed his 19th-century mansion and his Renaissance, Consular and First Empire collections of paintings and furniture to the Institut de France, and a museum was established. The focus of the museum changed in 1934 after the bequest by

↑ Claude Monet's glasses, Musée Marmottan Monet

Michel Monet of 65 paintings by his father, Claude Monet. Some of Monet's most famous paintings are here, among them *Impression, Sunrise*, a beautiful canvas from the *Rouen Cathedral* series, and several *Water Lilies*.

In addition, part of Monet's personal art collection passed to the museum, including paintings by Camille Pissarro and works by the Impressionists Pierre Auguste Renoir and Alfred Sisley. The museum also displays some exquisite medieval illuminated manuscripts.

↓ Shiny modern office blocks at La Défense business district

→

Tombs within the Basilique-Cathédrale de St-Denis

7

Basilique-Cathédrale de St-Denis

🏠 1 Rue de la Légion a'Honneur, 93200 St-Denis Ⓜ Basilique de St-Denis 🚆 St-Denis 🕐 Apr–Sep: 10am–6:15pm Mon–Sat, noon–6:15pm Sun; Oct–Mar: 10am–5:15pm Mon–Sat, noon–5:15pm Sun 🚫 1 Jan, 1 May, 25 Dec 🌐 saint-denis-basilique.fr

Constructed between 1137 and 1281, the cathedral is on the site of the tomb of St Denis, the first bishop of Paris, who was beheaded in 250. The building was the original influence for Gothic art. From Merovingian times, it was a burial place for rulers of France. During the Revolution, many tombs were desecrated and scattered, but the best were stored, and now represent a collection of funerary art. Memorials include those of Dagobert, Henri II and Catherine de Medici, and Louis XVI and Marie-Antoinette. Guided tours provide great views of the nave.

8

Potager du Roi

🏠 10 Rue du Maréchal-Joffre, 78000 Versailles 🕐 10am–6pm Tue–Fri (Apr–Oct: also Sat & Sun; Nov & Dec: also 10am–1pm Sat) 🚆 Versailles-Château-Rive Gauche 🌐 potager-du-roi.fr

When Louis XIV built Versailles, he decided that it would be prudent for a king to have his own vegetable garden (poisoning was a constant threat in the château). Jean-Baptiste de La Quintinie developed the *potager* – vegetable patch –

for Louis in 1678. At first, the swampy ground proved difficult to master, but eventually La Quintinie was producing all sorts of fruits and vegetables for the king, including summer produce in the winter. The garden continued to function in several capacities after the Revolution, becoming a centre for education and horticultural schools. In 1991, the Potager du Roi opened up to the public for visits. There is a shop, which sells seasonal produce pulled from the garden on Tuesdays.

9

Marché aux Puces de St-Ouen

🏠 Rue des Rosiers, 93400 St-Ouen Ⓜ Porte de Clignancourt, Garibaldi 🕐 10am–6pm Sat–Sun, 11am–5pm Mon, 8am–noon Wed 🌐 marcheauxpuces-saintouen.com

This is the oldest, most expensive and largest of the Paris flea markets, covering 6 ha (15 acres). In the 19th century, rag merchants and

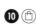

Did You Know?
Less than a quarter of Paris's 11.1 million inhabitants live within the 20 arrondissements.

tramps would gather outside the city limits and offer their wares for sale. By the 1920s, there was a proper market here, where masterpieces could sometimes be purchased cheaply from the often uninformed sellers. Today, it is divided into specialist markets, and is known especially for its profusion of furniture and ornaments from the Second Empire (1852–70). Few bargains are to be found these days, yet some 5 million people still flock here annually to browse among more than 2,500 stalls.

10

Marché aux Puces de la Porte de Vanves

🏠 Ave Georges Lafenestre & Ave Marc Sangnier 75014 Ⓜ Porte de Vanves 🕐 7am–2pm Sat & Sun 🌐 pucesde vanves.fr

Every Saturday and Sunday, bargain-hunters descend on this lively outdoor flea market. Visitors can pick through a wide selection of glassware, furniture and artworks, and a seemingly endless variety of odds and ends. There are always surprises. In 1989, the very first portrait ever taken by Louis Daguerre sold here at this market for the equivalent of €500, a modest sum for such a monumental piece of photographic history. There are real finds to be had if you look hard enough – go early to beat the crowds and prepare to spend a few hours browsing.

NEED TO KNOW

The Metro whizzing across the Pont de Bir Hakeim

BEFORE YOU GO

Things change, so plan ahead to make the most of your trip. Be prepared for all eventualities by considering the following points before you travel.

AT A GLANCE

CURRENCY
Euro (EUR)

AVERAGE DAILY SPEND

SAVE	SPEND	SPLURGE
€60	€165	€300+

BOTTLED WATER	COFFEE	BEER	DINNER FOR TWO
€1.50	€2.50	€6	€60

ESSENTIAL PHRASES

Hello	Bonjour
Goodbye	Au revoir
Please	S'il vous plaît
Thank you	Merci
Do you speak English	Parlez-vous anglais?
I don't understand...	Je ne comprends pas

ELECTRICITY SUPPLY

Power sockets are type C and E, fitting two-pronged plugs. Standard voltage is 230 volts.

Passports and Visas

For entry requirements, including visas, consult your nearest French embassy or check the **France-Visas** website. EU nationals do not need a visa for a stay of up to three months. Citizens of the UK, US, Canada, Australia and New Zealand do not need a visa for stays of up to three months but, from late 2023, must apply in advance for the European Travel Information and Authorization System **(ETIAS)**.
ETIAS
🔲 etiasvisa.com
France-Visas
🔲 france-visas.gouv.fr

Government Advice

Now more than ever, it is important to consult both your and the French government's advice before travelling. The **UK Foreign and Commonwealth Office**, the **US State Department**, the **Australian Department of Foreign Affairs and Trade** and **Gouvernement France** offer the latest information on security, health and local regulations.
Australian Department of Foreign Affairs and Trade
🔲 smartraveller.gov.au
Gouvernement France
🔲 gouvernement.fr
UK Foreign and Commonwealth Office
🔲 gov.uk/foreign-travel-advice
US State Department
🔲 travel.state.gov

Customs Information

You can find information on the laws relating to goods and currency taken in or out of France on the official **France Tourism** website.
France Tourism
🔲 ee.france.fr

Insurance

We recommend that you take out a comprehensive insurance policy covering theft, loss of belongings, medical care, cancellations and delays, and read the small print carefully.

EU citizens are eligible for free emergency medical care in France, provided they have a valid EHIC (European Health Insurance Card) or **GHIC** (UK Global Health Insurance Card).

GHIC

W ghic.org.uk

Vaccinations

No inoculations are needed for France.

Booking Accommodation

Paris offers a huge variety of accommodation, including luxury five-star hotels, family-run B&Bs, budget hostels and private apartments. Tourists pour in from May to September, but Parisians pour out en masse in August.

Money

Most establishments accept major credit, debit and prepaid currency cards, but it's always a good idea to carry some cash too. Contactless payments are widely accepted in Paris.

Tipping generally isn't required, but it is considered polite to leave a few coins in recognition of good service.

Travellers with Specific Requirements

Paris's historic buildings and cobbled streets can make the city tricky to navigate. However, there are many organizations working to improve accessibility in France's capital. The **Office du Tourisme et des Congrès** lists easily accessible sights and routes for visitors with mobility, visual or hearing impairment, while **Jaccede** has details of accessible museums, hotels, bars, restaurants and cinemas. The **Vianavigo** website provides information on accessible public transport, including a route planner that can be tailored to your specific needs, and **SNCF's** website has useful information on accessible train travel. **Les Compagnons du Voyage** will provide an escort for persons with limited mobility or visual impairment on public transport, for a small fee.

Jaccede

W jaccede.com

Les Compagnons du Voyage

W compagnons.com

Office du Tourisme et des Congrès

W parisinfo.com

SNCF

W asncf.com/fr

Vianavigo

W vianavigo.com

Language

French is the official language spoken in Paris. The French are fiercely proud of their language, but don't let this put you off. Mastering a few niceties goes a long way though you can get by without knowing the language at all.

Opening Hours

> The COVID-19 pandemic proved that situations can change suddenly. Always check before visiting attractions and hospitality venues for up-to-date hours and booking requirements.

Lunchtime Some shops and businesses close for an hour or two around noon.
Mondays Some museums, small shops, restaurants and bars are closed for the day.
Tuesdays National museums are closed for the day, except Versailles and the Musée d'Orsay, which are closed on Mondays.
Sundays Most shops are closed.
Public holidays Shops, museums and many attractions are usually closed.

PUBLIC HOLIDAYS

1 Jan	New Year's Day
Mar/Apr	Easter Monday
1 May	Labour Day
8 May	Victory 1945
14 Jul	Bastille Day
15 Aug	Assumption Day
1 Nov	All Saints' Day
11 Nov	Armistice 1918
25 Dec	Christmas Day

GETTING
AROUND

Paris has an efficient public transport system that will allow you to navigate the city's many sights with ease.

AT A GLANCE

PUBLIC TRANSPORT COSTS

Tickets are valid on all forms of public transport.

SINGLE

€1.90

(zones 1–3)

DAY TICKET

€13.20

(zones 1–3)

3-DAY TICKET

€29.40

(zones 1–3)

SPEED LIMIT

MOTORWAY

130 km/h (80 mph)

MAJOR ROADS

80 km/h (49 mph)

RING ROADS

70 km/h (43 mph)

URBAN AREAS

50 km/h (30 mph)

Arriving by Air

Paris has two major airports, Charles de Gaulle (also known as Roissy) and Orly, and one secondary airport, Beauvais, which serves mainly budget airlines. All three are well connected to the city centre by train, bus and taxi. Car rental facilities are also available, although driving in Paris is not recommended. For information on journey times and ticket prices between Paris's airports and the city centre, see the table opposite.

Airport Shuttles is a site that searches the best offers for services, including shared rides and private drivers, between the airports and your destination. It provides up-to-date prices for buses, taxis and all other options, allowing travellers to find what fits their budget.

The **RATP Roissybus** operates regular services from Charles de Gaulle, and RER trains (Line B) leave regularly every 5–15 minutes, calling at Gare du Nord, Châtelet-Les-Halles and several other major stations. The **Orlybus** shuttle links Orly with Denfert-Rochereau station.

The most direct way into Paris from Beauvais is by shuttle bus to Porte-Maillot. It is wise to book the 90-minute journey in advance online.

Airport Shuttles
W airportsshuttles.com
Le Bus Direct
W lebusdirect.com
Orlybus
W airport-orly.com/orly-bus.php

Train Travel

International Train Travel

Regular high-speed trains connect Paris's six international railway stations to numerous major cities across Europe. Reservations for these services are essential, as seats get booked up quickly, particularly during peak times.

You can buy tickets and passes for multiple international journeys from **Eurail** or **Interrail**; however, you may need to pay an additional reservation fee. Always check carefully before boarding that your pass is valid on the service you wish to use.

GETTING TO AND FROM THE AIRPORT

Airport	Transport	Journey Time	Price
Charles de Gaulle	Le Bus Direct Line 2	45–70 mins	€18
	Le Bus Direct Line 4	1 hr 20 mins	€18
	RATP Roissybus	1 hr 10 mins	€13.70
	RER	25–30 mins	€11.40
	Taxi	25–45 mins	€53–58
Orly	Le Bus Direct	20–60 mins	€12
	GO C	30 mins	€6.35
	RATP Orlybus	25–30 mins	€8.30
	Orlyval/RER	30–40 mins	€12.10
	Tram Line T7	30 mins	€1.90
	Taxi	25–45 mins	€32–37
Beauvais	Shuttle bus	1 hr 15 mins	€15.90
	Taxi	1 hr – 1 hr 30 mins	from €170

Eurostar runs a fast, regular service from London to central Paris via the Channel Tunnel.

Students and those under 26 can benefit from discounted rail travel both to and within France. For more information on discounted travel, visit the Eurail or Interrail website.

Thalys runs a high-speed service between Paris, Brussels and Amsterdam ten times a day, with a variety of special offers, package deals and half-price last-minute offers.

Eurail
W eurail.com
Eurostar
W eurostar.com
Interrail
W interrail.eu
Thalys
W thalys.com

Domestic Train Travel

Paris has six main train stations, located across the city, all of which serve different regions. The French state railway, **OUI SNCF**, has two services in Paris: the Banlieue suburban service and the Grandes Lignes, or long-distance service. Banlieue services operate within the five-zone network. Grandes Lignes operate throughout France. The TGV offers reliable high-speed routes which should be booked in advance. There are also a number of budget high-speed trains, such as **Ouigo**.

Before boarding a train, remember to time-punch (*composter*) tickets at the entrance to the train platform to validate your journey; this does not apply to e-tickets. Tickets for city transport cannot be used on Banlieue trains, with the exception of some RER tickets to stations with both SNCF and RER lines.

OUI SNCF
W oui.sncf.com
Ouigo
W ouigo.com

PARIS'S MAIN STATIONS

Station	Destinations Served
Gare de Lyon	Southern France, the Alps, Italy and Switzerland
Gare de l'Est	Eastern France, Austria, Switzerland and Germany.
Gare du Nord	Northeast France, Britain, Belgium, the Netherlands and Germany
Gare St-Lazare	Channel ports and Normandy
Gare d'Austerlitz	Southwest France, and the Loire Valley
Gare Montparnasse	Brittany and southwestern ports and Spain

Public Transport

The Metro, RER, buses and trams are all run by
RATP (Régie Autonome des Transports Parisiens).
Safety and hygiene measures, timetables, ticket
information, transport maps and more can be
found on their website.
RATP
w ratp.fr

Tickets

The Paris metropolitan area is divided into five
ticket zones. Central Paris is zone 1, Orly airport
and Versailles are in zone 4 and Charles de Gaulle
airport is in zone 5. The Metro serves zones 1–3.

To avoid buying paper tickets you can get a
Navigo pass, a rechargeable smart card that can
be used on the Metro, RER and buses. The
Navigo Easy costs €2 for the pass and can be
topped up with credit and with as many
standard fares as you like. The Passe Navigo
Découverte costs €5 for the pass and can then
be loaded with a week's unlimited travel in
zones 1–5. You will need a passport-sized photo
and to add your signature to the pass.

Visitors can also enjoy unlimited travel on the
Metro, RER and Paris buses with a Paris Visite
pass, valid for 1, 2, 3 or 5 consecutive days in
zones 1–3, or a Mobilis card, valid in the zones of
your choice for one day. Both of these are
available from the RATP. Children aged 4 and
under travel free, while children aged 10 and
under travel half price.

Bus-only tickets can be purchased on board
from the driver. All bus tickets must be validated
using the machine on the bus.
Navigo
w iledefrance-mobilites.fr/titres-et-tarifs

Metro and RER

The Paris Metro has 14 main lines and two
minor lines. The RER is a system of five lines
of commuter trains that travel underground in
central Paris and above ground in outlying areas.
The two systems overlap in the city centre.
RER trips outside the centre require special
tickets; fares to suburbs and nearby towns vary.

Buses and Trams

Most buses must be flagged down at
designated stops. Your ticket may be used for
transfers to other bus and tramway lines for
90 minutes (between the first and last
validation). Each time you change buses or
trams, you must validate your ticket again.
Exceptions to this rule are the Balabus, Orlybus
and Roissybus services, and lines 221, 297, 299,
350 and 351.

There are 48 night bus lines, called Noctilien,
serving Paris and its suburbs. The terminus for
most lines is Châtelet.

Eight tram lines, T1 to T8, operate in Paris,
mainly servicing the outskirts of the city. You can
travel on the trams using regular Metro tickets
and passes. They don't run past the most major
tourist attractions but can be a pleasant way to
see the outer reaches of Paris.

Long-Distance Bus Travel

Two major coach operators, **FlixBus** and
BlaBlaBus, link Paris to other towns in France
and destinations throughout Europe. Between
the two companies – low-cost alternatives to
planes and trains – travellers from Paris may
reach London, Brussels, Amsterdam, Milan and
Barcelona, as well as Warsaw, Zagreb and
Bucharest, among other cities.
BlaBlaBus
w blablacar.fr/bus
FlixBus
w global.flixbus.com

Taxis

Taxis can be hailed in the street or from one of
the 500 or so taxi ranks dotted around the city.
The meter will show an initial starting charge
(around €2.60). There is usually an additional
charge for more than three passengers.

Vélo taxis are motorized tricycle rickshaws
that offer a green alternative to traditional taxis.
G7 Taxis has a large fleet of electric and hybrid
cars. If you're after a motorcycle taxi, book with
CityBird. Taxi apps such as Uber, Free Now and
Bolt also operate in Paris.
Citybird
w city-bird.com
G7 Taxis
w g7.fr

Driving

Driving in Paris is not recommended. Traffic is
often heavy, there are many one-way streets and
parking is notoriously difficult and expensive.

Driving to Paris

Autoroutes (motorways) converge on Paris from
all directions. For those travelling from Britain
to Paris by road, the simplest way is to use
the Eurotunnel trains that run between the
terminals at Folkestone and Calais, which both
have direct motorway access.

Paris is surrounded by an outer ring road, the
Boulevard Périphérique. All motorways leading
to the capital link in to the Périphérique, which
separates the city from the suburbs. Each
former city gate (*porte*) corresponds to an exit
onto or from the Périphérique. Arriving
motorists should take time to check their
destination address and consult a map of central
Paris to find the closest corresponding *porte*.

Car Rental

To rent a car in France you must be 21 or over and have held a valid driver's licence for at least a year. You will also need to present a credit card to secure the rental deposit. Check the regulations regarding the type of driving licence you need to drive in France with your local automobile association before you travel.

Ada.Paris is a self-service car rental service that operates throughout Paris and the Paris region. You can pick up a car from one parking station, make your journey and park at any other station in the region.

Ada.Paris
🆆 ada.fr

Driving in Paris

Paris is a limited traffic zone and it is compulsory for all vehicles to display a Crit'Air sticker with a number ranging from 1 to 5, which denotes the level of pollution in ascending order. In the event of high pollution levels, vehicles with certain stickers may be banned from the road. The stickers can be purchased from the **Air Quality Certificate Service**.

Park in areas with a large "P" or *payant* sign on the pavement or road, and pay at the parking meter with *La Paris Carte* (available from any kiosk), a credit or debit card, or by using the **PaybyPhone** app *(p314)*.

Paris has numerous underground car parks, signposted by a white "P" on a blue background.

Air Quality Certificate Service
🆆 certificat-air.gouv.fr

Rules of the Road

Always drive on the right. Unless otherwise signposted, vehicles coming from the right have right of way. Cars on a roundabout usually have right of way, although the Arc de Triomphe is a hair-raising exception as cars give way to traffic on the right.

At all times, drivers must carry a valid driver's licence, registration and insurance documents. The wearing of seat belts is compulsory, and it is prohibited to sound your horn in the city. For motorbikes and scooters, the wearing of helmets and protective gloves is compulsory. In the city centre, it is against the law to use the bus lanes at any time of day. France strictly enforces its drink-drive limit *(p315)*.

Boats and Ferries

Arriving by Sea

A number of companies run passenger and vehicle ferry services from the UK.

P&O Ferries runs services from Dover to Calais, **Condor Ferries** operates between Poole and St-Malo and **DFDS Seaways** runs routes from Newhaven to Dieppe and from Dover

to Dunkirk and Calais. **Brittany Ferries** makes crossings from Plymouth to Roscoff, from Poole and Portsmouth to Cherbourg, and from Portsmouth to Le Havre and Caen. They also run an overnight service from Portsmouth to St-Malo.

Driving to Paris from Cherbourg takes about four hours; from Dieppe or Le Havre, about two and a half hours; and from Calais, two hours.

Brittany Ferries
🆆 brittany-ferries.co.uk
Condor Ferries
🆆 condorferries.co.uk
DFDS Seaways
🆆 dfdsseaways.co.uk
P&O Ferries
🆆 poferries.com

Paris by Boat

Paris's river-boat shuttle, the **Batobus**, runs every 20 to 45 minutes, with more frequent services in spring and summer. Tickets can be bought at Batobus stops and at RATP and tourist offices.

Batobus
🆆 batobus.com

Cycling

Paris is reasonably flat, manageably small and has many backstreets where traffic is restricted. The city now has around 1,000 km (620 miles) of cycle lanes, making exploring by bike easier and safer than ever. This is set to increase hugely over the next few years.

Bicycle Hire

The **Vélib'** shared bicycle scheme is available 24 hours a day. There are some 1,100 Vélib' docking terminals dotted throughout the city; payment is made via the smartphone app or by credit card at the terminals. For regular bikes, the first half-hour is €1, increasing by €1 for every additional half-hour; for electric bikes the first half-hour is €13, increasing by €2 for every additional half-hour.

Vélib'
🆆 velib-metropole.fr

Bicycle Tours

Bike About Tours offer trips to Paris's most famous landmarks, as well as "hidden Paris" and Versailles tours, in small groups or privately.

Bike About Tours
🆆 bikeabouttours.com

Walking

Walking is by far the most agreeable way to explore central Paris. Most sights are only a short distance apart. The Office du Tourisme et des Congrès has a number of walking itineraries on their website *(p309)*.

PRACTICAL
INFORMATION

A little local know-how goes a long way in Paris. Here you will find all the essential advice and information you will need during your stay.

AT A GLANCE

EMERGENCY NUMBERS

GENERAL EMERGENCY	FIRE SERVICE
112	**18**

POLICE	MEDICAL EMERGENCY
17	**15**

TIME ZONE
CET/CEST
Central European
Summer Time (CEST)
runs from end Mar
to end Oct.

TAP WATER
Unless stated
otherwise, tap
water in France
is safe to drink.

WEBSITES AND APPS

en.parisinfo.com
The official Paris tourist board website.
Le Fooding
No matter where you are in the city, find the nearest recommended restaurant in an instant.
PaybyPhone
Pay for on-street parking quickly and easily with this app.
Bonjour RATP
The official app from RATP, the city's public transport operator.

Personal Security

Paris is generally a safe city to visit. Petty theft is as common here as in most major cities. Pickpockets often frequent tourist spots and wander the Metro system and RER so guard your belongings at all times. To report a theft, go to the nearest police station (*commissariat de police*) within 24 hours, and bring ID with you. A list of police stations can be found on the Office du Tourisme et des Congrès website (*p309*). Get a copy of the crime report in order to make an insurance claim. If you have your passport stolen, or in the event of a serious crime or accident, contact your embassy.

When travelling late at night, avoid long transfers in Metro stations such as Châtelet-Les-Halles and Montparnasse. The last RER trains to and from outlying areas should also be avoided.

Paris is a diverse, mulitculutral city. As a rule, Parisians are accepting of all people, regardless of their race, gender or sexuality. Same-sex marriage was legalized in 2013 and France recognized the right to legally change your gender in 2016. Paris has a thriving LGBTQ+ scene, centred in the Marais district. The **Centre LGBT Paris Ile-de-France** offers advice and hosts regular events. It also has a library and bar.

Events in recent years have led to an increased army and police presence in Paris, which should be regarded as normal. Expect bag checks at most major attractions. Small groups of armed guards patrolling are common.
Centre LGBT Paris Ile-de-France
🔳 centrelgbtparis.org

Health

France has a world-class healthcare system. Emergency healthcare is free for all EU nationals with an EHIC card (*p308*). You may have to pay for treatment and reclaim the money later. For visitors from outside the EU, payment of medical expenses is the patient's responsibility. It is therefore important to arrange comprehensive medical insurance before travelling.

Paris hosptitals are listed on the **Assistance Publique** website. The most centrally located hospital is the Hôtel Dieu (Pl du Parvis Notre Dame). In the case of a dental emergency, **SOS Dentaire** will provide a prompt house call, but be prepared to pay a substantial fee. The **Centre Médical Europe** has a dental practice.

A green cross indicates a pharmacy. As well as selling medicines, pharmacies will advise on minor health problems and can give details of the nearest doctor. You can usually find details of the nearest 24-hour service on all pharmacy doors.

Assistance Publique
w aphp.fr

Centre Médical Europe
w centre-medical-europe.fr

SOS Dentaire
w sosdentaire.com

Smoking, Alcohol and Drugs

Smoking is prohibited in all public places, but is allowed on restaurant, café and pub terraces, as long as they are not enclosed.

The possession of narcotics is prohibited and could result in a prison sentence.

Unless stated otherwise, alcohol consumption on the streets is permitted. France has a strict limit of 0.05 per cent BAC (blood alcohol content) for drivers.

ID

There is no requirement for visitors to carry ID, but in the event of a routine check you may be asked to show your passport. If you don't have it with you, the police may escort you to wherever your passport is being kept.

Local Customs

Etiquette *(la politesse)* is important to Parisians. On entering a store or café, you are expected to say *"bonjour"* to staff, and when leaving to say *"au revoir"*. Be sure to add *"s'il vous plaît"* (please) when ordering something and *"pardon"* if you accidentally bump into someone.

The French usually shake hands on meeting someone for the first time. Friends and colleagues who know each other well greet each other with a kiss on each cheek. If you are unsure what's expected, wait to see if they proffer a hand or a cheek.

Visiting Churches and Cathedrals

Dress respectfully. Cover your torso and upper arms; ensure shorts and skirts cover your knees.

Mobile Phones and Wi-Fi

Free Wi-Fi hotspots provide fast internet access in more than 260 public places in Paris, including museums, parks and libraries. These are clearly signposted with the Paris Wi-Fi logo. Cafés and restaurants usually permit the use of their Wi-Fi on the condition that you make a purchase.

Visitors travelling to Paris with EU tariffs will be able to use their devices without being affected by data roaming charges. Users will be charged the same rates for data, SMS and voice calls as they would pay at home.

Post

Stamps *(timbres)* can be bought at post offices and *tabacs*. Most post offices have self-service machines to weigh and frank your mail.

Taxes and Refunds

VAT is around 20% in France. Non-EU residents can claim back tax on certain goods. Look out for the Global Refund Tax-Free sign, where the retailer will supply a form and issue a *détaxe* receipt. Present the goods receipt, *détaxe* receipt and passport at customs when you depart to receive your refund.

Discount Cards

Entry to some national and municipal museums is free on the first Sunday of each month.

Visitors under 18 years of age and EU passport holders aged 18–26 years are usually admitted free of charge to national museums, and there are sometimes discounts for students and over-60s who have ID showing their date of birth.

The **Paris Pass** offers access to over 60 attractions for 2, 3, 4 or 6 consecutive days. It also includes unlimited travel on the Metro, buses and RER within central Paris, and a ticket for a hop-on hop-off bus tour.

Paris Pass
w parispass.com

INDEX

Page numbers in **bold** type refer to main entries

PHRASE BOOK

IN AN EMERGENCY

Help!	Au secours!	oh sekoor
Stop!	Arrêtez!	aret-ay
Call a	Appelez un	apuh-lay uñ
doctor!	médecin!	medsañ
Call an	Appelez une	apuh-lay oon
ambulance!	ambulance!	oñboo-loñs
Call the	Appelez la	apuh-lay lah
police!	police!	poh-lees
Call the fire	Appelez les	apuh-lay leh
brigade!	pompiers!	poñ-peeyay
Where is the	Où est le téléphone	oo ay luh tehlehfon
nearest telephone?	le plus proche?	luh ploo prosh
Where is the	Où est l'hôpital	oo ay l'opeetal luh
nearest hospital?	le plus proche?	ploo prosh

COMMUNICATION ESSENTIALS

Yes	Oui	wee
No	Non	noñ
Please	S'il vous plaît	seel voo play
Thank you	Merci	mer-see
Excuse me	Excusez-moi	exkoo-zay mwah
Hello	Bonjour	boñzhoor
Goodbye	Au revoir	oh ruh-vwar
Good night	Bonsoir	boñ-swar
Morning	Le matin	matañ
Afternoon	L'après-midi	l'apreh-meedee
Evening	Le soir	swar
Yesterday	Hier	eeyehr
Today	Aujourd'hui	oh-zhoor-dwee
Tomorrow	Demain	duhmañ
Here	Ici	ee-see
There	Là	lah
What/which?	Quoi/quel, quelle?	kwah/kel, kel
When?	Quand?	koñ
Why?	Pourquoi?	poor-kwah
Where?	Où?	oo

USEFUL PHRASES

How are you?	Comment allez-vous?	kom-moñ talay voo
Very well, thank you.	Très bien, merci.	treh byañ, mer-see
Pleased to meet you.	Enchanté de faire votre connaissance.	oñshoñ-tay duh fehr votr kon-ay-sans
See you soon.	A bientôt.	byañ-toh
That's fine	C'est bon	say boñ
Where is/are...?	Où est/sont...?	ooay/soñ
How far is it to...?	Combien de kilomètres d'ici à...?	kom-byañ duh keelo-metr d'ee-see ah
Which way to...?	Quelle est la direction pour...?	kel ay lah deer-ek-syoñ poor
Do you speak English?	Parlez-vous anglais?	par-lay voo oñg-lay
I don't understand.	Je ne comprends pas.	zhuh nuh kom-proñ pah
Could you speak slowly please?	Pouvez-vous parler moins vite s'il vous plaît?	poo-vay voo par-lay mwañ veet seel voo play
I'm sorry.	Excusez-moi.	exkoo-zay mwah

USEFUL WORDS

big	grand	groñ
small	petit	puh-tee
hot	chaud	show
cold	froid	frwah
good	bon/bien	boñ/byañ
bad	mauvais	moh-veh
enough	assez	assay
well	bien	byañ
open	ouvert	oo-ver
closed	fermé	fer-meh
left	gauche	gohsh
right	droite	drwaht
straight on	tout droite	too drwaht
near	près	preh
far	loin	lwañ
up	en haut	oñ oh
down	en bas	oñ bah
early	de bonne heure	duh bon urr
late	en retard	oñ ruh-tar
entrance	l'entrée	l'on-tray
exit	la sortie	sor-tee
toilet	les toilettes, le WC	twah-let, vay-see
free, unoccupied	libre	leebr
free, no charge	gratuit	grah-twee

MAKING A TELEPHONE CALL

I'd like to place a long-distance call.	Je voudrais faire un appel à l'étranger.	zhuh voo-dreh fehr uñ apel a laytroñ-zhay
I'd like to make a reverse charge call.	Je voudrais faire une communication en PCV.	zhuh voo-dreh fehr oon komoonikah-syoñ oñ peh-seh-veh
I'll try again later.	Je rappelerai plus tard.	zhuh rappeleray ploo tar
Can I leave a message?	Est-ce que je peux laisser un message?	es-keh zhuh puh leh-say uñ mehsazh
Hold on.	Ne quittez pas, s'il vous plaît.	nuh kee-tay pah seel voo play
Could you speak up a little please?	Pouvez-vous parler un peu plus fort?	poo-vay voo parlay uñ puh ploo for
local call	la communication locale	komoonikahsyoñ low-kal

SHOPPING

How much does this cost?	C'est combien s'il vous plaît?	say kom-byañ seel voo play
I would like ...	Je voudrais...	zhuh voo-dray
Do you have?	Est-ce que vous avez	es-kuh voo zavay
I'm just looking.	Je regarde seulement.	zhuh ruhgar suhlmoñ
Do you take credit cards?	Est-ce que vous acceptez les cartes de crédit?	es-kuh voo zaksept-ay leh kart duh kreh-dee
Do you take traveller's cheques?	Est-ce que vous acceptez les cheques de voyages?	es-kuh voo zaksept-ay leh shek duh vwayazh
What time do you open?	A quelle heure vous êtes ouvert?	ah kel urr voo zet oo-ver
What time do you close?	A quelle heure vous êtes fermé?	ah kel urr voo zet fer-may
This one.	Celui-ci	suhl-wee-see
That one.	Celui-là	suhl-wee-lah
expensive	cher	shehr
cheap	pas cher, bon marché	pah shehr, boñ mar-shay
size, clothes	la taille	tye
size, shoes	la pointure	pwañ-tur
white	blanc	bloñ
black	noir	nwahr
red	rouge	roozh
yellow	jaune	zhohwn
green	vert	vehr
blue	bleu	bluh

TYPES OF SHOP

antique shop	le magasin d'antiquités	maga-zañ d'oñteekee-tay
bakery	la boulangerie	booloñ-zhuree
bank	la banque	boñk
bookshop	la librairie	lee-brehree
butcher	la boucherie	boo-shehree
cake shop	la pâtisserie	patee-sree
cheese shop	la fromagerie	fromazh-ree
chemist	la pharmacie	farmah-see
convenience store	l'alimentation	alee-moñta-syoñ
dairy	la crémerie	krem-ree
department store	le grand magasin	groñ maga-zañ
delicatessen	la charcuterie	sharkoot-ree
fishmonger	la poissonnerie	pwasson-ree
gift shop	le magasin de cadeaux	maga-zañ duh kadoh
greengrocer	le marchand de légumes	mar-shoñ duh lay-goom
hairdresser	le coiffeur	kwafuhr
market	le marché	marsh-ay
newsagent	le magasin de journaux	maga-zañ duh zhoor-no
post office	la poste, le bureau de poste, le PTT	pohst, booroh duh pohst, peh-teh-teh
shoe shop	le magasin de chaussures	maga-zañ duh show-soor
supermarket	le supermarché	soo pehr-marshay
tobacconist	le tabac	tabah
travel agent	l'agence de voyages	l'azhoñs duh vwayazh

SIGHTSEEING

abbey	l'abbaye	l'abay-ee
art gallery	la galerie d'art	galer-ree dart
bus station	la gare routière	gahr roo-tee-yehr
cathedral	la cathédrale	katay-dral
church	l'église	l'aygleez
garden	le jardin	zhar-dañ

library	la bibliothèque	beebleeo-tek
museum	le musée	moo-zay
railway station	la gare (SNCF)	gahr (es-en-say-ef)
tourist information office	les renseignements touristiques, le syndicat d'initiative	roñsayn-moñ toorees-teek, sandee-ka d'eenee-syateev
town hall	l'hôtel de ville	l'ohtel duh veel
closed for public holiday	fermeture jour férié	fehrmeh-tur zhoor fehree-ay

STAYING IN A HOTEL

Do you have a vacant room?	Est-ce que vous avez une chambre?	es-kuh voo-zavay oon shambr
double room, with double bed	la chambre à deux personnes, avec un grand lit	shambr ah duh pehr-son avek un groñf lee
twin room	la chambre à deux lits	shambr ah duh lee
single room	la chambre à une personne	shambr ah oon pehr-son
room with a bath, shower	la chambre avec salle de bains, une douche	shambr avek sal duh bañ, oon doosh
porter	le garçon	gar-soñ
key	la clé	klay
I have a reservation.	J'ai fait une réservation.	zhay fay oon rayzehrva-syoñ

EATING OUT

Have you got a table?	Avez-vous une table de libre?	avay-voo oon tahbl duh leebr
I want to reserve a table.	Je voudrais réserver une table.	zhuh voo-dray rayzehr-vay oon tahbl
The bill please.	L'addition s'il vous plaît.	l'adee-syoñ seel voo play
I am a vegetarian/vegan.	Je suis végétarien/végétalien.	zhuh swee vezhay-tehryañ/ vezgay-tahlyañ.
Waitress/waiter	Madame, Mademoiselle/Monsieur	mah-dam, mah-demwahzel/ muh-syuh
menu	le menu, la carte	men-oo, kart
fixed-price menu	le menu à prix fixe	men-oo ah pree feeks
cover charge	le couvert	koo-vehr
wine list	la carte des vins	kart-deh vañ
glass	le verre	vehr
bottle	la bouteille	boo-tay
knife	le couteau	koo-toh
fork	la fourchette	for-shet
spoon	la cuillère	kwee-yehr
breakfast	le petit déjeuner	puh-tee deh-zhuh-nay
lunch	le déjeuner	deh-zhuh-nay
dinner	le dîner	dee-nay
main course	le plat principal	plah prañsee-pal
starter, first course	l'entrée, le hors d'oeuvre	l'oñ-tray, or-duhvr
dish of the day	le plat du jour	plah doo zhoor
wine bar	le bar à vin	bar ah vañ
café	le café	ka-fay
rare	saignant	say-noñ
medium	à point	ah pwañ
well done	bien cuit	byañ kwee

MENU DECODER

apple	la pomme	pom
baked	cuit au four	kweet oh foor
banana	la banane	banan
beef	le boeuf	buhf
beer, draught beer	la bière, bière à la pression	bee-yehr, bee-yehr ah lah pres-syoñ
boiled	bouilli	boo-yee
bread	le pain	pan
butter	le beurre	burr
cake	le gâteau	gah-toh
cheese	le fromage	from-azh
chicken	le poulet	poo-lay
chips	les frites	freet
chocolate	le chocolat	shoko-lah
cocktail	le cocktail	cocktail
coffee	le café	kah-fay
dessert	le dessert	deh-ser
dry	sec	sek
duck	le canard	kanar
egg	l'oeuf	l'uf
fish	le poisson	pwah-ssoñ
fresh fruit	le fruit frais	frwee freh
garlic	l'ail	l'eye

grilled	grillé	gree-yay
ham	le jambon	zhoñ-boñ
ice, ice cream	la glace	glas
lamb	l'agneau	l'anyoh
lemon	le citron	see-troñ
lobster	le homard	omahr
meat	la viande	vee-yand
milk	le lait	leh
mineral water	l'eau minérale	l'oh meeney-ral
mustard	la moutarde	moo-tard
oil	l'huile	l'weel
olives	les olives	leh zoleev
onions	les oignons	leh zonyoñ
orange	l'orange	l'oroñzh
fresh orange juice	l'orange pressée	l'oroñzh press-eh
fresh lemon juice	le citron pressé	see-troñ press-eh
pepper	le poivre	pwavr
poached	poché	posh-ay
pork	le porc	por
potatoes	les pommes de terre	pom-duh tehr
prawns	les crevettes	kruh-vet
rice	le riz	ree
roast	rôti	row-tee
roll	le petit pain	puh-tee pañ
salt	le sel	sel
sauce	la sauce	sohs
sausage, fresh	la saucisse	sohsees
seafood	les fruits de mer	frwee duh mer
shellfish	les crustaces	kroos-tas
snails	les escargots	leh zes-kar-goh
soup	la soupe, le potage	soop, poh-tazh
steak	le bifteck, le steack	beef-tek, stek
sugar	le sucre	sookr
tea	le thé	tay
toast	pain grillé	pan greeyay
vegetables	les légumes	lay-goom
vinegar	le vinaigre	veenaygr
water	l'eau	l'oh
red wine	le vin rouge	vañ roozh
white wine	le vin blanc	vañ bloñ

NUMBERS

0	zéro	zeh-roh
1	un, une	uñ, oon
2	deux	duh
3	trois	trwah
4	quatre	katr
5	cinq	sañk
6	six	sees
7	sept	set
8	huit	weet
9	neuf	nerf
10	dix	dees
11	onze	oñz
12	douze	dooz
13	treize	trehz
14	quatorze	katorz
15	quinze	kañz
16	seize	sehz
17	dix-sept	dees-set
18	dix-huit	dees-weet
19	dix-neuf	dees-nerf
20	vingt	vañ
30	trente	tront
40	quarante	karoñt
50	cinquante	sañkoñt
60	soixante	swasoñt
70	soixante-dix	swasoñt-dees
80	quatre-vingts	katr-vañ
90	quatre-vingt-dix	katr-vañ-dees
100	cent	soñ
1,000	mille	meel

TIME

one minute	une minute	oon mee-noot
one hour	une heure	oon urr
half an hour	une demi-heure	oon duh-mee urr
Monday	lundi	luñ-dee
Tuesday	mardi	mar-dee
Wednesday	mercredi	mehrkruh-dee
Thursday	jeudi	zhuh-dee
Friday	vendredi	voñdruh-dee
Saturday	samedi	sam-dee
Sunday	dimanche	dee-moñsh

ACKNOWLEDGMENTS

DK would like to thank the following for their contribution to the previous edition: Elspeth Beidas, Alan Tillier, Bryan Pirolli, Zoe Ross

The publisher would like to thank the following for their kind permission to reproduce their photographs:

Key: a-above; b-below/bottom; c-centre; f-far; l-left; r-right; t-top

123RF.com: Jon Bilous 18tc, 114-5cl; Francesco Bucchi 303br; Nattee Chalermtiragool 32br; Christian Mueller 267bl; Inna Nerlich 89cra.

4Corners: Susanne Kremer 4.

Alamy Stock Photo: Agenzia Sintesi / Fiorani Fabio 267bc; Todd Anderson 186cr; Andrzej Gorzkowski Photography 299bl; ART Collection 60bl; Peter Barritt 185cr; Martin Beddall 303bl; Beucher / Andia 41tl; Tibor Bognar 83tr; Piere Bonbon 24tl, 262-3; Eden Breitz 217cb; Helen Cathcart 119tr; Chronicle 70br, 131tr; Daisy Corlett 49b; Crowdspark / Newzulu / Dan Pier 134tc; Cultura Creative Ltd / Aziz Ary Neto 63br; Directphoto Collection 23tl, 234-5; edpics 33b, 45t; Chad Ehlers 302cla; Everett Collection Inc 283cr; EyeEm / Cristian Bortes 10clb; PE Forsberg 99tc; Giovanni Guarino Photo 46-7b; GL Archive 60br, 131ca; Granger Historical Picture Archive 62cr; hitandrun / Greg Meeson / © Succession Brancusi - All rights reserved. ADAGP, Paris and DACS, London 2018 *Brancusi's studio being exhibited at the Pompidou Centre in Paris* 91crb; hemis.fr / Arnaud Chicurel 247tl, / Bertrand Gardel 36b, 43tr, 98bl, 106-7b, 143tr, 219cra, 219crb, / Henri Bouchard *Apollo* © ADAGP, Paris and DACS, London 2018 220tr, / Franck Guiziou 25, 112bl, 113t, 290-1, / René Mattes 28crb, 289tl, / Bertrand Rieger 137br, 245br, / Gilles Rigoulet 270bl, / Sylvain Sonnet 96tl, / © Succession Picasso / DACS, London 2018 *Femmes à leur toilette (Women washing)* 88-9b; Heritage Image Partnership Ltd / The Print Collector 61tl; IanDagnall Computing 131crb; imageBROKER / Daniel Schoenen 57cr; JaiHoneybrook 294cr; Boris Karpinski 8cla; John Kellerman 17bl, 92-3b, 100-1, 121t, 165br, 242b, 242-3t; Keystone Pictures USA 131br; Elena Korchenko 297t; Lautaro 219bl; Chris Lawrence 258b; Lebrecht Music and Arts Photo Library 104br; Elizabeth Leyden 8-9b; lugris 105; Luciano Mortula / *Centre Pompidou in Paris: Studio Piano & Rogers*, courtesy of Fondazione Renzo Piano and Rogers Stirk Harbour + Partners 90-1b; Perry van Munster 37br, 48tc; National Geographic Creative 81tl; Niday Picture Library 61bc; John Norman 28cr; Samantha Ohlsen 259t; Paris 94crb; Pawel Libera Images 300-1t; Photo 12 / Gilles Targat 136cr, 176bl; PhotoAlto / es Cuisine / Laurence Mouton 58cla; Photononstop / Christophe Lehenaff 42-3b,/ Daniel Thierry 270-1; Pierre Pochan 136t; Premium Stock Photography GmbH / Scattolin 190-1bc; Prisma by Dukas Presseagentur GmbH / Raga Jose Fuste 230bl; Paul Quayle / *Henri Cochet Statue outside Roland Garros, Paris* 293br; National Museum of Modern Art in the Pompidou Centre, Paris / Mervyn Rees / Xavier Veilhan © Veilhan / ADAGP, Paris and DACS, London 2018 *Le Rhinocéros* 91cra; Robertharding ,/ Stuart Dee 46-7t, / Julian Elliott 233tr, / Godong 33ca, / H P Merten 104clb, / De Rocker 156cra; RossHelen editorial 221; Francois Roux 11cr; Peter Schickert 96-7b; Science History Images 61cla; Shawshots 217crb; Sipa USA / Lev Radin 35cl; SJH Photography 301bl; Sergey Sklznev 267cr; William Stevens 40b; Street Art 18bl, 126-7; Claude Thibault 121br; Tuul and Bruno Morandi / © Succession Picasso / DACS, London 2018 *Head of a Woman* 88tr; Frédéric Vielcanet 51br; Viennaslide 120b; Tracey Whitefoot 287br; Gari Wyn Williams 274bc; ZUMA Press, Inc. / Pierre Stevenin 34bl.

AWL Images: Jon Arnold 119tl, / Tour eiffel- Illuminations Pierre Bideau 21t, 196-7cl; Jan Christopher Becke 8clb, 173cla, 189tr, 239tr; Walter Bibikow 39cr; Danita Delimont Stock 297cl; Bertrand Gardel 12-3bc.

Candelaria: Fabien Voileau 53b.

Cité Des Sciences et de L'industrie: EPPD CSI / JP 145bl, / E Luider 144-5t.

La Cuisine Cooking: 8cl.

Depositphotos Inc: packshot 299clb; wjarek 208tr.

Disneyland® Paris: © Disney / Pixar: 301clb, 301br.

Dorling Kindersley: Neil Lukas 283clb, / © Succession Brancusi - All rights reserved. ADAGP, Paris and DACS, London 2018 *The Kiss* 282br;

Musee Bourdelle: Dorine Potel 286bl.

Musee de Cluny: M. Chassat 254tl.

Musée de Louvre: ©Pyramide du Louvre, arch. I. M. Pei 11tl, 20cb, 32br, 180, 184-5t, 185bl.

Musée de Montmartre: Jean-Pierre Delagarde 161b.

Parc de la Villette: William Beaucardet 142-3b, 143cla; Pierre-Emmanuel Rastoin 150-1t.

Philharmonie de Paris: William Beaucardet / Architect Jean Nouvel © ADAGP, Paris and DACS, London 2018 147t.

Picfair.com: Benis Arapovic 260bl.

RMN: Grand Palais (Musée du Louvre) / Peter Willi / Trésor de l'abbaye de Saint-Denis 187tl.

Robert Harding Picture Library: Stuart Dee 239cl; Jakob+MacFarlane - Cite de la mode et du design, Quai de Austerlitz, Paris / Javier Gil 272-3b.

Shutterstock.com: Frederic Legrand - COMEO 34-35t; Granger 62bc; Moviestore Collection 44tl; VanderWolf Images 58crb.

SuperStock: 4X5 COLLECTION / Musee Picasso / © Succession Picasso / DACS, London 2018 *The Kiss* (1969) by Pablo Picasso 89br; Francisco de Zurbaran *Lying in State of St Bonaventura* (c.1629) 186tl; age fotostock / Heinz-Dieter Falkenstein 75br, / T. Papageorgiou 42tl, / Carlos S. Pereyra 26cr; Javier Larrea / Centre George Pompidou / Vassily Kandinsky *With the Black Arc (1912)* 91tl; agf photo 53cla; eps / Marka 62-3tr; hemis / Maurizio Borgese 218br, / Bertrand Gardel 57br, 59tl, 63tr, 294bl, 295, / Architect Jean Nouvel © ADAGP, Paris and DACS, London 2018 *Le Parc de la Villette, Philharmonie de Paris* 19tl, 138-9 and *Paris Philharmonic Concert Hall* 148-9, / Jean-Pierre Degas 56tl, / Hervé Hughes 150br, / Stéphane Lemaire 297cra, / Lionel Montico /Architect Adrien Fainsilber © ADAGP, Paris and DACS, London 2018 *La Geode*, Parc de la Villette 145br, / Hervé Tardy 267crb; imageBROKER / Stephan Gabriel / Architect Jean Nouvel © ADAGP, Paris and DACS, London 2018 Exterior of Musee Du Quai Branley - Jacques Chirac 203tl; Photononstop / Architect Adrien Fainsilber © ADAGP, Paris and DACS, London 2018 Cite des Sciences et de L'industrie 145clb; Universal Images 299crb.

Front Flap:
Alamy Stock Photo: Piere Bonbon t; Elena Korchenko cla. **AWL Images:** Jan Christopher Becke bl. **Dreamstime.com:** Ionut David br. **iStockphoto.com:** shishic cra. **SuperStock:** hemis.fr / Jean-Pierre Degas c.

Sheet Map Cover:
iStockphoto.com: GlobalP.

Cover images:
Front and Spine: **iStockphoto.com:** GlobalP. *Back:* **Alamy Stock Photo:** John Kellerman tr; **La Cuisine Cooking:** c; **Dreamstime.com:** Rosshelen cla; **iStockphoto.com:** GlobalP b.

For further information see: www.dkimages.com

Cartographic Data ERA-Maptec Ltd (Dublin) adapted with permission from original survey and mapping by Shobunsha (Japan)

Illustrators Stephen Conlin, Stephen Gyapay, Maltings Partnership, John Fox Nick Gibbard, David Harris, Kevin Jones Associates, John Woodcock

This edition updated by

Contributor Emma Gibbs
Senior Editor Alison McGill
Senior Designers Laura O'Brien,
Vinita Venugopal
Editor Alex Pathe
Picture Research Administrator Vagisha Pushp
Picture Research Manager Taiyaba Khatoon
Publishing Assistant Halima Mohammed
Jacket Designer Jordan Lambley
Cartographer Ashif
Cartography Manager Suresh Kumar
Senior DTP Designer Tanveer Zaidi
Senior Production Editor Jason Little
Senior Production Controller Samantha Cross
Managing Editors Shikha Kulkarni, Beverly
Smart, Hollie Teague
Managing Art Editor Sarah Snelling
Senior Managing Art Editor Priyanka Thakur
Art Director Maxine Pedliham
Publishing Director Georgina Dee

First edition 1993

Published in Great Britain by Dorling Kindersley Limited,
One Embassy Gardens, 8 Viaduct Gardens,
London SW11 7BW, UK

The authorised representative in the EEA is Dorling Kindersley
Verlag GmbH. Arnulfstr. 124, 80636 Munich, Germany

Published in the United States by DK Publishing,
1745 Broadway, 20th Floor, New York, NY 10019, USA

The publishers cannot accept responsibility for any consequences
arising from the use of this book, nor for any material on third
party websites, and cannot guarantee that any website address
in this book will be a suitable source of travel information.

A CIP catalogue record for this book
is available from the British Library.

A catalogue record for this book is available
from the Library of Congress.

ISSN: 1542 1554
ISBN: 978 0 2416 1929 2

Printed and bound in China

www.dk.com

MIX
Paper | Supporting
responsible forestry
FSC™ C018179
www.fsc.org

This book was made with
Forest Stewardship Council™
certified paper – one small
step in DK's commitment
to a sustainable future.
**For more information go to
www.dk.com/our-green-pledge**

A NOTE FROM DK EYEWITNESS

The rapid rate at which the world is changing is
constantly keeping the DK Eyewitness team on our
toes. While we've worked hard to ensure that this
edition of Paris is accurate and up-to-date, we know
that opening hours alter, standards shift, prices
fluctuate, places close and new ones pop up in their
stead. So, if you notice we've got something wrong
or left something out, we want to hear about it.
Please get in touch at travelguides@dk.com